Deep Learning with

Implementing deep learning models and neural networks with the power of Python

Antonio Gulli

Sujit Pal

BIRMINGHAM - MUMBAI

Deep Learning with Keras

First published: April 2017

Production reference: 1240417

Published by Packt Publishing Ltd.
Livery Place
35 Livery Street
Birmingham
B3 2PB, UK.
ISBN 978-1-78712-842-2

www.packtpub.com

Credits

Authors

Antonio Gulli

Sujit Pal

Reviewers

Mike Dahlin

Nick McClure

Corrado Zocollo

Commissioning Editor

Amey Varangaonkar

Acquisition Editor

Divya Poojari

Content Development Editor

Cheryl Dsa

Technical Editor

Dinesh Pawar

Copy Editor

Vikrant Phadkay

Project Coordinator

Nidhi Joshi

Proofreader

Safis Editing

Indexer

Francy Puthiry

Graphics

Tania Dutta

Production Coordinator

Arvindkumar Gupta

About the Authors

Antonio Gulli is a software executive and business leader with a passion for establishing and managing global technological talent, innovation, and execution. He is an expert in search engines, online services, machine learning, information retrieval, analytics, and cloud computing. So far, he has been lucky enough to gain professional experience in four different countries in Europe and managed people in six different countries in Europe and America. Antonio served as CEO, GM, CTO, VP, director, and site lead in multiple fields spanning from publishing (Elsevier) to consumer internet (Ask.com and Tiscali) and high-tech R&D (Microsoft and Google).

I would like to thank my coauthor, Sujit Pal, for being a such talented colleague, always willing to help with a humble spirit. I constantly appreciate his dedication to teamwork, which made this book a real thing.

I would like to thank Francois Chollet (and the many Keras contributors) for taking the time and effort to build an awesome deep learning toolkit that is easy to use without sacrificing too much power.

I would also like to thank our editors from Packt, Divya Poojari, Cheryl Dsa, and Dinesh Pawar, and our reviewers from Packt and Google, for their support and valuable suggestions. This book would not have been possible without you.

I would like to thank my manager, Brad, and my colleagues Mike and Corrado at Google for encouraging me to write this book, and for their constant help in reviewing the content.

I would like to thank Same Fusy, Herbaciarnia i Kawiarnia in Warsaw. I got the initial inspiration to write this book in front of a cup of tea chosen among hundreds of different offers. This place is magic and I strongly recommend visiting it if you are in search of a place to stimulate creativeness (http://www.samefusy.pl/).

Then I would like to thank HRBP at Google for supporting my wish to donate all of this book's royalties in favor of a minority/diversity scholarship.

I would like to thank my friends Eric, Laura, Francesco, Ettore, and Antonella for supporting me when I was in need. Long-term friendship is a real thing, and you are true friends to me.

I would like to thank my son Lorenzo for encouraging me to join Google, my son Leonardo for his constant passion to discover new things, and my daughter Aurora for making me smile every day of my life. Finally thanks to my father Elio and my mother Maria for their love.

Sujit Pal is a technology research director at Elsevier Labs, working on building intelligent systems around research content and metadata. His primary interests are information retrieval, ontologies, natural language processing, machine learning, and distributed processing. He is currently working on image classification and similarity using deep learning models. Prior to this, he worked in the consumer healthcare industry, where he helped build ontology-backed semantic search, contextual advertising, and EMR data processing platforms. He writes about technology on his blog at *Salmon Run*.

I would like to thank my coauthor, Antonio Gulli, for asking me to join him in writing this book. This was an incredible opportunity and a great learning experience for me. Besides, had he not done so, I quite literally wouldn't have been here today.

I would like to thank Ron Daniel, the director of Elsevier Labs, and Bradley P Allen, chief architect at Elsevier, for introducing me to deep learning and making me a believer in its capabilities.

I would also like to thank Francois Chollet (and the many Keras contributors) for taking the time and effort to build an awesome deep learning toolkit that is easy to use without sacrificing too much power.

Thanks to our editors from Packt, Divya Poojari, Cheryl Dsa, and Dinesh Pawar, and our reviewers from Packt and Google, for their support and valuable suggestions. This book would not have been possible without you.

I would like to thank my colleagues and managers over the years, especially the ones who took their chances with me and helped me make discontinuous changes in my career.

Finally, I would like to thank my family for putting up with me these past few months as I juggled work, this book, and family, in that order. I hope you will agree that it was all worth it.

About the Reviewer

Nick McClure is currently a senior data scientist at PayScale Inc. in Seattle, Washington, USA. Prior to that, he worked at Zillow and Caesars Entertainment. He got his degrees in applied mathematics from the University of Montana and the College of Saint Benedict and Saint John's University. Nick has also authored *TensorFlow Machine Learning Cookbook* by Packt Publishing.

He has a passion for learning and advocating for analytics, machine learning, and artificial intelligence. Nick occasionally puts his thoughts and musing on his blog, `fromdata.org`, or through his Twitter account at `@nfmcclure`.

www.PacktPub.com

For support files and downloads related to your book, please visit www.PacktPub.com.

Did you know that Packt offers eBook versions of every book published, with PDF and ePub files available? You can upgrade to the eBook version at www.PacktPub.com and as a print book customer, you are entitled to a discount on the eBook copy. Get in touch with us at service@packtpub.com for more details.

At www.PacktPub.com, you can also read a collection of free technical articles, sign up for a range of free newsletters and receive exclusive discounts and offers on Packt books and eBooks.

https://www.packtpub.com/mapt

Get the most in-demand software skills with Mapt. Mapt gives you full access to all Packt books and video courses, as well as industry-leading tools to help you plan your personal development and advance your career.

Why subscribe?

- Fully searchable across every book published by Packt
- Copy and paste, print, and bookmark content
- On demand and accessible via a web browser

Customer Feedback

Thanks for purchasing this Packt book. At Packt, quality is at the heart of our editorial process. To help us improve, please leave us an honest review on this book's Amazon page at `https://www.amazon.com/dp/1787128423`.

If you'd like to join our team of regular reviewers, you can e-mail us at `customerreviews@packtpub.com`. We award our regular reviewers with free eBooks and videos in exchange for their valuable feedback. Help us be relentless in improving our products!

Table of Contents

Preface

Hands-on deep learning with Keras is a concise yet thorough introduction to modern neural networks, artificial intelligence, and deep learning technologies designed especially for software engineers and data scientists.

Mission

The book presents more than 20 working deep neural networks coded in Python using Keras, a modular neural network library that runs on top of either Google's TensorFlow or Lisa Lab's Theano backends.

The reader is introduced step by step to supervised learning algorithms such as simple linear regression, classical multilayer perceptron, and more sophisticated deep convolutional networks and generative adversarial networks. In addition, the book covers unsupervised learning algorithms such as autoencoders and generative networks. Recurrent networks and **long short-term memory (LSTM)** networks are also explained in detail. The book goes on to cover the Keras functional API and how to customize Keras in case the reader's use case is not covered by Keras's extensive functionality. It also looks at larger, more complex systems composed of the building blocks covered previously. The book concludes with an introduction to deep reinforcement learning and how it can be used to build game playing AIs.

Practical applications include code for the classification of news articles into predefined categories, syntactic analysis of texts, sentiment analysis, synthetic generation of texts, and parts of speech annotation. Image processing is also explored, with recognition of handwritten digit images, classification of images into different categories, and advanced object recognition with related image annotations. An example of identification of salient points for face detection will be also provided. Sound analysis comprises recognition of discrete speeches from multiple speakers. Reinforcement learning is used to build a deep Q-learning network capable of playing games autonomously.

Experiments are the essence of the book. Each net is augmented by multiple variants that progressively improve the learning performance by changing the input parameters, the shape of the network, loss functions, and algorithms used for optimizations. Several comparisons between training on CPUs and GPUs are also provided.

How deep learning is different from machine learning and artificial intelligence

Artificial intelligence (**AI**) is a very large research field, where machines show *cognitive* capabilities such as learning behaviours, proactive interaction with the environment, inference and deduction, computer vision, speech recognition, problem solving, knowledge representation, perception, and many others (for more information, refer to this article: *Artificial Intelligence: A Modern Approach*, by S. Russell and P. Norvig, Prentice Hall, 2003). More colloquially, AI denotes any activity where machines mimic *intelligent* behaviors typically shown by humans. Artificial intelligence takes inspiration from elements of computer science, mathematics, and statistics.

Machine learning (**ML**) is a subbranch of AI that focuses on teaching computers how to learn without the need to be programmed for specific tasks (for more information refer to *Pattern Recognition and Machine Learning*, by C. M. Bishop, Springer, 2006). In fact, the key idea behind ML is that it is possible to create algorithms that learn from and make predictions on data. There are three different broad categories of ML. In supervised learning, the machine is presented with input data and desired output, and the goal is to learn from those training examples in such a way that meaningful predictions can be made for fresh unseen data. In unsupervised learning, the machine is presented with input data only and the machine has to find some meaningful structure by itself with no external supervision. In reinforcement learning, the machine acts as an agent interacting with the environment and learning what are the behaviours that generate rewards.

Deep learning (**DL**) is a particular subset of ML methodologies using **artificial neural networks** (**ANN**) slightly inspired by the structure of neurons located in the human brain (for more information, refer to the article *Learning Deep Architectures for AI*, by Y. Bengio, Found. Trends, vol. 2, 2009). Informally, the word *deep* refers to the presence of many layers in the artificial neural network, but this meaning has changed over time. While 4 years ago, 10 layers were already sufficient to consider a network as *deep*, today it is more common to consider a network as *deep* when it has hundreds of layers.

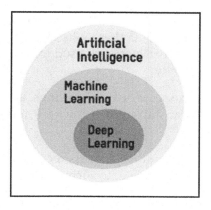

DL is a real tsunami (for more information, refer to *Computational Linguistics and Deep Learning* by C. D. Manning, "Computational Linguistics", vol. 41, 2015) for machine learning in that a relatively small number of clever methodologies have been very successfully applied to so many different domains (image, text, video, speech, and vision), significantly improving previous state-of-the-art results achieved over dozens of years. The success of DL is also due to the availability of more training data (such as ImageNet for images) and the relatively low-cost availability of GPUs for very efficient numerical computation. Google, Microsoft, Amazon, Apple, Facebook, and many others use those deep learning techniques every day for analyzing massive amounts of data. However, this kind of expertise is not limited any more to the domain of pure academic research and to large industrial companies. It has become an integral part of modern software production and therefore something that the reader should definitively master. The book does not require any particular mathematical background. However, it assumes that the reader is already a Python programmer.

What this book covers

Chapter 1, *Neural Networks Foundations*, teaches the basics of neural networks.

Chapter 2, *Keras Installation and API*, shows how to install Keras on AWS, Microsoft Azure, Google Cloud, and your own machine. In addition to that, we provide an overview of the Keras APIs.

Chapter 3, *Deep Learning with ConvNets*, introduces the concept of convolutional networks. It is a fundamental innovation in deep learning that has been used with success in multiple domains, from text to video to speech, going well beyond the initial image processing domain where it was originally conceived.

Chapter 4, *Generative Adversarial Networks and WaveNet*, introduces generative adversarial networks used to reproduce synthetic data that looks like data generated by humans. And we will present WaveNet, a deep neural network used for reproducing human voice and musical instruments with high quality.

Chapter 5, *Word Embeddings*, discusses word embeddings, a set of deep learning methodologies for detecting relationships between words and grouping together similar words.

Chapter 6, *Recurrent Neural Networks – RNN*, covers recurrent neural networks, a class of network optimized for handling sequence data such as text.

Chapter 7, *Additional Deep Learning Models*, gives a brief look into the Keras functional API, regression networks, autoencoders, and so on.

Chapter 8, *AI Game Playing*, teaches you deep reinforcement learning and how it can be used to build deep learning networks with Keras that learn how to play arcade games based on reward feedback.

Appendix, *Conclusion*, is a crisp refresher of the topics covered in this book and walks the users through what is new in Keras 2.0.

What you need for this book

To be able to smoothly follow through the chapters, you will need the following pieces of software:

- TensorFlow 1.0.0 or higher
- Keras 2.0.2 or higher
- Matplotlib 1.5.3 or higher
- Scikit-learn 0.18.1 or higher
- NumPy 1.12.1 or higher

The hardware specifications are as follows:

- Either 32-bit or 64-bit architecture
- 2+ GHz CPU
- 4 GB RAM
- At least 10 GB of hard disk space available

Who this book is for

If you are a data scientist with experience in machine learning or an AI programmer with some exposure to neural networks, you will find this book a useful entry point to deep learning with Keras. Knowledge of Python is required for this book.

Conventions

In this book, you will find a number of text styles that distinguish between different kinds of information. Here are some examples of these styles and an explanation of their meaning.

Code words in text, database table names, folder names, filenames, file extensions, pathnames, dummy URLs, user input, and Twitter handles are shown as follows: "In addition, we load the true labels into Y_train and Y_test respectively and perform a one-hot encoding on them."

A block of code is set as follows:

```
from keras.models import Sequential
model = Sequential()
model.add(Dense(12, input_dim=8, kernel_initializer='random_uniform'))
```

When we wish to draw your attention to a particular part of a code block, the relevant lines or items are set in bold:

```
# 10 outputs
# final stage is softmax
model = Sequential()
model.add(Dense(NB_CLASSES, input_shape=(RESHAPED,)))
model.add(Activation('softmax'))
model.summary()
```

Any command-line input or output is written as follows:

```
pip install quiver_engine
```

New terms and **important words** are shown in bold. Words that you see on the screen, for example, in menus or dialog boxes, appear in the text like this: "Our simple net started with an accuracy of **92.22%**, which means that about eight handwritten characters out of 100 are not correctly recognized."

Warnings or important notes appear in a box like this.

Tips and tricks appear like this.

Reader feedback

Feedback from our readers is always welcome. Let us know what you think about this book-what you liked or disliked. Reader feedback is important for us as it helps us develop titles that you will really get the most out of.

To send us general feedback, simply e-mail `feedback@packtpub.com`, and mention the book's title in the subject of your message.

If there is a topic that you have expertise in and you are interested in either writing or contributing to a book, see our author guide at `www.packtpub.com/authors`.

Customer support

Now that you are the proud owner of a Packt book, we have a number of things to help you to get the most from your purchase.

Downloading the example code

You can download the example code files for this book from your account at `http://www.packtpub.com`. If you purchased this book elsewhere, you can visit `http://www.packtpub.com/support` and register to have the files e-mailed directly to you.

You can download the code files by following these steps:

1. Log in or register to our website using your e-mail address and password.
2. Hover the mouse pointer on the **SUPPORT** tab at the top.
3. Click on **Code Downloads & Errata**.
4. Enter the name of the book in the **Search** box.
5. Select the book for which you're looking to download the code files.
6. Choose from the drop-down menu where you purchased this book from.
7. Click on **Code Download**.

Once the file is downloaded, please make sure that you unzip or extract the folder using the latest version of:

* WinRAR / 7-Zip for Windows
* Zipeg / iZip / UnRarX for Mac
* 7-Zip / PeaZip for Linux

The code bundle for the book is also hosted on GitHub at https://github.com/PacktPublishing/Deep-Learning-with-Keras. We also have other code bundles from our rich catalog of books and videos available at https://github.com/PacktPublishing/. Check them out!

Downloading the color images of this book

We also provide you with a PDF file that has color images of the screenshots/diagrams used in this book. The color images will help you better understand the changes in the output. You can download this file from https://www.packtpub.com/sites/default/files/downloads/DeepLearningwithKeras_ColorImages.pdf.

Errata

Although we have taken every care to ensure the accuracy of our content, mistakes do happen. If you find a mistake in one of our books-maybe a mistake in the text or the code-we would be grateful if you could report this to us. By doing so, you can save other readers from frustration and help us improve subsequent versions of this book. If you find any errata, please report them by visiting http://www.packtpub.com/submit-errata, selecting your book, clicking on the **Errata Submission Form** link, and entering the details of your errata. Once your errata are verified, your submission will be accepted and the errata will be uploaded to our website or added to any list of existing errata under the Errata section of that title.

To view the previously submitted errata, go to https://www.packtpub.com/books/content/support and enter the name of the book in the search field. The required information will appear under the **Errata** section.

Piracy

Piracy of copyrighted material on the Internet is an ongoing problem across all media. At Packt, we take the protection of our copyright and licenses very seriously. If you come across any illegal copies of our works in any form on the Internet, please provide us with the location address or website name immediately so that we can pursue a remedy.

Please contact us at copyright@packtpub.com with a link to the suspected pirated material.

We appreciate your help in protecting our authors and our ability to bring you valuable content.

Questions

If you have a problem with any aspect of this book, you can contact us at questions@packtpub.com, and we will do our best to address the problem.

1
Neural Networks Foundations

Artificial neural networks (briefly, *nets*) represent a class of machine learning models, loosely inspired by studies about the central nervous systems of mammals. Each net is made up of several interconnected *neurons*, organized in *layers*, which exchange messages (they *fire*, in jargon) when certain conditions happen. Initial studies were started in the late 1950s with the introduction of the perceptron (for more information, refer to the article: *The Perceptron: A Probabilistic Model for Information Storage and Organization in the Brain*, by F. Rosenblatt, Psychological Review, vol. 65, pp. 386 - 408, 1958), a two-layer network used for simple operations, and further expanded in the late 1960s with the introduction of the *backpropagation algorithm*, used for efficient multilayer networks training (according to the articles: *Backpropagation through Time: What It Does and How to Do It*, by P. J. Werbos, Proceedings of the IEEE, vol. 78, pp. 1550 - 1560, 1990, and *A Fast Learning Algorithm for Deep Belief Nets*, by G. E. Hinton, S. Osindero, and Y. W. Teh, Neural Computing, vol. 18, pp. 1527 - 1554, 2006). Some studies argue that these techniques have roots dating further back than normally cited (for more information, refer to the article: *Deep Learning in Neural Networks: An Overview*, by J. Schmidhuber, vol. 61, pp. 85 - 117, 2015). Neural networks were a topic of intensive academic studies until the 1980s, when other simpler approaches became more relevant. However, there has been a resurrection of interest starting from the mid-2000s, thanks to both a breakthrough fast-learning algorithm proposed by G. Hinton (for more information, refer to the articles: *The Roots of Backpropagation: From Ordered Derivatives to Neural Networks and Political Forecasting, Neural Networks*, by S. Leven, vol. 9, 1996 and *Learning Representations by Backpropagating Errors*, by D. E. Rumelhart, G. E. Hinton, and R. J. Williams, vol. 323, 1986) and the introduction of GPUs, roughly in 2011, for massive numeric computation.

These improvements opened the route for modern *deep learning*, a class of neural networks characterized by a significant number of layers of neurons, which are able to learn rather sophisticated models based on progressive levels of abstraction. People called it *deep* with 3-5 layers a few years ago, and now it has gone up to 100-200.

This learning via progressive abstraction resembles vision models that have evolved over millions of years in the human brain. The human visual system is indeed organized into different layers. Our eyes are connected to an area of the brain called the **visual cortex V1**, which is located in the lower posterior part of our brain. This area is common to many mammals and has the role of discriminating basic properties and small changes in visual orientation, spatial frequencies, and colors. It has been estimated that V1 consists of about 140 million neurons, with 10 billion connections between them. V1 is then connected with other areas V2, V3, V4, V5, and V6, doing progressively more complex image processing and recognition of more sophisticated concepts, such as shapes, faces, animals, and many more. This organization in layers is the result of a huge number of attempts tuned over several 100 million years. It has been estimated that there are ~16 billion human cortical neurons, and about 10%-25% of the human cortex is devoted to vision (for more information, refer to the article: *The Human Brain in Numbers: A Linearly Scaled-up Primate Brain*, by S. Herculano-Houzel, vol. 3, 2009). Deep learning has taken some inspiration from this layer-based organization of the human visual system: early artificial neuron layers learn basic properties of images, while deeper layers learn more sophisticated concepts.

This book covers several major aspects of neural networks by providing working nets coded in Keras, a minimalist and efficient Python library for deep learning computations running on the top of either Google's TensorFlow (for more information, refer to `https://www.tensorflow.org/`) or University of Montreal's Theano (for more information, refer to `http://deeplearning.net/software/theano/`) backend. So, let's start.

In this chapter, we will cover the following topics:

- Perceptron
- Multilayer perceptron
- Activation functions
- Gradient descent
- Stochastic gradient descent
- Backpropagation

Perceptron

The perceptron is a simple algorithm which, given an input vector x of m values (x_1, x_2, ..., x_n) often called input features or simply features, outputs either *1* (yes) or *0* (no). Mathematically, we define a function:

$$f(x) = \begin{cases} 1 & wx + b > 0 \\ 0 & otherwise \end{cases}$$

Here, w is a vector of weights, wx is the dot product $\sum_{j=1}^{m} w_j x_j$, and b is a bias. If you remember elementary geometry, $wx + b$ defines a boundary hyperplane that changes position according to the values assigned to w and b. If x lies above the straight line, then the answer is positive, otherwise it is negative. Very simple algorithm! The perception cannot express a *maybe* answer. It can answer *yes* (*1*) or *no* (*0*) if we understand how to define w and b, that is the training process that will be discussed in the following paragraphs.

The first example of Keras code

The initial building block of Keras is a model, and the simplest model is called **sequential**. A sequential Keras model is a linear pipeline (a stack) of neural networks layers. This code fragment defines a single layer with `12` artificial neurons, and it expects `8` input variables (also known as features):

```
from keras.models import Sequential
model = Sequential()
model.add(Dense(12, input_dim=8, kernel_initializer='random_uniform'))
```

Each neuron can be initialized with specific weights. Keras provides a few choices, the most common of which are listed as follows:

- `random_uniform`: Weights are initialized to uniformly random small values in (*-0.05*, *0.05*). In other words, any value within the given interval is equally likely to be drawn.
- `random_normal`: Weights are initialized according to a Gaussian, with a zero mean and small standard deviation of *0.05*. For those of you who are not familiar with a Gaussian, think about a symmetric *bell curve* shape.
- `zero`: All weights are initialized to zero.

A full list is available at `https://keras.io/initializations/`.

Multilayer perceptron — the first example of a network

In this chapter, we define the first example of a network with multiple linear layers. Historically, perceptron was the name given to a model having one single linear layer, and as a consequence, if it has multiple layers, you would call it **multilayer perceptron** (**MLP**). The following image represents a generic neural network with one input layer, one intermediate layer and one output layer.

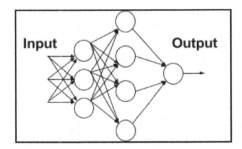

In the preceding diagram, each node in the first layer receives an input and fires according to the predefined local decision boundaries. Then the output of the first layer is passed to the second layer, the results of which are passed to the final output layer consisting of one single neuron. It is interesting to note that this layered organization vaguely resembles the patterns of human vision we discussed earlier.

The *net* is dense, meaning that each neuron in a layer is connected to all neurons located in the previous layer and to all the neurons in the following layer.

Problems in training the perceptron and a solution

Let's consider a single neuron; what are the best choices for the weight w and the bias b? Ideally, we would like to provide a set of training examples and let the computer adjust the weight and the bias in such a way that the errors produced in the output are minimized. In order to make this a bit more concrete, let's suppose we have a set of images of cats and another separate set of images not containing cats. For the sake of simplicity, assume that each neuron looks at a single input pixel value. While the computer processes these images, we would like our neuron to adjust its weights and bias so that we have fewer and fewer images wrongly recognized as non-cats. This approach seems very intuitive, but it requires that a small change in weights (and/or bias) causes only a small change in outputs.

If we have a big output jump, we cannot *progressively* learn (rather than trying things in all possible directions—a process known as exhaustive search—without knowing if we are improving). After all, kids learn little by little. Unfortunately, the perceptron does not show this little-by-little behavior. A perceptron is either *0* or *1* and that is a big jump and it will not help it to learn, as shown in the following graph:

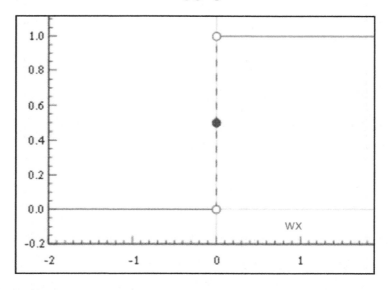

We need something different, smoother. We need a function that progressively changes from *0* to *1* with no discontinuity. Mathematically, this means that we need a continuous function that allows us to compute the derivative.

Activation function — sigmoid

The sigmoid function is defined as follows:

$$\sigma(x) = \frac{1}{1 + e^{-x}}$$

As represented in the following graph, it has small output changes in *(0, 1)* when the input varies in $(-\infty, \infty)$. Mathematically, the function is continuous. A typical sigmoid function is represented in the following graph:

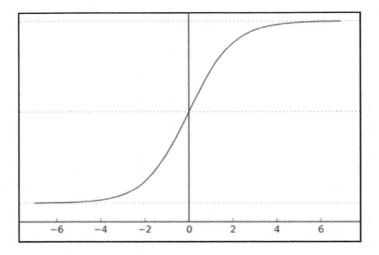

A neuron can use the sigmoid for computing the nonlinear function $\sigma(z = wx + b)$. Note that, if $z = wx + b$ is very large and positive, then $e^{-z} \to 0$, so $\sigma(z) \to 1$, while $z = wx + b$ if is very large and negative $e^{-z} \to \infty$ so $\sigma(z) \to 0$. In other words, a neuron with sigmoid activation has a behavior similar to the perceptron, but the changes are gradual and output values, such as *0.5539* or *0.123191*, are perfectly legitimate. In this sense, a sigmoid neuron can answer *maybe*.

Activation function — ReLU

The sigmoid is not the only kind of smooth activation function used for neural networks. Recently, a very simple function called **rectified linear unit (ReLU)** became very popular because it generates very good experimental results. A ReLU is simply defined as $f(x) = \max(0, x)$, and the nonlinear function is represented in the following graph. As you can see in the following graph, the function is zero for negative values, and it grows linearly for positive values:

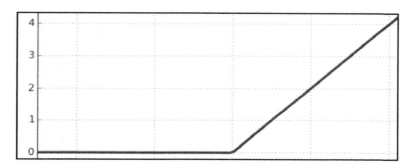

Activation functions

Sigmoid and ReLU are generally called *activation functions* in neural network jargon. In the *Testing different optimizers in Keras* section, we will see that those gradual changes, typical of sigmoid and ReLU functions, are the basic building blocks to developing a learning algorithm which adapts little by little, by progressively reducing the mistakes made by our nets. An example of using the activation function σ with the $(x_1, x_2, ..., x_m)$ input vector, $(w_1, w_2, ..., w_m)$ weight vector, b bias, and Σ summation is given in the following diagram:

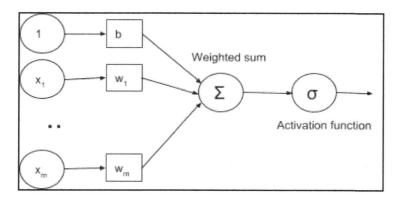

Keras supports a number of activation functions, and a full list is available at `https://kera`
`s.io/activations/`.

A real example — recognizing handwritten digits

In this section, we will build a network that can recognize handwritten numbers. For
achieving this goal, we use MNIST (for more information, refer to `http://yann.lecun.com`
`/exdb/mnist/`), a database of handwritten digits made up of a training set of 60,000
examples and a test set of 10,000 examples. The training examples are annotated by humans
with the correct answer. For instance, if the handwritten digit is the number three, then
three is simply the label associated with that example.

In machine learning, when a dataset with correct answers is available, we say that we can
perform a form of *supervised learning*. In this case, we can use training examples for tuning
up our net. Testing examples also have the correct answer associated with each digit. In this
case, however, the idea is to pretend that the label is unknown, let the network do the
prediction, and then later on, reconsider the label to evaluate how well our neural network
has learned to recognize digits. So, not unsurprisingly, testing examples are just used to test
our net.

Each MNIST image is in gray scale, and it consists of 28 x 28 pixels. A subset of these
numbers is represented in the following diagram:

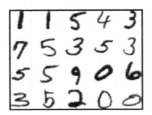

One-hot encoding — OHE

In many applications, it is convenient to transform categorical (non-numerical) features into numerical variables. For instance, the categorical feature digit with the value *d* in *[0-9]* can be encoded into a binary vector with *10* positions, which always has *0* value, except the *d*-th position where a *1* is present. This type of representation is called **one-hot encoding (OHE)** and is very common in data mining when the learning algorithm is specialized for dealing with numerical functions.

Defining a simple neural net in Keras

Here, we use Keras to define a network that recognizes MNIST handwritten digits. We start with a very simple neural network and then progressively improve it.

Keras provides suitable libraries to load the dataset and split it into training sets X_train, used for fine-tuning our net, and tests set X_test, used for assessing the performance. Data is converted into float32 for supporting GPU computation and normalized to *[0, 1]*. In addition, we load the true labels into Y_train and Y_test respectively and perform a one-hot encoding on them. Let's see the code:

```
from __future__ import print_function
import numpy as np
from keras.datasets import mnist
from keras.models import Sequential
from keras.layers.core import Dense, Activation
from keras.optimizers import SGD
from keras.utils import np_utils
np.random.seed(1671)  # for reproducibility

# network and training
NB_EPOCH = 200
BATCH_SIZE = 128
VERBOSE = 1
NB_CLASSES = 10 # number of outputs = number of digits
OPTIMIZER = SGD() # SGD optimizer, explained later in this chapter
N_HIDDEN = 128
VALIDATION_SPLIT=0.2 # how much TRAIN is reserved for VALIDATION

# data: shuffled and split between train and test sets
#
(X_train, y_train), (X_test, y_test) = mnist.load_data()
#X_train is 60000 rows of 28x28 values --> reshaped in 60000 x 784
RESHAPED = 784
#
```

```
X_train = X_train.reshape(60000, RESHAPED)
X_test = X_test.reshape(10000, RESHAPED)
X_train = X_train.astype('float32')
X_test = X_test.astype('float32')
# normalize
#
X_train /= 255
X_test /= 255
print(X_train.shape[0], 'train samples')
print(X_test.shape[0], 'test samples')
# convert class vectors to binary class matrices
Y_train = np_utils.to_categorical(y_train, NB_CLASSES)
Y_test = np_utils.to_categorical(y_test, NB_CLASSES)
```

The input layer has a neuron associated with each pixel in the image for a total of *28 x 28 = 784* neurons, one for each pixel in the MNIST images.

Typically, the values associated with each pixel are normalized in the range *[0, 1]* (which means that the intensity of each pixel is divided by 255, the maximum intensity value). The output is 10 classes, one for each digit.

The final layer is a single neuron with activation function softmax, which is a generalization of the sigmoid function. Softmax *squashes* a k-dimensional vector of arbitrary real values into a k-dimensional vector of real values in the range *(0, 1)*. In our case, it aggregates 10 answers provided by the previous layer with 10 neurons:

```
# 10 outputs
# final stage is softmax
model = Sequential()
model.add(Dense(NB_CLASSES, input_shape=(RESHAPED,)))
model.add(Activation('softmax'))
model.summary()
```

Once we define the model, we have to compile it so that it can be executed by the Keras backend (either Theano or TensorFlow). There are a few choices to be made during compilation:

- We need to select the *optimizer* that is the specific algorithm used to update weights while we train our model
- We need to select the *objective function* that is used by the optimizer to navigate the space of weights (frequently, objective functions are called *loss function*, and the process of optimization is defined as a process of loss *minimization*)
- We need to evaluate the trained model

Some common choices for the objective function (a complete list of Keras objective functions is at `https://keras.io/objectives/`) are as follows:

- **MSE**: This is the mean squared error between the predictions and the true values. Mathematically, if Υ is a vector of n predictions, and Y is the vector of n observed values, then they satisfy the following equation:

$$MSE = \frac{1}{n}\Sigma_{i=1}^{n}(\Upsilon - Y)^2$$

These objective functions average all the mistakes made for each prediction, and if the prediction is far from the true value, then this distance is made more evident by the squaring operation.

- **Binary cross-entropy**: This is the binary logarithmic loss. Suppose that our model predicts p while the target is t, then the binary cross-entropy is defined as follows:

$$-t\log(p) - (1 - t)log(1 - p)$$

This objective function is suitable for binary labels prediction.

- **Categorical cross-entropy**: This is the multiclass logarithmic loss. If the target is $t_{i,j}$ and the prediction is $p_{i,j}$, then the categorical cross-entropy is this:

$$L_i = -\Sigma_j t_{i,j} \log(p_{i,j})$$

This objective function is suitable for multiclass labels predictions. It is also the default choice in association with softmax activation.

Some common choices for metrics (a complete list of Keras metrics is at `https://keras.io/metrics/`) are as follows:

- **Accuracy**: This is the proportion of correct predictions with respect to the targets
- **Precision**: This denotes how many selected items are relevant for a multilabel classification
- **Recall**: This denotes how many selected items are relevant for a multilabel classification

Metrics are similar to objective functions, with the only difference that they are not used for training a model but only for evaluating a model. Compiling a model in Keras is easy:

```
model.compile(loss='categorical_crossentropy', optimizer=OPTIMIZER,
metrics=['accuracy'])
```

Once the model is compiled, it can be then trained with the `fit()` function, which specifies a few parameters:

- `epochs`: This is the number of times the model is exposed to the training set. At each iteration, the optimizer tries to adjust the weights so that the objective function is minimized.
- `batch_size`: This is the number of training instances observed before the optimizer performs a weight update.

Training a model in Keras is very simple. Suppose we want to iterate for NB_EPOCH steps:

```
history = model.fit(X_train, Y_train,
batch_size=BATCH_SIZE, epochs=NB_EPOCH,
verbose=VERBOSE, validation_split=VALIDATION_SPLIT)
```

 We reserved part of the training set for validation. The key idea is that we reserve a part of the training data for measuring the performance on the validation while training. This is a good practice to follow for any machine learning task, which we will adopt in all our examples.

Once the model is trained, we can evaluate it on the test set that contains new unseen examples. In this way, we can get the minimal value reached by the objective function and best value reached by the evaluation metric.

Note that the training set and the test set are, of course, rigorously separated. There is no point in evaluating a model on an example that has already been used for training. Learning is essentially a process intended to generalize unseen observations and not to memorize what is already known:

```
score = model.evaluate(X_test, Y_test, verbose=VERBOSE)
print("Test score:", score[0])
print('Test accuracy:', score[1])
```

So, congratulations, you have just defined your first neural network in Keras. A few lines of code, and your computer is able to recognize handwritten numbers. Let's run the code and see what the performance is.

Running a simple Keras net and establishing a baseline

So let's see what will happen when we run the code in the following screenshot:

```
● ● ●                         code — -bash — 118×71
gulli-macbookpro:code gulli$ python keras_MINST_V1.py
Using TensorFlow backend.
60000 train samples
10000 test samples

Layer (type)                  Output Shape          Param #     Connected to
==============================================================================
dense_1 (Dense)               (None, 10)            7850        dense_input_1[0][0]

activation_1 (Activation)     (None, 10)            0           dense_1[0][0]
==============================================================================
Total params: 7850

Train on 48000 samples, validate on 12000 samples
Epoch 1/200
48000/48000 [==============================] - 0s - loss: 1.4102 - acc: 0.6554 - val_loss: 0.9073 - val_acc: 0.8244
Epoch 2/200
48000/48000 [==============================] - 0s - loss: 0.8006 - acc: 0.8279 - val_loss: 0.6625 - val_acc: 0.8567
Epoch 3/200
48000/48000 [==============================] - 0s - loss: 0.6467 - acc: 0.8495 - val_loss: 0.5650 - val_acc: 0.8704
Epoch 4/200
48000/48000 [==============================] - 0s - loss: 0.5728 - acc: 0.8600 - val_loss: 0.5112 - val_acc: 0.8778
Epoch 5/200
48000/48000 [==============================] - 0s - loss: 0.5280 - acc: 0.8677 - val_loss: 0.4767 - val_acc: 0.8822
```

First, the net architecture is dumped, and we can see the different types of layers used, their output shape, how many parameters they need to optimize, and how they are connected. Then, the network is trained on 48,000 samples, and 12,000 are reserved for validation. Once the neural model is built, it is then tested on 10,000 samples. As you can see, Keras is internally using TensorFlow as a backend system for computation. For now, we don't go into the internals on how the training happens, but we can notice that the program runs for 200 iterations, and each time, the accuracy improves.

When the training ends, we test our model on the test set and achieve about 92.36% accuracy on training, 92.27% on validation, and 92.22% on the test.

This means that a bit less than one handwritten character out of ten is not correctly recognized. We can certainly do better than that. In the following screenshot, we can see the test accuracy:

```
Epoch 198/200
48000/48000 [==============================] - 0s - loss: 0.2761 - acc: 0.9230 - val_loss: 0.2762 - val_acc: 0.9224
Epoch 199/200
48000/48000 [==============================] - 0s - loss: 0.2760 - acc: 0.9231 - val_loss: 0.2762 - val_acc: 0.9223
Epoch 200/200
48000/48000 [==============================] - 0s - loss: 0.2758 - acc: 0.9236 - val_loss: 0.2761 - val_acc: 0.9227
 9888/10000 [==========================>.] - ETA: 0s
Test score: 0.277792117235
Test accuracy: 0.9222
gulli-macbookpro:code gulli$ ▊
```

Improving the simple net in Keras with hidden layers

We have a baseline accuracy of 92.36% on training, 92.27% on validation, and 92.22% on the test. This is a good starting point, but we can certainly improve it. Let's see how.

A first improvement is to add additional layers to our network. So, after the input layer, we have a first dense layer with the N_HIDDEN neurons and an activation function relu. This additional layer is considered *hidden* because it is not directly connected to either the input or the output. After the first hidden layer, we have a second hidden layer, again with the N_HIDDEN neurons, followed by an output layer with 10 neurons, each of which will fire when the relative digit is recognized. The following code defines this new network:

```
from __future__ import print_function
import numpy as np
from keras.datasets import mnist
from keras.models import Sequential
from keras.layers.core import Dense, Activation
from keras.optimizers import SGD
from keras.utils import np_utils
np.random.seed(1671) # for reproducibility
# network and training
NB_EPOCH = 20
BATCH_SIZE = 128
VERBOSE = 1
NB_CLASSES = 10 # number of outputs = number of digits
OPTIMIZER = SGD() # optimizer, explained later in this chapter
N_HIDDEN = 128
```

```
VALIDATION_SPLIT=0.2 # how much TRAIN is reserved for VALIDATION
# data: shuffled and split between train and test sets
(X_train, y_train), (X_test, y_test) = mnist.load_data()
#X_train is 60000 rows of 28x28 values --> reshaped in 60000 x 784
RESHAPED = 784
#
X_train = X_train.reshape(60000, RESHAPED)
X_test = X_test.reshape(10000, RESHAPED)
X_train = X_train.astype('float32')
X_test = X_test.astype('float32')
# normalize
X_train /= 255
X_test /= 255
print(X_train.shape[0], 'train samples')
print(X_test.shape[0], 'test samples')
# convert class vectors to binary class matrices
Y_train = np_utils.to_categorical(y_train, NB_CLASSES)
Y_test = np_utils.to_categorical(y_test, NB_CLASSES)
# M_HIDDEN hidden layers
# 10 outputs
# final stage is softmax
model = Sequential()
model.add(Dense(N_HIDDEN, input_shape=(RESHAPED,)))
model.add(Activation('relu'))
model.add(Dense(N_HIDDEN))
model.add(Activation('relu'))
model.add(Dense(NB_CLASSES))
model.add(Activation('softmax'))
model.summary()
model.compile(loss='categorical_crossentropy',
optimizer=OPTIMIZER,
metrics=['accuracy'])
history = model.fit(X_train, Y_train,
batch_size=BATCH_SIZE, epochs=NB_EPOCH,
verbose=VERBOSE, validation_split=VALIDATION_SPLIT)
score = model.evaluate(X_test, Y_test, verbose=VERBOSE)
print("Test score:", score[0])
print('Test accuracy:', score[1])
```

Let's run the code and see which result we get with this multilayer network. Not bad. By adding two hidden layers, we reached 94.50% on the training set, 94.63% on validation, and 94.41% on the test. This means that we gained an additional 2.2% accuracy on the test with respect to the previous network. However, we dramatically reduced the number of iterations from 200 to 20. That's good, but we want more.

If you want, you can play by yourself and see what happens if you add only one hidden layer instead of two, or if you add more than two layers. I leave this experiment as an exercise. The following screenshot shows the output of the preceding example:

```
● ● ●                        code — -bash — 118×66
gulli-macbookpro:code gulli$ python keras_MINST_V2.py
Using TensorFlow backend.
60000 train samples
10000 test samples

Layer (type)                    Output Shape        Param #     Connected to
==================================================================================================
dense_1 (Dense)                 (None, 128)         100480      dense_input_1[0][0]
_____
activation_1 (Activation)       (None, 128)         0           dense_1[0][0]
_____
dense_2 (Dense)                 (None, 128)         16512       activation_1[0][0]
_____
activation_2 (Activation)       (None, 128)         0           dense_2[0][0]
_____
dense_3 (Dense)                 (None, 10)          1290        activation_2[0][0]
_____
activation_3 (Activation)       (None, 10)          0           dense_3[0][0]
==================================================================================================
Total params: 118282

Train on 48000 samples, validate on 12000 samples
Epoch 1/20
48000/48000 [==============================] - 1s - loss: 1.5266 - acc: 0.6101 - val_loss: 0.7839 - val_acc: 0.8296
Epoch 2/20
48000/48000 [==============================] - 1s - loss: 0.6108 - acc: 0.8464 - val_loss: 0.4603 - val_acc: 0.8796
Epoch 3/20
48000/48000 [==============================] - 1s - loss: 0.4422 - acc: 0.8794 - val_loss: 0.3765 - val_acc: 0.8963
Epoch 4/20
48000/48000 [==============================] - 1s - loss: 0.3796 - acc: 0.8946 - val_loss: 0.3374 - val_acc: 0.9065
Epoch 5/20
48000/48000 [==============================] - 1s - loss: 0.3450 - acc: 0.9027 - val_loss: 0.3119 - val_acc: 0.9116
Epoch 6/20
48000/48000 [==============================] - 1s - loss: 0.3214 - acc: 0.9090 - val_loss: 0.2940 - val_acc: 0.9165
Epoch 7/20
48000/48000 [==============================] - 1s - loss: 0.3033 - acc: 0.9148 - val_loss: 0.2794 - val_acc: 0.9213
Epoch 8/20
48000/48000 [==============================] - 1s - loss: 0.2885 - acc: 0.9181 - val_loss: 0.2668 - val_acc: 0.9251
Epoch 9/20
48000/48000 [==============================] - 1s - loss: 0.2763 - acc: 0.9220 - val_loss: 0.2569 - val_acc: 0.9287
Epoch 10/20
48000/48000 [==============================] - 1s - loss: 0.2654 - acc: 0.9245 - val_loss: 0.2491 - val_acc: 0.9304
Epoch 11/20
48000/48000 [==============================] - 1s - loss: 0.2556 - acc: 0.9274 - val_loss: 0.2400 - val_acc: 0.9335
Epoch 12/20
48000/48000 [==============================] - 1s - loss: 0.2464 - acc: 0.9299 - val_loss: 0.2329 - val_acc: 0.9355
Epoch 13/20
48000/48000 [==============================] - 1s - loss: 0.2382 - acc: 0.9321 - val_loss: 0.2279 - val_acc: 0.9369
Epoch 14/20
48000/48000 [==============================] - 1s - loss: 0.2309 - acc: 0.9342 - val_loss: 0.2208 - val_acc: 0.9388
Epoch 15/20
48000/48000 [==============================] - 1s - loss: 0.2237 - acc: 0.9365 - val_loss: 0.2140 - val_acc: 0.9413
Epoch 16/20
48000/48000 [==============================] - 1s - loss: 0.2172 - acc: 0.9380 - val_loss: 0.2085 - val_acc: 0.9423
Epoch 17/20
48000/48000 [==============================] - 1s - loss: 0.2110 - acc: 0.9397 - val_loss: 0.2035 - val_acc: 0.9435
Epoch 18/20
48000/48000 [==============================] - 1s - loss: 0.2051 - acc: 0.9415 - val_loss: 0.1993 - val_acc: 0.9445
Epoch 19/20
48000/48000 [==============================] - 1s - loss: 0.1997 - acc: 0.9427 - val_loss: 0.1954 - val_acc: 0.9461
Epoch 20/20
48000/48000 [==============================] - 1s - loss: 0.1947 - acc: 0.9450 - val_loss: 0.1914 - val_acc: 0.9463
 9696/10000 [=========================>.] - ETA: 0s
Test score: 0.191052276902
Test accuracy: 0.9441
gulli-macbookpro:code gulli$ █
```

Further improving the simple net in Keras with dropout

Now our baseline is 94.50% on the training set, 94.63% on validation, and 94.41% on the test. A second improvement is very simple. We decide to randomly drop with the dropout probability some of the values propagated inside our internal dense network of hidden layers. In machine learning, this is a well-known form of regularization. Surprisingly enough, this idea of randomly dropping a few values can improve our performance:

```python
from __future__ import print_function
import numpy as np
from keras.datasets import mnist
from keras.models import Sequential
from keras.layers.core import Dense, Dropout, Activation
from keras.optimizers import SGD
from keras.utils import np_utils
np.random.seed(1671) # for reproducibility
# network and training
NB_EPOCH = 250
BATCH_SIZE = 128
VERBOSE = 1
NB_CLASSES = 10 # number of outputs = number of digits
OPTIMIZER = SGD() # optimizer, explained later in this chapter
N_HIDDEN = 128
VALIDATION_SPLIT=0.2 # how much TRAIN is reserved for VALIDATION
DROPOUT = 0.3
# data: shuffled and split between train and test sets
(X_train, y_train), (X_test, y_test) = mnist.load_data()
#X_train is 60000 rows of 28x28 values --> reshaped in 60000 x 784
RESHAPED = 784
#
X_train = X_train.reshape(60000, RESHAPED)
X_test = X_test.reshape(10000, RESHAPED)
X_train = X_train.astype('float32')
X_test = X_test.astype('float32')
# normalize
X_train /= 255
X_test /= 255
# convert class vectors to binary class matrices
Y_train = np_utils.to_categorical(y_train, NB_CLASSES)
Y_test = np_utils.to_categorical(y_test, NB_CLASSES)
# M_HIDDEN hidden layers 10 outputs
model = Sequential()
model.add(Dense(N_HIDDEN, input_shape=(RESHAPED,)))
model.add(Activation('relu'))
model.add(Dropout(DROPOUT))
```

```
model.add(Dense(N_HIDDEN))
model.add(Activation('relu'))
model.add(Dropout(DROPOUT))
model.add(Dense(NB_CLASSES))
model.add(Activation('softmax'))
model.summary()
model.compile(loss='categorical_crossentropy',
optimizer=OPTIMIZER,
metrics=['accuracy'])
history = model.fit(X_train, Y_train,
batch_size=BATCH_SIZE, epochs=NB_EPOCH,
verbose=VERBOSE, validation_split=VALIDATION_SPLIT)
score = model.evaluate(X_test, Y_test, verbose=VERBOSE)
print("Test score:", score[0])
print('Test accuracy:', score[1])
```

Let's run the code for 20 iterations as previously done, and we will see that this net achieves an accuracy of 91.54% on the training, 94.48% on validation, and 94.25% on the test:

```
● ● ●                              code — -bash — 118×70
gulli-macbookpro:code gulli$ python keras_MINST_V3_1.py
Using TensorFlow backend.
60000 train samples
10000 test samples

Layer (type)                    Output Shape          Param #      Connected to
====================================================================================================
dense_1 (Dense)                 (None, 128)           100480       dense_input_1[0][0]
_____
activation_1 (Activation)       (None, 128)           0            dense_1[0][0]
_____
dropout_1 (Dropout)             (None, 128)           0            activation_1[0][0]
_____
dense_2 (Dense)                 (None, 128)           16512        dropout_1[0][0]
_____
activation_2 (Activation)       (None, 128)           0            dense_2[0][0]
_____
dropout_2 (Dropout)             (None, 128)           0            activation_2[0][0]
_____
dense_3 (Dense)                 (None, 10)            1290         dropout_2[0][0]
_____
activation_3 (Activation)       (None, 10)            0            dense_3[0][0]
====================================================================================================
Total params: 118282
_____
Train on 48000 samples, validate on 12000 samples
Epoch 1/20
48000/48000 [==============================] - 1s - loss: 1.7206 - acc: 0.4625 - val_loss: 0.9125 - val_acc: 0.8036
Epoch 2/20
48000/48000 [==============================] - 1s - loss: 0.9254 - acc: 0.7149 - val_loss: 0.5374 - val_acc: 0.8621
Epoch 3/20
48000/48000 [==============================] - 1s - loss: 0.6938 - acc: 0.7883 - val_loss: 0.4240 - val_acc: 0.8872
Epoch 4/20
48000/48000 [==============================] - 1s - loss: 0.5917 - acc: 0.8205 - val_loss: 0.3724 - val_acc: 0.8958
Epoch 5/20
48000/48000 [==============================] - 1s - loss: 0.5307 - acc: 0.8398 - val_loss: 0.3370 - val_acc: 0.9038
Epoch 6/20
48000/48000 [==============================] - 1s - loss: 0.4868 - acc: 0.8546 - val_loss: 0.3126 - val_acc: 0.9084
Epoch 7/20
48000/48000 [==============================] - 1s - loss: 0.4563 - acc: 0.8654 - val_loss: 0.2939 - val_acc: 0.9126
Epoch 8/20
48000/48000 [==============================] - 1s - loss: 0.4322 - acc: 0.8726 - val_loss: 0.2789 - val_acc: 0.9173
Epoch 9/20
48000/48000 [==============================] - 1s - loss: 0.4061 - acc: 0.8799 - val_loss: 0.2666 - val_acc: 0.9196
Epoch 10/20
48000/48000 [==============================] - 1s - loss: 0.3908 - acc: 0.8848 - val_loss: 0.2556 - val_acc: 0.9236
Epoch 11/20
48000/48000 [==============================] - 1s - loss: 0.3758 - acc: 0.8893 - val_loss: 0.2463 - val_acc: 0.9263
Epoch 12/20
48000/48000 [==============================] - 1s - loss: 0.3592 - acc: 0.8938 - val_loss: 0.2372 - val_acc: 0.9297
Epoch 13/20
48000/48000 [==============================] - 1s - loss: 0.3491 - acc: 0.8970 - val_loss: 0.2294 - val_acc: 0.9323
Epoch 14/20
48000/48000 [==============================] - 1s - loss: 0.3361 - acc: 0.9009 - val_loss: 0.2224 - val_acc: 0.9344
Epoch 15/20
48000/48000 [==============================] - 1s - loss: 0.3266 - acc: 0.9036 - val_loss: 0.2165 - val_acc: 0.9348
Epoch 16/20
48000/48000 [==============================] - 1s - loss: 0.3182 - acc: 0.9064 - val_loss: 0.2102 - val_acc: 0.9371
Epoch 17/20
48000/48000 [==============================] - 1s - loss: 0.3073 - acc: 0.9103 - val_loss: 0.2035 - val_acc: 0.9395
Epoch 18/20
48000/48000 [==============================] - 1s - loss: 0.2998 - acc: 0.9109 - val_loss: 0.1987 - val_acc: 0.9418
Epoch 19/20
48000/48000 [==============================] - 1s - loss: 0.2930 - acc: 0.9131 - val_loss: 0.1930 - val_acc: 0.9423
Epoch 20/20
48000/48000 [==============================] - 1s - loss: 0.2855 - acc: 0.9154 - val_loss: 0.1893 - val_acc: 0.9448
 9888/10000 [==========================>.] - ETA: 0s
Test score: 0.191873697177
Test accuracy: 0.9425
gulli-macbookpro:code gulli$ ▉
```

Note that training accuracy should still be above the test accuracy, otherwise we are not training long enough. So let's try to increase significantly the number of epochs up to 250, and we get 98.1% accuracy on training, 97.73% on validation, and 97.7% on the test:

```
Epoch 248/250
48000/48000 [==============================] - 1s - loss: 0.0630 - acc: 0.9804 - val_loss: 0.0785 - val_acc: 0.9769
Epoch 249/250
48000/48000 [==============================] - 1s - loss: 0.0634 - acc: 0.9799 - val_loss: 0.0789 - val_acc: 0.9775
Epoch 250/250
48000/48000 [==============================] - 1s - loss: 0.0616 - acc: 0.9810 - val_loss: 0.0787 - val_acc: 0.9773
 9696/10000 [===========================>.] - ETA: 0s
Test score: 0.0726828922328
Test accuracy: 0.9777
gulli-macbookpro:code gulli$ ▋
```

It is useful to observe how accuracy increases on training and test sets when the number of epochs increases. As you can see in the following graph, these two curves touch at about 250 epochs, and therefore, there is no need to train further after that point:

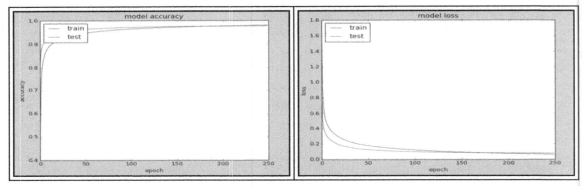

Note that it has been frequently observed that networks with random dropout in internal hidden layers can generalize better on unseen examples contained in test sets. Intuitively, one can think of this as each neuron becoming more capable because it knows it cannot depend on its neighbors. During testing, there is no dropout, so we are now using all our highly tuned neurons. In short, it is generally a good approach to test how a net performs when some dropout function is adopted.

Testing different optimizers in Keras

We have defined and used a network; it is useful to start giving an intuition about how networks are trained. Let's focus on one popular training technique known as **gradient descent** (**GD**). Imagine a generic cost function $C(w)$ in one single variable w like in the following graph:

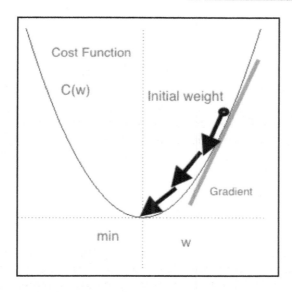

The gradient descent can be seen as a hiker who aims at climbing down a mountain into a valley. The mountain represents the function C, while the valley represents the minimum C_{min}. The hiker has a starting point w_0. The hiker moves little by little. At each step r, the gradient is the direction of maximum increase. Mathematically, this direction is the value of the partial derivative $\frac{ac}{\partial w}$ evaluated at point w_r reached at step r. Therefore by taking the opposite direction, $-\frac{ac}{\partial w}(w_r)$, the hiker can move towards the valley. At each step, the hiker can decide what the leg length is before the next step. This is the *learning rate* $\eta \geq 0$ in gradient descent jargon. Note that if η is too small, then the hiker will move slowly. However, if η is too high, then the hiker will possibly miss the valley.

Now you should remember that a sigmoid is a continuous function, and it is possible to compute the derivative. It can be proven that the sigmoid is shown as follows:

$$\sigma(x) = \frac{1}{1 + e^{-x}}$$

It has the following derivative:

$$\frac{d\sigma(x)}{d(x)} = \sigma(x)(1 - \sigma(x))$$

ReLU is not differentiable in *0*. We can, however, extend the first derivative in *0* to a function over the whole domain by choosing it to be either *0* or *1*. The point-wise derivative of ReLU $y = \max(0, x)$ is as follows:

$$\frac{dy}{dx} = \begin{cases} 0 & x \leq 0 \\ 1 & x > 0 \end{cases}$$

Once we have the derivative, it is possible to optimize the nets with a gradient descent technique. Keras uses its backend (either TensorFlow or Theano) for computing the derivative on our behalf so we don't need to worry about implementing or computing it. We just choose the activation function, and Keras computes its derivative on our behalf.

A neural network is essentially a composition of multiple functions with thousands, and sometimes millions, of parameters. Each network layer computes a function whose error should be minimized in order to improve the accuracy observed during the learning phase. When we discuss backpropagation, we will discover that the minimization game is a bit more complex than our toy example. However, it is still based on the same intuition of descending a valley.

Keras implements a fast variant of gradient descent known as **stochastic gradient descent (SGD)** and two more advanced optimization techniques known as **RMSprop** and **Adam**. RMSprop and Adam include the concept of momentum (a velocity component) in addition to the acceleration component that SGD has. This allows faster convergence at the cost of more computation. A full list of Keras-supported optimizers is at `https://keras.io/optim izers/`. SGD was our default choice so far. So now let's try the other two. It is very simple, we just need to change few lines:

```
from keras.optimizers import RMSprop, Adam
...
OPTIMIZER = RMSprop() # optimizer,
```

That's it. Let's test it as shown in the following screenshot:

```
code — python keras_MINST_V4.py — 118×71
gulli-macbookpro:code gulli$ python keras_MINST_V4.py
Using TensorFlow backend.
60000 train samples
10000 test samples

Layer (type)                     Output Shape          Param #     Connected to
====================================================================================================
dense_1 (Dense)                  (None, 128)           100480      dense_input_1[0][0]
_____
activation_1 (Activation)        (None, 128)           0           dense_1[0][0]
_____
dropout_1 (Dropout)              (None, 128)           0           activation_1[0][0]
_____
dense_2 (Dense)                  (None, 128)           16512       dropout_1[0][0]
_____
activation_2 (Activation)        (None, 128)           0           dense_2[0][0]
_____
dropout_2 (Dropout)              (None, 128)           0           activation_2[0][0]
_____
dense_3 (Dense)                  (None, 10)            1290        dropout_2[0][0]
_____
activation_3 (Activation)        (None, 10)            0           dense_3[0][0]
====================================================================================================
Total params: 118282
Train on 48000 samples, validate on 12000 samples
Epoch 1/20
48000/48000 [==============================] - 2s - loss: 0.4714 - acc: 0.8571 - val_loss: 0.1780 - val_acc: 0.9478
Epoch 2/20
48000/48000 [==============================] - 1s - loss: 0.2257 - acc: 0.9328 - val_loss: 0.1350 - val_acc: 0.9608
Epoch 3/20
48000/48000 [==============================] - 1s - loss: 0.1737 - acc: 0.9477 - val_loss: 0.1217 - val_acc: 0.9643
Epoch 4/20
48000/48000 [==============================] - 1s - loss: 0.1522 - acc: 0.9542 - val_loss: 0.1095 - val_acc: 0.9687
Epoch 5/20
48000/48000 [==============================] - 1s - loss: 0.1312 - acc: 0.9609 - val_loss: 0.1039 - val_acc: 0.9703
Epoch 6/20
48000/48000 [==============================] - 1s - loss: 0.1222 - acc: 0.9640 - val_loss: 0.1004 - val_acc: 0.9710
Epoch 7/20
48000/48000 [==============================] - 1s - loss: 0.1134 - acc: 0.9660 - val_loss: 0.0985 - val_acc: 0.9730
Epoch 8/20
48000/48000 [==============================] - 1s - loss: 0.1046 - acc: 0.9688 - val_loss: 0.0975 - val_acc: 0.9739
Epoch 9/20
48000/48000 [==============================] - 1s - loss: 0.1009 - acc: 0.9705 - val_loss: 0.1014 - val_acc: 0.9732
Epoch 10/20
48000/48000 [==============================] - 1s - loss: 0.0970 - acc: 0.9717 - val_loss: 0.0967 - val_acc: 0.9748
Epoch 11/20
48000/48000 [==============================] - 1s - loss: 0.0922 - acc: 0.9726 - val_loss: 0.0956 - val_acc: 0.9764
Epoch 12/20
48000/48000 [==============================] - 1s - loss: 0.0874 - acc: 0.9751 - val_loss: 0.0975 - val_acc: 0.9747
Epoch 13/20
48000/48000 [==============================] - 1s - loss: 0.0853 - acc: 0.9750 - val_loss: 0.0980 - val_acc: 0.9760
Epoch 14/20
48000/48000 [==============================] - 1s - loss: 0.0807 - acc: 0.9754 - val_loss: 0.1003 - val_acc: 0.9760
Epoch 15/20
48000/48000 [==============================] - 1s - loss: 0.0777 - acc: 0.9771 - val_loss: 0.1025 - val_acc: 0.9766
Epoch 16/20
48000/48000 [==============================] - 1s.- loss: 0.0742 - acc: 0.9778 - val_loss: 0.1074 - val_acc: 0.9765
Epoch 17/20
48000/48000 [==============================] - 1s - loss: 0.0746 - acc: 0.9786 - val_loss: 0.1104 - val_acc: 0.9750
Epoch 18/20
48000/48000 [==============================] - 1s - loss: 0.0730 - acc: 0.9788 - val_loss: 0.1046 - val_acc: 0.9776
Epoch 19/20
48000/48000 [==============================] - 1s - loss: 0.0711 - acc: 0.9793 - val_loss: 0.1112 - val_acc: 0.9769
Epoch 20/20
48000/48000 [==============================] - 1s - loss: 0.0725 - acc: 0.9797 - val_loss: 0.1060 - val_acc: 0.9759
 9888/10000 [=============================>.] - ETA: 0s
Test score: 0.0962571567255
Test accuracy: 0.9784
['acc', 'loss', 'val_acc', 'val_loss']
```

As you can see in the preceding screenshot, RMSprop is faster than SDG since we are able to achieve an accuracy of 97.97% on training, 97.59% on validation, and 97.84% on the test improving SDG with only 20 iterations. For the sake of completeness, let's see how the accuracy and loss change with the number of epochs, as shown in the following graphs:

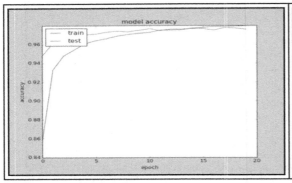 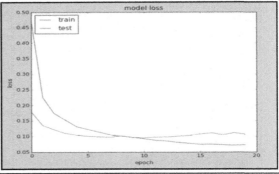

OK, let's try the other optimizer, `Adam()`. It is pretty simple, as follows:

```
OPTIMIZER = Adam() # optimizer
```

As we have seen, Adam is slightly better. With Adam, we achieve 98.28% accuracy on training, 98.03% on validation, and 97.93% on the test with 20 iterations, as shown in the following graphs:

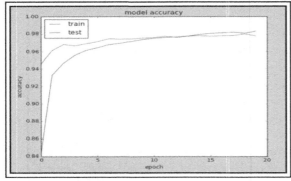 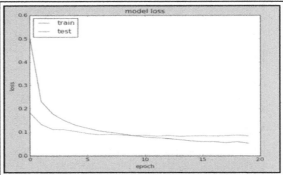

This is our fifth variant, and remember that our initial baseline was at 92.36%.

So far, we made progressive improvements; however, the gains are now more and more difficult. Note that we are optimizing with a dropout of 30%. For the sake of completeness, it could be useful to report the accuracy on the test only for other dropout values with `Adam()` chosen as optimizer, as shown in the following graph:

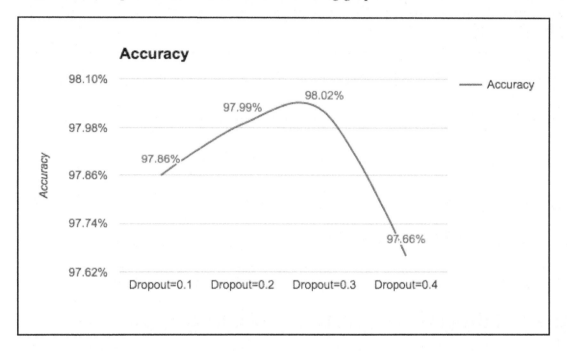

Increasing the number of epochs

Let's make another attempt and increase the number of epochs used for training from 20 to 200. Unfortunately, this choice increases our computation time by 10, but it gives us no gain. The experiment is unsuccessful, but we have learned that if we spend more time learning, we will not necessarily improve. Learning is more about adopting smart techniques and not necessarily about the time spent in computations. Let's keep track of our sixth variant in the following graph:

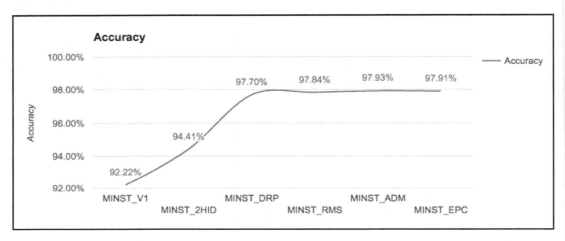

Controlling the optimizer learning rate

There is another attempt we can make, which is changing the learning parameter for our optimizer. As you can see in the following graph, the optimal value is somewhere close to *0.001*, which is the default learning rate for the optimer. Good! Adam works well out of the box:

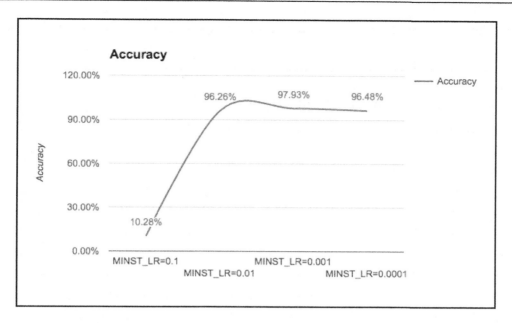

Increasing the number of internal hidden neurons

We can make yet another attempt, that is, changing the number of internal hidden neurons. We report the results of the experiments with an increasing number of hidden neurons. We can see in the following graph that by increasing the complexity of the model, the run time increases significantly because there are more and more parameters to optimize. However, the gains that we are getting by increasing the size of the network decrease more and more as the network grows:

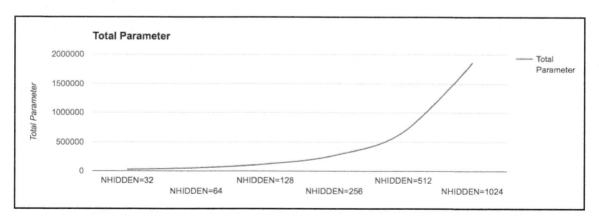

In the following graph, we show the time needed for each iteration as the number of hidden neurons grow:

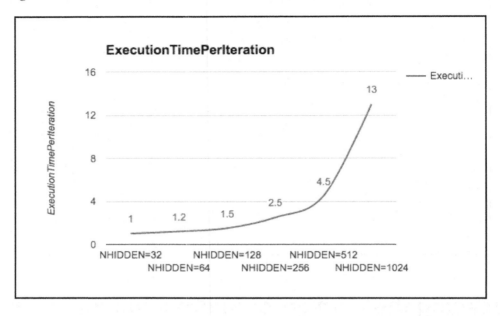

The following graph shows the accuracy as the number of hidden neurons grow:

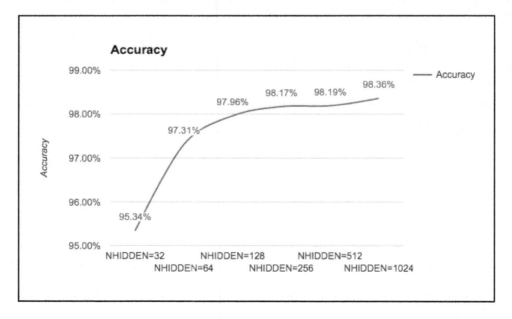

Increasing the size of batch computation

Gradient descent tries to minimize the cost function on all the examples provided in the training sets and, at the same time, for all the features provided in the input. Stochastic gradient descent is a much less expensive variant, which considers only `BATCH_SIZE` examples. So, let's see what the behavior is by changing this parameter. As you can see, the optimal accuracy value is reached for `BATCH_SIZE=128`:

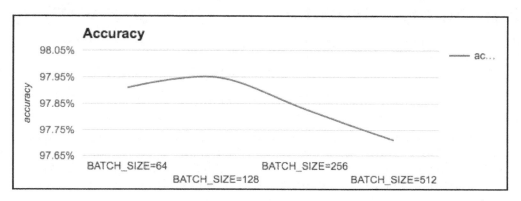

Summarizing the experiments run for recognizing handwritten charts

So, let's summarize: with five different variants, we were able to improve our performance from 92.36% to 97.93%. First, we defined a simple layer network in Keras. Then, we improved the performance by adding some hidden layers. After that, we improved the performance on the test set by adding a few random dropouts to our network and by experimenting with different types of optimizers. Current results are summarized in the following table:

Model/Accuracy	Training	Validation	Test
Simple	92.36%	92.37%	92.22%
Two hidden (128)	94.50%	94.63%	94.41%
Dropout (30%)	98.10%	97.73%	97.7% (200 epochs)
RMSprop	97.97%	97.59%	97.84% (20 epochs)
Adam	98.28%	98.03%	97.93% (20 epochs)

However, the next two experiments did not provide significant improvements. Increasing the number of internal neurons creates more complex models and requires more expensive computations, but it provides only marginal gains. We get the same experience if we increase the number of training epochs. A final experiment consisted in changing the `BATCH_SIZE` for our optimizer.

Adopting regularization for avoiding overfitting

Intuitively, a good machine learning model should achieve low error on training data. Mathematically, this is equivalent to minimizing the loss function on the training data given the machine learning model built. This is expressed by the following formula.:

$$\min : \{loss(Training\ Data | Model)\}$$

However, this might not be enough. A model can become excessively complex in order to capture all the relations inherently expressed by the training data. This increase of complexity might have two negative consequences. First, a complex model might require a significant amount of time to be executed. Second, a complex model can achieve very good performance on training data—because all the inherent relations in trained data are memorized, but not so good performance on validation data—as the model is not able to generalize on fresh unseen data. Again, learning is more about generalization than memorization. The following graph represents a typical loss function decreasing on both validation and training sets. However, a certain point the loss on validation starts to increase because of overfitting:

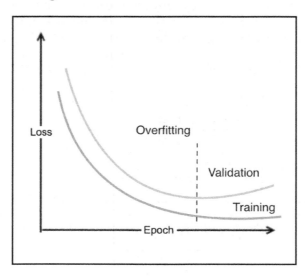

As a rule of thumb, if during the training we see that the loss increases on validation, after an initial decrease, then we have a problem of model complexity that overfits training. Indeed, overfitting is the word used in machine learning for concisely describing this phenomenon.

In order to solve the overfitting problem, we need a way to capture the complexity of a model, that is, how complex a model can be. What could be the solution? Well, a model is nothing more than a vector of weights. Therefore the complexity of a model can be conveniently represented as the number of nonzero weights. In other words, if we have two models, *M1* and *M2*, achieving pretty much the same performance in terms of loss function, then we should choose the simplest model that has the minimum number of nonzero weights. We can use a hyperparameter *λ>=0* for controlling what the importance of having a simple model is, as in this formula:

$$\min : \{loss(Training\ Data|Model)\} + \lambda * complexity(Model)$$

There are three different types of regularizations used in machine learning:

- **L1 regularization** (also known as **lasso**): The complexity of the model is expressed as the sum of the absolute values of the weights
- **L2 regularization** (also known as **ridge**): The complexity of the model is expressed as the sum of the squares of the weights
- **Elastic net regularization**: The complexity of the model is captured by a combination of the two preceding techniques

Note that the same idea of regularization can be applied independently to the weights, to the model, and to the activation.

Therefore, playing with regularization can be a good way to increase the performance of a network, in particular when there is an evident situation of overfitting. This set of experiments is left as an exercise for the interested reader.

Note that Keras supports both l1, l2, and elastic net regularizations. Adding regularization is easy; for instance, here we have a 12 regularizer for kernel (the weight *W*):

```
from keras import regularizers model.add(Dense(64, input_dim=64,
kernel_regularizer=regularizers.l2(0.01)))
```

A full description of the available parameters is available at: https://keras.io/regulariz ers/.

Hyperparameters tuning

The preceding experiments gave a sense of what the opportunities for fine-tuning a net are. However, what is working for this example is not necessarily working for other examples. For a given net, there are indeed multiple parameters that can be optimized (such as the number of `hidden neurons`, `BATCH_SIZE`, number of `epochs`, and many more according to the complexity of the net itself).

Hyperparameter tuning is the process of finding the optimal combination of those parameters that minimize cost functions. The key idea is that if we have n parameters, then we can imagine that they define a space with n dimensions, and the goal is to find the point in this space which corresponds to an optimal value for the cost function. One way to achieve this goal is to create a grid in this space and systematically check for each grid vertex what the value assumed by the cost function is. In other words, the parameters are divided into buckets, and different combinations of values are checked via a brute force approach.

Predicting output

When a net is trained, it can be course be used for predictions. In Keras, this is very simple. We can use the following method:

```
# calculate predictions
predictions = model.predict(X)
```

For a given input, several types of output can be computed, including a method:

- `model.evaluate()`: This is used to compute the loss values
- `model.predict_classes()`: This is used to compute category outputs
- `model.predict_proba()`: This is used to compute class probabilities

A practical overview of backpropagation

Multilayer perceptrons learn from training data through a process called backpropagation. The process can be described as a way of progressively correcting mistakes as soon as they are detected. Let's see how this works.

Remember that each neural network layer has an associated set of weights that determines the output values for a given set of inputs. In addition to that, remember that a neural network can have multiple hidden layers.

In the beginning, all the weights have some random assignment. Then the net is activated for each input in the training set: values are propagated *forward* from the input stage through the hidden stages to the output stage where a prediction is made (note that we have kept the following diagram simple by only representing a few values with green dotted lines, but in reality, all the values are propagated forward through the network):

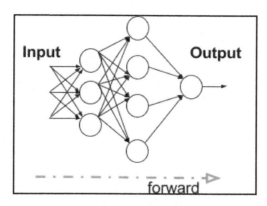

Since we know the true observed value in the training set, it is possible to calculate the error made in prediction. The key intuition for backtracking is to propagate the error back and use an appropriate optimizer algorithm, such as a gradient descent, to adjust the neural network weights with the goal of reducing the error (again for the sake of simplicity, only a few error values are represented):

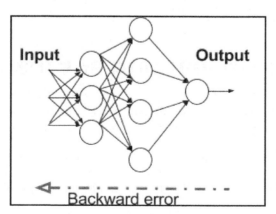

The process of forward propagation from input to output and backward propagation of errors is repeated several times until the error gets below a predefined threshold. The whole process is represented in the following diagram:

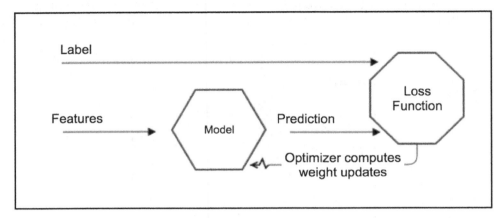

The features represent the input and the labels are here used to drive the learning process. The model is updated in such a way that the loss function is progressively minimized. In a neural network, what really matters is not the output of a single neuron but the collective weights adjusted in each layer. Therefore, the network progressively adjusts its internal weights in such a way that the prediction increases the number of labels correctly forecasted. Of course, using the right set features and having a quality labeled data is fundamental to minimizing the bias during the learning process.

Towards a deep learning approach

While playing with handwritten digit recognition, we came to the conclusion that the closer we get to the accuracy of 99%, the more difficult it is to improve. If we want to have more improvements, we definitely need a new idea. What are we missing? Think about it.

The fundamental intuition is that, so far, we lost all the information related to the local spatiality of the images. In particular, this piece of code transforms the bitmap, representing each written digit into a flat vector where the spatial locality is gone:

```
#X_train is 60000 rows of 28x28 values --> reshaped in 60000 x 784
X_train = X_train.reshape(60000, 784)
X_test = X_test.reshape(10000, 784)
```

However, this is not how our brain works. Remember that our vision is based on multiple cortex levels, each one recognizing more and more structured information, still preserving the locality. First we see single pixels, then from that, we recognize simple geometric forms and then more and more sophisticated elements such as objects, faces, human bodies, animals and so on.

In Chapter 3, *Deep Learning with ConvNets*, we will see that a particular type of deep learning network known as **convolutional neural network** (**CNN**) has been developed by taking into account both the idea of preserving the spatial locality in images (and, more generally, in any type of information) and the idea of learning via progressive levels of abstraction: with one layer, you can only learn simple patterns; with more than one layer, you can learn multiple patterns. Before discussing CNN, we need to discuss some aspects of Keras architecture and have a practical introduction to a few additional machine learning concepts. This will be the topic of the next chapters.

Summary

In this chapter, you learned the basics of neural networks, more specifically, what a perceptron is, what a multilayer perceptron is, how to define neural networks in Keras, how to progressively improve metrics once a good baseline is established, and how to fine-tune the hyperparameter's space. In addition to that, you now also have an intuitive idea of what some useful activation functions (sigmoid and ReLU) are, and how to train a network with backpropagation algorithms based on either gradient descent, on stochastic gradient descent, or on more sophisticated approaches, such as Adam and RMSprop.

In the next chapter, we will see how to install Keras on AWS, Microsoft Azure, Google Cloud, and on your own machine. In addition to that, we will provide an overview of Keras APIs.

2
Keras Installation and API

In the previous chapter, we discussed the basic principles of neural networks and provided a few examples of nets that are able to recognize MNIST handwritten numbers.

This chapter explains how to install Keras, Theano, and TensorFlow. Step by step, we will look at how to get the environment working and move from intuition to working nets in very little time. Then we will discuss how to install on a dockerized infrastructure based on containers, and in the cloud with Google GCP, Amazon AWS, and Microsoft Azure. In addition to that, we will present an overview of Keras APIs, and some commonly useful operations such as loading and saving neural networks' architectures and weights, early stopping, history saving, checkpointing, and interactions with TensorBoard and Quiver. Let us start.

By the end of this chapter, we will have covered the following topics:

- Installing and configuring Keras
- Keras architecture

Installing Keras

In the sections to follow, we will show how to install Keras on multiple platforms.

Step 1 — install some useful dependencies

First, we install the numpy package, which provides support for large, multidimensional arrays and matrices as well as high-level mathematical functions. Then we install scipy, a library used for scientific computation. After that, it might be appropriate to install scikit-learn, a package considered the Python Swiss army knife for machine learning. In this case, we will use it for data exploration. Optionally, it could be useful to install pillow, a library useful for image processing, and h5py, a library useful for data serialization used by Keras for model saving. A single command line is enough for installing what is needed. Alternatively, one can install Anaconda Python, which will automatically install numpy, scipy, scikit-learn, h5py, pillow, and a lot of other libraries that are needed for scientific computing (for more information, refer to: *Batch Normalization: Accelerating Deep Network Training by Reducing Internal Covariate Shift*, by S. Ioffe and C. Szegedy, arXiv.org/abs/1502.03167, 2015). You can find the packages available in Anaconda Python at https://docs.continuum.io/anaconda/pkg-docs. The following screenshot shows how to install the packages for our work:

```
● ● ●                         code — -bash — 103×20
gulli-macbookpro:code gulli$ pip install numpy scipy scikit-learn pillow h5py
Collecting numpy
  Using cached numpy-1.11.2-cp27-cp27m-macosx_10_6_intel.macosx_10_9_intel.macosx_10_9_x86_64.macosx_10
_10_intel.macosx_10_10_x86_64.whl
Collecting scipy
  Using cached scipy-0.18.1-cp27-cp27m-macosx_10_6_intel.macosx_10_9_intel.macosx_10_9_x86_64.macosx_10
_10_intel.macosx_10_10_x86_64.whl
Collecting scikit-learn
  Using cached scikit_learn-0.18.1-cp27-cp27m-macosx_10_6_intel.macosx_10_9_intel.macosx_10_9_x86_64.ma
cosx_10_10_intel.macosx_10_10_x86_64.whl
Collecting pillow
  Using cached Pillow-3.4.2-cp27-cp27m-macosx_10_6_intel.macosx_10_9_intel.macosx_10_9_x86_64.macosx_10
_10_intel.macosx_10_10_x86_64.whl
Collecting h5py
  Using cached h5py-2.6.0-cp27-cp27m-macosx_10_6_intel.macosx_10_9_intel.macosx_10_9_x86_64.macosx_10_1
0_intel.macosx_10_10_x86_64.whl
Requirement already satisfied: six in /Users/gulli/miniconda2/lib/python2.7/site-packages (from h5py)
Installing collected packages: numpy, scipy, scikit-learn, pillow, h5py
Successfully installed h5py-2.6.0 numpy-1.11.2 pillow-3.4.2 scikit-learn-0.18.1 scipy-0.18.1
gulli-macbookpro:code gulli$
```

Step 2 — install Theano

We can use `pip` to install Theano, as shown in the following screenshot:

```
● ● ●                    google-cloud-sdk — root@7b599d0dcaeb: / — -bash — 117×8
gulli-macbookpro:google-cloud-sdk gulli$ pip install Theano
Collecting Theano
Requirement already satisfied: numpy>=1.7.1 in /Users/gulli/miniconda2/lib/python2.7/site-packages (from Theano)
Requirement already satisfied: scipy>=0.11 in /Users/gulli/miniconda2/lib/python2.7/site-packages (from Theano)
Requirement already satisfied: six>=1.9.0 in /Users/gulli/miniconda2/lib/python2.7/site-packages (from Theano)
Installing collected packages: Theano
Successfully installed Theano-0.8.2
gulli-macbookpro:google-cloud-sdk gulli$ █
```

Step 3 — install TensorFlow

Now we can install TensorFlow using the instructions found on the TensorFlow website at `https://www.tensorflow.org/versions/r0.11/get_started/os_setup.html#pip-installation`. Again, we simply use `pip` for installing the correct package, as shown in the following screenshot. For instance, if we need to use GPUs, it is important to pick the appropriate package:

```
● ● ●                        code — -bash — 103×27
gulli-macbookpro:code gulli$ export TF_BINARY_URL=https://storage.googleapis.com/tensorflow/mac/cpu/ten
sorflow-0.11.0-py2-none-any.whl
gulli-macbookpro:code gulli$ sudo pip install --upgrade $TF_BINARY_URL --ignore-installed
Collecting tensorflow==0.11.0 from https://storage.googleapis.com/tensorflow/mac/cpu/tensorflow-0.11.0-
py2-none-any.whl
  Using cached https://storage.googleapis.com/tensorflow/mac/cpu/tensorflow-0.11.0-py2-none-any.whl
Collecting mock>=2.0.0 (from tensorflow==0.11.0)
  Using cached mock-2.0.0-py2.py3-none-any.whl
Collecting protobuf==3.0.0 (from tensorflow==0.11.0)
  Using cached protobuf-3.0.0-py2.py3-none-any.whl
Collecting numpy>=1.11.0 (from tensorflow==0.11.0)
  Using cached numpy-1.11.2-cp27-cp27m-macosx_10_6_intel.macosx_10_9_intel.macosx_10_9_x86_64.macosx_10
_10_intel.macosx_10_10_x86_64.whl
Collecting wheel (from tensorflow==0.11.0)
  Using cached wheel-0.29.0-py2.py3-none-any.whl
Collecting six>=1.10.0 (from tensorflow==0.11.0)
  Using cached six-1.10.0-py2.py3-none-any.whl
Collecting funcsigs>=1; python_version < "3.3" (from mock>=2.0.0->tensorflow==0.11.0)
  Using cached funcsigs-1.0.2-py2.py3-none-any.whl
Collecting pbr>=0.11 (from mock>=2.0.0->tensorflow==0.11.0)
  Using cached pbr-1.10.0-py2.py3-none-any.whl
Collecting setuptools (from protobuf==3.0.0->tensorflow==0.11.0)
  Using cached setuptools-28.8.0-py2.py3-none-any.whl
Installing collected packages: six, funcsigs, pbr, mock, setuptools, protobuf, numpy, wheel, tensorflow
Successfully installed funcsigs-1.0.2 mock-2.0.0 numpy-1.11.2 pbr-1.10.0 protobuf-3.0.0 setuptools-28.8
.0 six-1.10.0 tensorflow-0.11.0 wheel-0.29.0
gulli-macbookpro:code gulli$ █
```

Step 4 — install Keras

Now we can simply install Keras and start testing the installed environment. Pretty simple; let's use `pip` again, as shown in this screenshot:

```
● ● ●                    code — -bash — 103×14
gulli-macbookpro:code gulli$ pip install keras
Collecting keras
Requirement already satisfied: theano in /Users/gulli/miniconda2/lib/python2.7/site-packages (from kera
s)
Requirement already satisfied: pyyaml in /Users/gulli/miniconda2/lib/python2.7/site-packages (from kera
s)
Requirement already satisfied: six in /Users/gulli/miniconda2/lib/python2.7/site-packages (from keras)
Requirement already satisfied: numpy>=1.9.1 in /Users/gulli/miniconda2/lib/python2.7/site-packages (fro
m theano->keras)
Requirement already satisfied: scipy>=0.14 in /Users/gulli/miniconda2/lib/python2.7/site-packages (from
 theano->keras)
Installing collected packages: keras
Successfully installed keras-1.1.1
gulli-macbookpro:code gulli$
```

Step 5 — testing Theano, TensorFlow, and Keras

Now let's test the environment. First let's look at how to define the sigmoid function in Theano. As you see, it is very simple; we just write the mathematical formula and compute the function element-wise on a matrix. Just run the Python Shell and write the code as shown in the following screenshot to get the result:

```
● ● ●                    code — python — 103×9
>>> import theano
>>> import theano.tensor as T
>>> x = T.dmatrix('x')
>>> s = 1 / (1 + T.exp(-x))
>>> logistic = theano.function([x], s)
>>> logistic([[0, 1], [-1, -2]])
array([[ 0.5       ,  0.73105858],
       [ 0.26894142,  0.11920292]])
>>>
```

So, Theano works. Let's test TensorFlow by simply importing the MNIST dataset as shown in the following screenshot. We have already seen, in Chapter 1, *Neural Networks Foundations*, a few working examples of the Keras network:

```
gulli-macbookpro:code gulli$ python
Python 2.7.12 |Continuum Analytics, Inc.| (default, Jul  2 2016, 17:43:17)
[GCC 4.2.1 (Based on Apple Inc. build 5658) (LLVM build 2336.11.00)] on darwin
Type "help", "copyright", "credits" or "license" for more information.
Anaconda is brought to you by Continuum Analytics.
Please check out: http://continuum.io/thanks and https://anaconda.org
>>> from tensorflow.examples.tutorials.mnist import input_data
>>> mnist = input_data.read_data_sets("MNIST_data/", one_hot=True)
Successfully downloaded train-images-idx3-ubyte.gz 9912422 bytes.
Extracting MNIST_data/train-images-idx3-ubyte.gz
Successfully downloaded train-labels-idx1-ubyte.gz 28881 bytes.
Extracting MNIST_data/train-labels-idx1-ubyte.gz
Successfully downloaded t10k-images-idx3-ubyte.gz 1648877 bytes.
Extracting MNIST_data/t10k-images-idx3-ubyte.gz
Successfully downloaded t10k-labels-idx1-ubyte.gz 4542 bytes.
Extracting MNIST_data/t10k-labels-idx1-ubyte.gz
>>>
```

Configuring Keras

Keras has a very minimalist configuration file. Let's load it with a vi session. The parameters are very simple:

Parameters	Values
image_dim_ordering	Can be either tf for the TensorFlow image ordering or th for Theano image ordering
epsilon	The epsilon value used during computation
floatx	Can be either float32 or float64
backend	Can be either tensorflow or theano

The `image_dim_ordering` of `th` value gives you a somewhat non-intuitive dimension ordering for images (depth, width, and height), instead of (width, height, and depth), for `tf`. The following are the default parameters in my machine:

```
code — vi ~/.keras/keras.json — 103×8
{
    "image_dim_ordering": "th",
    "epsilon": 1e-07,
    "floatx": "float32",
    "backend": "tensorflow"
}
~
"~/.keras/keras.json" [noeol] 6L, 113C
```

 If you install a GPU-enabled TensorFlow version, then Keras will automatically use your configured GPU when TensorFlow is selected as the backend.

Installing Keras on Docker

One of the easiest ways to get started with TensorFlow and Keras is running in a Docker container. A convenient solution is to use a predefined Docker image for deep learning created by the community that contains all the popular DL frameworks (TensorFlow, Theano, Torch, Caffe, and so on). Refer to the GitHub repository at `https://github.com/s aiprashanths/dl-docker` for the code files. Assuming that you already have Docker up and running (for more information, refer to `https://www.docker.com/products/overview`), installing it is pretty simple and is shown as follows:

```
gulli-macbookpro:dl-docker gulli$ git clone https://github.com/saiprashanths/dl-docker
.git
Cloning into 'dl-docker'...
remote: Counting objects: 89, done.
remote: Total 89 (delta 0), reused 0 (delta 0), pack-reused 89
Unpacking objects: 100% (89/89), done.
gulli-macbookpro:dl-docker gulli$ ▮
```

The following screenshot, says something like, after getting the image from Git, we build the Docker image:

```
[gulli-macbookpro:dl-docker gulli$ cd dl-docker/
[gulli-macbookpro:dl-docker gulli$ docker build -t floydhub/dl-docker:cpu -f Dockerfile]
.cpu .
Sending build context to Docker daemon 284.2 kB
Step 1 : FROM ubuntu:14.04
 ---> 3f755ca42730
Step 2 : MAINTAINER Sai Soundararaj <saip@outlook.com>
 ---> Using cache
 ---> af02b42bde1c
Step 3 : ARG THEANO_VERSION=rel-0.8.2
 ---> Using cache
 ---> c8d03ba70cff
Step 4 : ARG TENSORFLOW_VERSION=0.8.0
 ---> Using cache
 ---> de0ed51e5732
Step 5 : ARG TENSORFLOW_ARCH=cpu
 ---> Using cache
 ---> 270d4bfbccaa
Step 6 : ARG KERAS_VERSION=1.0.3
 ---> Using cache
 ---> 61219a95474f
Step 7 : ARG LASAGNE_VERSION=v0.1
 ---> Using cache
 ---> 585e125f1e76
Step 8 : ARG TORCH_VERSION=latest
 ---> Using cache
 ---> fa5c4246c2ec
Step 9 : ARG CAFFE_VERSION=master
 ---> Using cache
 ---> 989ad8491f04
Step 10 : RUN apt-get update && apt-get install -y          bc          build-
```

In this screenshot, we see how to run it:

```
[gulli-macbookpro:dl-docker gulli$ docker run -it -p 8888:8888 -p 6006:6006 floydhub/dl]
-docker:cpu bash
[root@780e0d54bfc0:~# ls
caffe  iTorch  run_jupyter.sh  torch
root@780e0d54bfc0:~#
```

From within the container, it is possible to activate support for Jupyter Notebooks (for more information, refer to `http://jupyter.org/`):

```
root@780e0d54bfc0:~# sh run_jupyter.sh
[I 10:51:17.489 NotebookApp] Copying /root/.ipython/kernels -> /root/.local/share/jupy
ter/kernels
[I 10:51:17.498 NotebookApp] Writing notebook server cookie secret to /root/.local/sha
re/jupyter/runtime/notebook_cookie_secret
[W 10:51:17.520 NotebookApp] WARNING: The notebook server is listening on all IP addre
sses and not using encryption. This is not recommended.
[I 10:51:17.536 NotebookApp] Serving notebooks from local directory: /root
[I 10:51:17.536 NotebookApp] 0 active kernels
[I 10:51:17.537 NotebookApp] The Jupyter Notebook is running at: http://[all ip addres
ses on your system]:8888/?token=503b59dc969d43f588638e3bd153dd1525837ff46d7b1eb9
[I 10:51:17.537 NotebookApp] Use Control-C to stop this server and shut down all kerne
ls (twice to skip confirmation).
[C 10:51:17.539 NotebookApp]

    Copy/paste this URL into your browser when you connect for the first time,
    to login with a token:
        http://localhost:8888/?token=503b59dc969d43f588638e3bd153dd1525837ff46d7b1eb9
[I 10:51:32.547 NotebookApp] 302 GET / (172.17.0.1) 0.60ms
[I 10:51:32.553 NotebookApp] 302 GET /tree? (172.17.0.1) 0.86ms
[I 10:51:40.207 NotebookApp] 302 GET /?token=503b59dc969d43f588638e3bd153dd1525837ff46
d7b1eb9 (172.17.0.1) 0.36ms
```

Access it directly from the host machine on port:

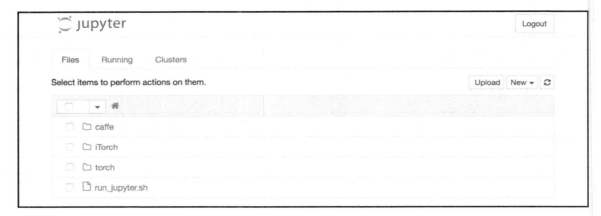

It is also possible to access TensorBoard (for more information, refer to `https://www.tenso rflow.org/how_tos/summaries_and_tensorboard/`) with the help of the command in the screenshot that follows, which is discussed in the next section:

```
root@7b599d0dcaeb:~# tensorboard --logdir .
```

After running the preceding command, you will be redirected to the following page:

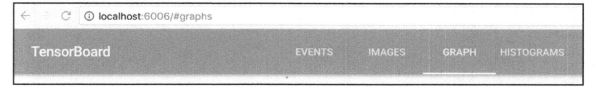

Installing Keras on Google Cloud ML

Installing Keras on Google Cloud is very simple. First, we can install Google Cloud (for the downloadable file, refer to `https://cloud.google.com/sdk/`), a command-line interface for Google Cloud Platform; then we can use CloudML, a managed service that enables us to easily build machine, learning models with TensorFlow. Before using Keras, let's use Google Cloud with TensorFlow to train an MNIST example available on GitHub. The code is local and training happens in the cloud:

```
gulli-macbookpro:google-cloud-sdk gulli$ git clone https://github.com/GoogleCloudPlatform/cloudml-samples/
Cloning into 'cloudml-samples'...
remote: Counting objects: 118, done.
remote: Total 118 (delta 0), reused 0 (delta 0), pack-reused 118
Receiving objects: 100% (118/118), 84.40 KiB | 0 bytes/s, done.
Resolving deltas: 100% (49/49), done.
gulli-macbookpro:google-cloud-sdk gulli$
```

In the following screenshot, you can see how to run a training session:

```
gulli-macbookpro:codeBook gulli$ cd cloudml-samples/mnist/trainable/
gulli-macbookpro:trainable gulli$ ls
trainer
gulli-macbookpro:trainable gulli$ gcloud beta ml local train   --package-path=trainer   --module-name=trainer.task
Successfully downloaded train-images-idx3-ubyte.gz 9912422 bytes.
Extracting /var/folders/dx/s5b40ll92sz_sls6btf35mjr00cn0l/T/tmpcARkfj/train-images-idx3-ubyte.gz
Successfully downloaded train-labels-idx1-ubyte.gz 28881 bytes.
Extracting /var/folders/dx/s5b40ll92sz_sls6btf35mjr00cn0l/T/tmpcARkfj/train-labels-idx1-ubyte.gz
Successfully downloaded t10k-images-idx3-ubyte.gz 1648877 bytes.
Extracting /var/folders/dx/s5b40ll92sz_sls6btf35mjr00cn0l/T/tmpcARkfj/t10k-images-idx3-ubyte.gz
Successfully downloaded t10k-labels-idx1-ubyte.gz 4542 bytes.
Extracting /var/folders/dx/s5b40ll92sz_sls6btf35mjr00cn0l/T/tmpcARkfj/t10k-labels-idx1-ubyte.gz
Step 0: loss = 2.32 (0.018 sec)
Step 100: loss = 2.19 (0.002 sec)
Step 200: loss = 1.94 (0.002 sec)
Step 300: loss = 1.64 (0.002 sec)
Step 400: loss = 1.30 (0.002 sec)
Step 500: loss = 0.95 (0.002 sec)
Step 600: loss = 0.80 (0.002 sec)
Step 700: loss = 0.67 (0.002 sec)
Step 800: loss = 0.62 (0.002 sec)
Step 900: loss = 0.48 (0.002 sec)
Training Data Eval:
  Num examples: 55000  Num correct: 47295  Precision @ 1: 0.8599
Validation Data Eval:
  Num examples: 5000  Num correct: 4347  Precision @ 1: 0.8694
Test Data Eval:
  Num examples: 10000  Num correct: 8649  Precision @ 1: 0.8649
Step 1000: loss = 0.58 (0.018 sec)
Step 1100: loss = 0.49 (0.115 sec)
Step 1200: loss = 0.49 (0.002 sec)
Step 1300: loss = 0.48 (0.002 sec)
Step 1400: loss = 0.46 (0.002 sec)
Step 1500: loss = 0.34 (0.002 sec)
Step 1600: loss = 0.49 (0.002 sec)
Step 1700: loss = 0.29 (0.002 sec)
Step 1800: loss = 0.35 (0.002 sec)
Step 1900: loss = 0.39 (0.002 sec)
Training Data Eval:
  Num examples: 55000  Num correct: 49243  Precision @ 1: 0.8953
Validation Data Eval:
  Num examples: 5000  Num correct: 4519  Precision @ 1: 0.9038
Test Data Eval:
  Num examples: 10000  Num correct: 9000  Precision @ 1: 0.9000
gulli-macbookpro:trainable gulli$ ▊
```

We can use TensorBoard to show how cross-entropy decreases across iterations:

```
gulli-macbookpro:trainable gulli$ tensorboard --logdir=data/ --port=8080
Starting TensorBoard 29 on port 8080
```

In the next screenshot, we see the graph of cross-entropy:

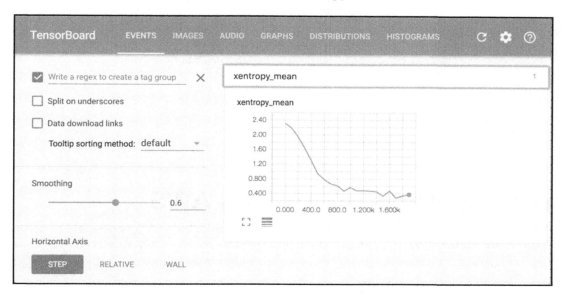

Now, if we want to use Keras on the top of TensorFlow, we simply download the Keras source from PyPI (for the downloadable file, refer to `https://pypi.Python.org/pypi/Ker as/1.2.0` or later versions) and then directly use Keras as a CloudML package solution, as in the following example:

```
gulli-macbookpro:trainable gulli$ gcloud beta ml local train   --package-path=trainer --package-path=../../../CloudML/fchol
let-keras-1.2.0-0-g12d068f.tar.gz  --module-name=trainer.task2
Using TensorFlow backend.
(0, 'input_1', (None, 224, 224, 3))
(1, 'block1_conv1', (None, 224, 224, 64))
(2, 'block1_conv2', (None, 224, 224, 64))
(3, 'block1_pool', (None, 112, 112, 64))
(4, 'block2_conv1', (None, 112, 112, 128))
(5, 'block2_conv2', (None, 112, 112, 128))
(6, 'block2_pool', (None, 56, 56, 128))
(7, 'block3_conv1', (None, 56, 56, 256))
(8, 'block3_conv2', (None, 56, 56, 256))
(9, 'block3_conv3', (None, 56, 56, 256))
(10, 'block3_pool', (None, 28, 28, 256))
(11, 'block4_conv1', (None, 28, 28, 512))
(12, 'block4_conv2', (None, 28, 28, 512))
(13, 'block4_conv3', (None, 28, 28, 512))
(14, 'block4_pool', (None, 14, 14, 512))
(15, 'block5_conv1', (None, 14, 14, 512))
(16, 'block5_conv2', (None, 14, 14, 512))
(17, 'block5_conv3', (None, 14, 14, 512))
(18, 'block5_pool', (None, 7, 7, 512))
(19, 'flatten', (None, 25088))
(20, 'fc1', (None, 4096))
(21, 'fc2', (None, 4096))
(22, 'predictions', (None, 1000))
gulli-macbookpro:trainable gulli$ ls
data    trainer
gulli-macbookpro:trainable gulli$ 
```

Here, `trainer.task2.py` is an example script:

```
from keras.applications.vgg16 import VGG16
from keras.models import Model
from keras.preprocessing import image
from keras.applications.vgg16 import preprocess_input
import numpy as np

# pre-built and pre-trained deep learning VGG16 model
base_model = VGG16(weights='imagenet', include_top=True)
for i, layer in enumerate(base_model.layers):
  print (i, layer.name, layer.output_shape)
```

Installing Keras on Amazon AWS

Installing TensorFlow and Keras on Amazon is very simple. Indeed, it is possible to use a prebuilt AMI named `TFAMI.v3` that is open and free (for more information, refer to `https ://github.com/ritchieng/tensorflow-aws-ami`), shown as follows:

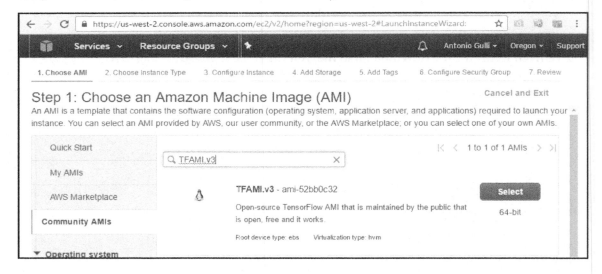

This AMI runs TensorFlow in less than five minutes and supports TensorFlow, Keras, OpenAI Gym, and all dependencies. As of January 2017, it supports the following:

- TensorFlow 0.12
- Keras 1.1.0
- TensorLayer 1.2.7
- CUDA 8.0
- CuDNN 5.1
- Python 2.7
- Ubuntu 16.04

In addition, `TFAMI.v3` works on P2 computing instances (for more information, refer to `htt ps://aws.amazon.com/ec2/instance-types/#p2`), as shown in the following screenshot:

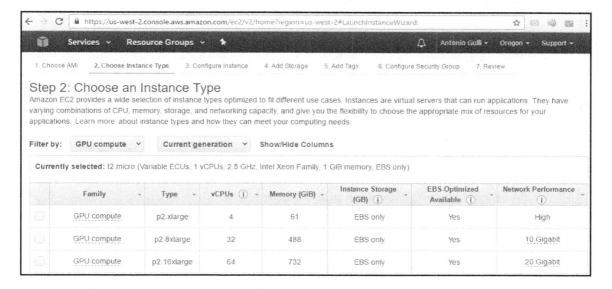

Some features of P2 instances are as follows:

- Intel Xeon E5-2686v4 (Broadwell) processors
- NVIDIA K80 GPUs, each with 2,496 parallel cores and 12 GB of GPU memory
- Supports peer-to-peer GPU communication
- Provides enhanced networking (for more information, refer to `https://aws.amaz on.com/ec2/faqs/#What_networking_capabilities_are_included_in_this_f eature`) with 20 Gbps of aggregate network bandwidth

The `TFAMI.v3` also works on G2 computing instances (for more information, refer to `https://aws.amazon.com/ec2/instance-types/#g2`). Some features of G2 instances are as follows:

- Intel Xeon E5-2670 (Sandy Bridge) processors
- NVIDIA GPUs, each with 1,536 CUDA cores and 4 GB of video memory

Installing Keras on Microsoft Azure

One way to install Keras on Azure is to install the support for Docker and then get a containerized version of TensorFlow plus Keras. Online, it is also possible to find a detailed set of instructions on how to install Keras and TensorFlow with Docker, but this is essentially what we have seen already in a previous section (for more information, refer to `https://blogs.msdn.microsoft.com/uk_faculty_connection/2016/09/26/tensorflow-on-docker-with-microsoft-azure/`).

If you use Theano as the only backend, then Keras can run with just a click by loading a pre-built package available on Cortana Intelligence Gallery (for more information, refer to `https://gallery.cortanaintelligence.com/Experiment/Theano-Keras-1`).

The following sample shows how to import Theano and Keras into Azure ML directly as a ZIP file and use them in the Execute Python Script module. This example is due to Hai Ning (for more information, refer to `https://goo.gl/VLR25o`), and it essentially runs the Keras code within the `azureml_main()` method:

```
# The script MUST contain a function named azureml_main
# which is the entry point for this module.

# imports up here can be used to
import pandas as pd
import theano
import theano.tensor as T
from theano import function
from keras.models import Sequential
from keras.layers import Dense, Activation
import numpy as np
# The entry point function can contain up to two input arguments:
#   Param<dataframe1>: a pandas.DataFrame
#   Param<dataframe2>: a pandas.DataFrame
def azureml_main(dataframe1 = None, dataframe2 = None):
    # Execution logic goes here
    # print('Input pandas.DataFrame #1:rnrn{0}'.format(dataframe1))

    # If a zip file is connected to the third input port is connected,
```

```
# it is unzipped under ".Script Bundle". This directory is added
# to sys.path. Therefore, if your zip file contains a Python file
# mymodule.py you can import it using:
# import mymodule
model = Sequential()
model.add(Dense(1, input_dim=784, activation="relu"))
model.compile(optimizer='rmsprop', loss='binary_crossentropy',
metrics=['accuracy'])
data = np.random.random((1000,784))
labels = np.random.randint(2, size=(1000,1))
model.fit(data, labels, nb_epoch=10, batch_size=32)
model.evaluate(data, labels)

return dataframe1,
```

In this screenshot, you see an example use of Microsoft Azure ML to run Theano and Keras:

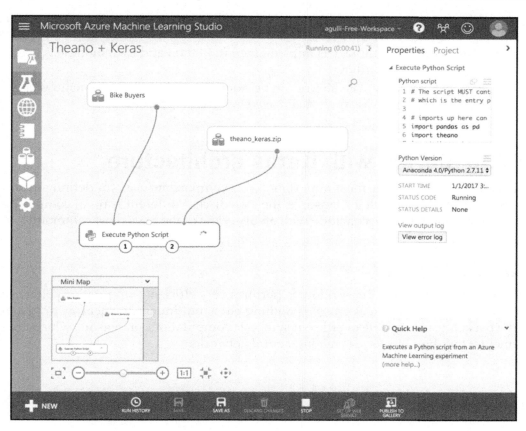

Keras API

Keras has a modular, minimalist, and easy extendable architecture. Francois Chollet, the author of Keras, says:

> *The library was developed with a focus on enabling fast experimentation. Being able to go from idea to result with the least possible delay is key to doing good research.*

Keras defines high-level neural networks running on top of either TensorFlow (for more information, refer to `https://github.com/tensorflow/tensorflow`) or Theano (for more information, refer to `https://github.com/Theano/Theano`). In details:

- **Modularity**: A model is either a sequence or a graph of standalone modules that can be combined together like LEGO blocks for building neural networks. Namely, the library predefines a very large number of modules implementing different types of neural layers, cost functions, optimizers, initialization schemes, activation functions, and regularization schemes.
- **Minimalism**: The library is implemented in Python and each module is kept short and self-describing.
- **Easy extensibility**: The library can be extended with new functionalities, as we will describe in `Chapter 7`, *Additional Deep Learning Models*.

Getting started with Keras architecture

In this section, we review the most important Keras components used for defining neural networks. First, we define what a tensor is, then we discuss different ways of composing predefined modules, and we conclude with an overview of the ones most commonly used.

What is a tensor?

Keras uses either Theano or TensorFlow to perform very efficient computations on tensors. But what is a tensor anyway? A tensor is nothing but a multidimensional array or matrix. Both the backends are capable of efficient symbolic computations on tensors, which are the fundamental building blocks for creating neural networks.

Composing models in Keras

There are two ways of composing models in Keras. They are as follows:

- Sequential composition
- Functional composition

Let us take a look at each one in detail.

Sequential composition

The first one is the sequential composition, where different predefined models are stacked together in a linear pipeline of layers similar to a stack or a queue. In Chapter 1, *Neural Networks Foundations*, we saw a few examples of sequential pipelines. For instance:

```
model = Sequential()
model.add(Dense(N_HIDDEN, input_shape=(784,)))
model.add(Activation('relu'))
model.add(Dropout(DROPOUT))
model.add(Dense(N_HIDDEN))
model.add(Activation('relu'))
model.add(Dropout(DROPOUT))
model.add(Dense(nb_classes))
model.add(Activation('softmax'))
model.summary()
```

Functional composition

The second way of composing modules is via the functional API, where it is possible to define complex models, such as directed acyclic graphs, models with shared layers, or multi-output models. We will see such examples in Chapter 7, *Additional Deep Learning Models*.

An overview of predefined neural network layers

Keras has a number of prebuilt layers. Let us review the most commonly used ones and highlight in which chapter these layers are mostly used.

Regular dense

A dense model is a fully connected neural network layer. We have already seen examples of usage in `Chapter 1`, *Neural Networks Foundations*. Here is the prototype with a definition of the parameters:

```
keras.layers.core.Dense(units, activation=None, use_bias=True,
kernel_initializer='glorot_uniform', bias_initializer='zeros',
kernel_regularizer=None, bias_regularizer=None, activity_regularizer=None,
kernel_constraint=None, bias_constraint=None)
```

Recurrent neural networks — simple, LSTM, and GRU

Recurrent neural networks are a class of neural networks that exploit the sequential nature of their input. Such inputs could be a text, a speech, time series, and anything else where the occurrence of an element in the sequence is dependent on the elements that appeared before it. We will discuss simple, LSTM, and GRU recurrent neural networks in `Chapter 6`, *Recurrent Neural Network — RNN*. Here you can see some prototypes with a definition of the parameters:

```
keras.layers.recurrent.Recurrent(return_sequences=False,
go_backwards=False, stateful=False, unroll=False, implementation=0)

keras.layers.recurrent.SimpleRNN(units, activation='tanh', use_bias=True,
kernel_initializer='glorot_uniform', recurrent_initializer='orthogonal',
bias_initializer='zeros', kernel_regularizer=None,
recurrent_regularizer=None, bias_regularizer=None,
activity_regularizer=None, kernel_constraint=None,
recurrent_constraint=None, bias_constraint=None, dropout=0.0,
recurrent_dropout=0.0)

keras.layers.recurrent.GRU(units, activation='tanh',
recurrent_activation='hard_sigmoid', use_bias=True,
kernel_initializer='glorot_uniform', recurrent_initializer='orthogonal',
bias_initializer='zeros', kernel_regularizer=None,
recurrent_regularizer=None, bias_regularizer=None,
activity_regularizer=None, kernel_constraint=None,
recurrent_constraint=None, bias_constraint=None, dropout=0.0,
recurrent_dropout=0.0)

keras.layers.recurrent.LSTM(units, activation='tanh',
recurrent_activation='hard_sigmoid', use_bias=True,
kernel_initializer='glorot_uniform', recurrent_initializer='orthogonal',
bias_initializer='zeros', unit_forget_bias=True, kernel_regularizer=None,
recurrent_regularizer=None, bias_regularizer=None,
activity_regularizer=None, kernel_constraint=None,
```

```
recurrent_constraint=None, bias_constraint=None, dropout=0.0,
recurrent_dropout=0.0)
```

Convolutional and pooling layers

ConvNets are a class of neural networks using convolutional and pooling operations for progressively learning rather sophisticated models based on progressive levels of abstraction. This learning via progressive abstraction resembles vision models that have evolved over millions of years inside the human brain. People called it *deep* with 3-5 layers a few years ago, and now it has gone up to 100-200. We will discuss convolutional neural networks in Chapter 3, *Deep Learning with ConvNets*. Here are some prototypes with a definition of the parameters:

```
keras.layers.convolutional.Conv1D(filters, kernel_size, strides=1,
padding='valid', dilation_rate=1, activation=None, use_bias=True,
kernel_initializer='glorot_uniform', bias_initializer='zeros',
kernel_regularizer=None, bias_regularizer=None, activity_regularizer=None,
kernel_constraint=None, bias_constraint=None)

keras.layers.convolutional.Conv2D(filters, kernel_size, strides=(1, 1),
padding='valid', data_format=None, dilation_rate=(1, 1), activation=None,
use_bias=True, kernel_initializer='glorot_uniform',
bias_initializer='zeros', kernel_regularizer=None, bias_regularizer=None,
activity_regularizer=None, kernel_constraint=None, bias_constraint=None)

keras.layers.pooling.MaxPooling1D(pool_size=2, strides=None,
padding='valid')

keras.layers.pooling.MaxPooling2D(pool_size=(2, 2), strides=None,
padding='valid', data_format=None)
```

Regularization

Regularization is a way to prevent overfitting. We have already seen examples of usage in Chapter 1, *Neural Networks Foundations*. Multiple layers have parameters for regularization. The following is the list of regularization parameters commonly used for dense, and convolutional modules:

- kernel_regularizer: Regularizer function applied to the weight matrix
- bias_regularizer: Regularizer function applied to the bias vector
- activity_regularizer: Regularizer function applied to the output of the layer (its activation)

In addition is possible to use Dropout for regularization and that is frequently a very effective choice

```
keras.layers.core.Dropout(rate, noise_shape=None, seed=None)
```

Where:

- `rate`: It is a float between 0 and 1 which represents the fraction of the input units to drop
- `noise_shape`: It is a 1D integer tensor which represents the shape of the binary dropout mask that will be multiplied with the input
- `seed`: It is a integer which is used use as random seed

Batch normalization

Batch normalization (for more information, refer to https://www.colwiz.com/cite-in-go ogle-docs/cid=f20f9683aaf69ce) is a way to accelerate learning and generally achieve better accuracy. We will look at examples of usage in Chapter 4, *Generative Adversarial Networks and WaveNet,* when we discuss GANs. Here is the prototype with a definition of the parameters:

```
keras.layers.normalization.BatchNormalization(axis=-1, momentum=0.99,
epsilon=0.001, center=True, scale=True, beta_initializer='zeros',
gamma_initializer='ones', moving_mean_initializer='zeros',
moving_variance_initializer='ones', beta_regularizer=None,
gamma_regularizer=None, beta_constraint=None, gamma_constraint=None)
```

An overview of predefined activation functions

Activation includes commonly used functions such as sigmoid, linear, hyperbolic tangent, and ReLU. We have seen a few examples of activation functions in Chapter 1, *Neural Networks Foundations,* and more examples will be presented in the next chapters. The following diagrams are examples of sigmoid, linear, hyperbolic tangent, and ReLU activation functions:

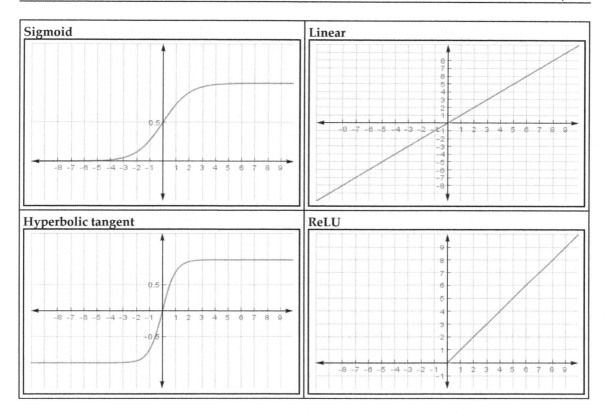

An overview of losses functions

Losses functions (or objective functions, or optimization score function; for more information, refer to https://keras.io/losses/) can be classified into four categories:

- Accuracy which is used for classification problems. There are multiple choices: binary_accuracy (mean accuracy rate across all predictions for binary classification problems), categorical_accuracy (mean accuracy rate across all predictions for multiclass classification problems), sparse_categorical_accuracy (useful for sparse targets), and top_k_categorical_accuracy (success when the target class is within the top_k predictions provided).

- Error loss, which measures the difference between the values predicted and the values actually observed. There are multiple choices: `mse` (mean square error between predicted and target values), `rmse` (root square error between predicted and target values), `mae` (mean absolute error between predicted and target values), `mape` (mean percentage error between predicted and target values), and `msle` (mean squared logarithmic error between predicted and target values).

- Hinge loss, which is generally used for training classifiers. There are two versions: *hinge* defined as $max(1 - y_{true} * y_{pred}, 0)$ and *squared hinge* defined as the the squared value of the hinge loss.

- Class loss is used to calculate the cross-entropy for classification problems. There are multiple versions, including binary cross-entropy (for more information, refer to `https://en.wikipedia.org/wiki/Cross_entropy`), and categorical cross-entropy.

We have seen a few examples of objective functions in `Chapter 1`, *Neural Networks Foundations*, and more examples will be presented in the next chapters.

An overview of metrics

A metric function (for more information, refer to `https://keras.io/metrics/`) is similar to an objective function. The only difference is that the results from evaluating a metric are not used when training the model. We have seen a few examples of metrics in `Chapter 1`, *Neural Networks Foundations*, and more examples will be presented in the next chapters.

An overview of optimizers

Optimizers include SGD, RMSprop, and Adam. We have seen a few examples of optimizers in `Chapter 1`, *Neural Networks Foundations*, and more examples (Adagrad and Adadelta; for more information, refer to `https://keras.io/optimizers/`) will be presented in the next chapters.

Some useful operations

Here we report some utility operations that can be carried out with Keras APIs. The goal is to facilitate the creation of networks, the training process, and the saving of intermediate results.

Saving and loading the weights and the architecture of a model

Model architectures can be easily saved and loaded as follows:

```
# save as JSON json_string = model.to_json()
# save as YAML yaml_string = model.to_yaml()
# model reconstruction from JSON: from keras.models import model_from_json
model = model_from_json(json_string) # model reconstruction from YAML model
= model_from_yaml(yaml_string)
```

Model parameters (weights) can be easily saved and loaded as follows:

```
from keras.models import load_model model.save('my_model.h5')
# creates a HDF5 file 'my_model.h5' del model
# deletes the existing model
# returns a compiled model
# identical to the previous one model = load_model('my_model.h5')
```

Callbacks for customizing the training process

The training process can be stopped when a metric has stopped improving by using an appropriate `callback`:

```
keras.callbacks.EarlyStopping(monitor='val_loss', min_delta=0,
patience=0, verbose=0, mode='auto')
```

Loss history can be saved by defining a `callback` like the following:

```
class LossHistory(keras.callbacks.Callback):      def on_train_begin(self,
logs={}):          self.losses = []      def on_batch_end(self, batch,
logs={}):          self.losses.append(logs.get('loss')) model = Sequential()
model.add(Dense(10, input_dim=784, init='uniform'))
model.add(Activation('softmax'))
model.compile(loss='categorical_crossentropy', optimizer='rmsprop') history
= LossHistory() model.fit(X_train,Y_train, batch_size=128, nb_epoch=20,
verbose=0, callbacks=[history]) print history.losses
```

Checkpointing

Checkpointing is a process that saves a snapshot of the application's state at regular intervals, so the application can be restarted from the last saved state in case of failure. This is useful during training of deep learning models, which can often be a time-consuming task. The state of a deep learning model at any point in time is the weights of the model at that time. Keras saves these weights in HDF5 format (for more information, refer to `https://www.hdfgroup.org/`) and provides checkpointing using its callback API.

Some scenarios where checkpointing can be useful include the following:

- If you want the ability to restart from your last checkpoint after your AWS Spot instance (for more information, refer to `http://docs.aws.amazon.com/AWSEC2/latest/UserGuide/how-spot-instances-work.html`) or Google preemptible virtual machine (for more information, refer to `https://cloud.google.com/compute/docs/instances/preemptible`) is unexpectedly terminated
- If you want to stop training, perhaps to test your model on test data, then continue training from the last checkpoint
- If you want to retain the best version (by some metric such as validation loss) as it trains over multiple epochs

The first and second scenarios can be handled by saving a checkpoint after each epoch, which is handled by the default usage of the `ModelCheckpoint` callback. The following code illustrates how to add checkpointing during training of your deep learning model in Keras:

```
from __future__ import division, print_function
from keras.callbacks import ModelCheckpoint
from keras.datasets import mnist
from keras.models import Sequential
from keras.layers.core import Dense, Dropout
from keras.utils import np_utils
import numpy as np
import os

BATCH_SIZE = 128
NUM_EPOCHS = 20
MODEL_DIR = "/tmp"

(Xtrain, ytrain), (Xtest, ytest) = mnist.load_data()
Xtrain = Xtrain.reshape(60000, 784).astype("float32") / 255
Xtest = Xtest.reshape(10000, 784).astype("float32") / 255
Ytrain = np_utils.to_categorical(ytrain, 10)
Ytest = np_utils.to_categorical(ytest, 10)
```

```
print(Xtrain.shape, Xtest.shape, Ytrain.shape, Ytest.shape)

model = Sequential()
model.add(Dense(512, input_shape=(784,), activation="relu"))
model.add(Dropout(0.2))
model.add(Dense(512, activation="relu"))
model.add(Dropout(0.2))
model.add(Dense(10, activation="softmax"))

model.compile(optimizer="rmsprop", loss="categorical_crossentropy",
              metrics=["accuracy"])

# save best model
checkpoint = ModelCheckpoint(
    filepath=os.path.join(MODEL_DIR, "model-{epoch:02d}.h5"))
model.fit(Xtrain, Ytrain, batch_size=BATCH_SIZE, nb_epoch=NUM_EPOCHS,
          validation_split=0.1, callbacks=[checkpoint])
```

The third scenario involves monitoring a metric, such as validation accuracy or loss, and only saving a checkpoint if the current metric is better than the previously saved checkpoint. Keras provides an additional parameter, save_best_only, which needs to be set to true when instantiating the checkpoint object in order to support this functionality.

Using TensorBoard and Keras

Keras provides a callback for saving your training and test metrics, as well as activation histograms for the different layers in your model:

```
keras.callbacks.TensorBoard(log_dir='./logs', histogram_freq=0,
write_graph=True, write_images=False)
```

Saved data can then be visualized with TensorBoad launched at the command line:

```
tensorboard --logdir=/full_path_to_your_logs
```

Using Quiver and Keras

In Chapter 3, *Deep Learning with ConvNets*, we will discuss ConvNets, which are an advanced deep learning technique for dealing with images. Here we give a preview of Quiver (for more information, refer to https://github.com/jakebian/quiver), a tool useful for visualizing ConvNets features in an interactive way. The installation is pretty simple, and after that Quiver can be used with one single line:

```
pip install quiver_engine

from quiver_engine import server       server.launch(model)
```

This will launch the visualization at localhost:5000. Quiver allows you to visually inspect a neural network, as in the following example:

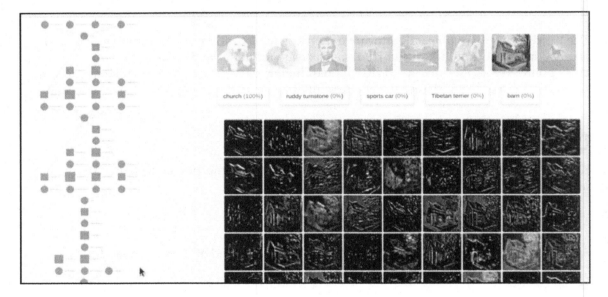

Summary

In this chapter, we discussed how to install Theano, TensorFlow, and Keras on the following:

- Your local machine
- A dockerized infrastructure based on containers
- In the cloud with Google GCP, Amazon AWS, and Microsoft Azure

In addition to that, we looked at a few modules defining Keras APIs and some commonly useful operations such as loading and saving neural networks' architectures and weights, early stopping, history saving, checkpointing, interactions with TensorBoard, and interactions with Quiver.

In the next chapter, we will introduce the concept of convolutional networks a fundamental innovation in deep learning which has been used with success in multiple domains from text, to video, to speech going well beyond the initial image processing domain where they were originally conceived.

3
Deep Learning with ConvNets

In previous chapters, we discussed dense nets, in which each layer is fully connected to the adjacent layers. We applied those dense networks to classify the MNIST handwritten characters dataset. In that context, each pixel in the input image is assigned to a neuron for a total of 784 (28 x 28 pixels) input neurons. However, this strategy does not leverage the spatial structure and relations of each image. In particular, this piece of code transforms the bitmap representing each written digit into a flat vector, where the spatial locality is gone:

```
#X_train is 60000 rows of 28x28 values --> reshaped in 60000 x 784
X_train = X_train.reshape(60000, 784)
X_test = X_test.reshape(10000, 784)
o
```

Convolutional neural networks (also called ConvNet) leverage spatial information and are therefore very well suited for classifying images. These nets use an ad hoc architecture inspired by biological data taken from physiological experiments done on the visual cortex. As discussed, our vision is based on multiple cortex levels, each one recognizing more and more structured information. First, we see single pixels; then from them, we recognize simple geometric forms. And then... more and more sophisticated elements such as objects, faces, human bodies, animals, and so on.

Convolutional neural networks are indeed fascinating. Over a short period of time, they become a *disruptive* technology, breaking all the state-of-the-art results in multiple domains, from text, to video, to speech going well beyond the initial image processing domain where they were originally conceived.

In this chapter, we will cover the following topics:

- Deep convolutional neural networks
- Image classification

Deep convolutional neural network — DCNN

A **deep convolutional neural network (DCNN)** consists of many neural network layers. Two different types of layers, convolutional and pooling, are typically alternated. The depth of each filter increases from left to right in the network. The last stage is typically made of one or more fully connected layers:

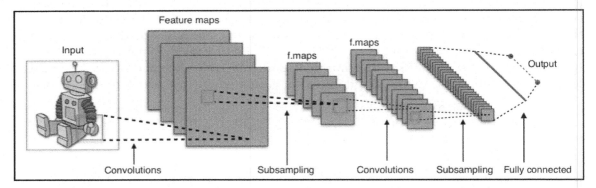

There are three key intuitions beyond ConvNets:

- Local receptive fields
- Shared weights
- Pooling

Let's review them.

Local receptive fields

If we want to preserve spatial information, then it is convenient to represent each image with a matrix of pixels. Then, a simple way to encode the local structure is to connect a submatrix of adjacent input neurons into one single hidden neuron belonging to the next layer. That single hidden neuron represents one local receptive field. Note that this operation is named convolution and it gives the name to this type of network.

Of course, we can encode more information by having overlapping submatrices. For instance, let's suppose that the size of each single submatrix is 5 x 5 and that those submatrices are used with MNIST images of 28 x 28 pixels. Then we will be able to generate 23 x 23 local receptive field neurons in the next hidden layer. In fact it is possible to slide the submatrices by only 23 positions before touching the borders of the images. In Keras, the size of each single submatrix is called **stride length**, and this is a hyperparameter that can be fine-tuned during the construction of our nets.

Let's define the feature map from one layer to another layer. Of course, we can have multiple feature maps that learn independently from each hidden layer. For instance, we can start with 28 x 28 input neurons for processing MINST images and then recall k feature maps of size 23 x 23 neurons each (again with a stride of 5 x 5) in the next hidden layer.

Shared weights and bias

Let's suppose that we want to move away from the pixel representation in a row by gaining the ability to detect the same feature independently from the location where it is placed in the input image. A simple intuition is to use the same set of weights and bias for all the neurons in the hidden layers. In this way, each layer will learn a set of position-independent latent features derived from the image.

Assuming that the input image has shape *(256, 256)* on three channels with *tf* (TensorFlow) ordering, this is represented as *(256, 256, 3)*. Note that with th (Theano) mode, the channel's dimension (the depth) is at index *1*; in *tf* (TensoFlow) mode, it is at index *3*.

In Keras, if we want to add a convolutional layer with dimensionality of the output 32 and extension of each filter 3 x 3, we will write:

```
model = Sequential()
model.add(Conv2D(32, (3, 3), input_shape=(256, 256, 3))
```

Alternatively, we will write:

```
model = Sequential()
model.add(Conv2D(32, kernel_size=3, input_shape=(256, 256, 3))
```

This means that we are applying a 3 x 3 convolution on a 256 x 256 image with three input channels (or input filters), resulting in 32 output channels (or output filters).

An example of convolution is provided in the following diagram:

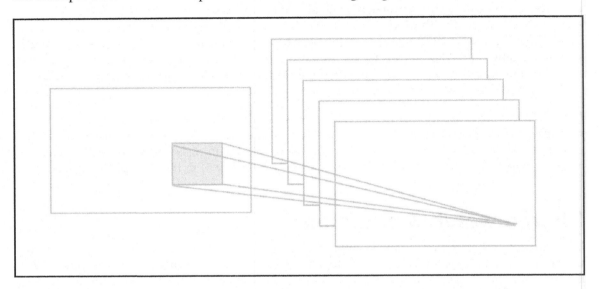

Pooling layers

Let's suppose that we want to summarize the output of a feature map. Again, we can use the spatial contiguity of the output produced from a single feature map and aggregate the values of a submatrix into a single output value that synthetically describes the *meaning* associated with that physical region.

Max-pooling

One easy and common choice is *max-pooling*, which simply outputs the maximum activation as observed in the region. In Keras, if we want to define a max-pooling layer of size 2 x 2, we will write:

```
model.add(MaxPooling2D(pool_size = (2, 2)))
```

An example of max-pooling is shown in the following diagram:

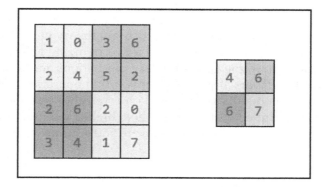

Average pooling

Another choice is average pooling, which simply aggregates a region into the average values of the activations observed in that region.

Note that Keras implements a large number of pooling layers and a complete list is available at: `https://keras.io/layers/pooling/`. In short, all pooling operations are nothing more than a summary operation on a given region.

ConvNets summary

So far, we have described the basic concepts of ConvNets. CNNs apply convolution and pooling operations in one dimension for audio and text data along the time dimension, in two dimensions for images along the (height x width) dimensions, and in three dimensions for videos along the (height x width x time) dimensions. For images, sliding the filter over input volume produces a map that gives the responses of the filter for each spatial position. In other words, a ConvNet has multiple filters stacked together which learn to recognize specific visual features independently of the location in the image. Those visual features are simple in the initial layers of the network, and then more and more sophisticated deeper in the network.

An example of DCNN — LeNet

Yann le Cun proposed (for more information refer to: *Convolutional Networks for Images, Speech, and Time-Series*, by Y. LeCun and Y. Bengio, brain theory neural networks, vol. 3361, 1995) a family of ConvNets named LeNet trained for recognizing MNIST handwritten characters with robustness to simple geometric transformations and to distortion. The key intuition here is to have low-layers alternating convolution operations with max-pooling operations. The convolution operations are based on carefully chosen local receptive fields with shared weights for multiple feature maps. Then, higher levels are fully connected layers based on a traditional MLP with hidden layers and softmax as the output layer.

LeNet code in Keras

To define LeNet code, we use a convolutional 2D module, which is:

```
keras.layers.convolutional.Conv2D(filters, kernel_size, padding='valid')
```

Here, `filters` is the number of convolution kernels to use (for example, the dimensionality of the output), `kernel_size` is an integer or tuple/list of two integers, specifying the width and height of the 2D convolution window (can be a single integer to specify the same value for all spatial dimensions), and `padding='same'` means that padding is used. There are two options: `padding='valid'` means that the convolution is only computed where the input and the filter fully overlap, and therefore the output is smaller than the input, while `padding='same'` means that we have an output that is the *same* size as the input, for which the area around the input is padded with zeros.

In addition, we use a `MaxPooling2D` module:

```
keras.layers.pooling.MaxPooling2D(pool_size=(2, 2), strides=(2, 2))
```

Here, `pool_size=(2, 2)` is a tuple of two integers representing the factors by which the image is vertically and horizontally downscaled. So *(2, 2)* will halve the image in each dimension, and `strides=(2, 2)` is the stride used for processing.

Now, let us review the code. First we import a number of modules:

```
from keras import backend as K
from keras.models import Sequential
from keras.layers.convolutional import Conv2D
from keras.layers.convolutional import MaxPooling2D
from keras.layers.core import Activation
from keras.layers.core import Flatten
from keras.layers.core import Dense
from keras.datasets import mnist
from keras.utils import np_utils
from keras.optimizers import SGD, RMSprop, Adam
import numpy as np
import matplotlib.pyplot as plt
```

Then we define the LeNet network:

```
#define the ConvNet
class LeNet:
    @staticmethod
    def build(input_shape, classes):
        model = Sequential()
        # CONV => RELU => POOL
```

We have a first convolutional stage with ReLU activations followed by a max-pooling. Our net will learn 20 convolutional filters, each one of which has a size of 5 x 5. The output dimension is the same one of the input shape, so it will be 28 x 28. Note that since the Convolution2D is the first stage of our pipeline, we are also required to define its input_shape. The max-pooling operation implements a sliding window that slides over the layer and takes the maximum of each region with a step of two pixels vertically and horizontally:

```
model.add(Convolution2D(20, kernel_size=5, padding="same",
input_shape=input_shape))
model.add(Activation("relu"))
model.add(MaxPooling2D(pool_size=(2, 2), strides=(2, 2)))
# CONV => RELU => POOL
```

Then a second convolutional stage with ReLU activations follows, again by a max-pooling. In this case, we increase the number of convolutional filters learned to 50 from the previous 20. Increasing the number of filters in deeper layers is a common technique used in deep learning:

```
model.add(Conv2D(50, kernel_size=5, border_mode="same"))
model.add(Activation("relu"))
model.add(MaxPooling2D(pool_size=(2, 2), strides=(2, 2)))
```

Then we have a pretty standard flattening and a dense network of 500 neurons, followed by a softmax classifier with 10 classes:

```
# Flatten => RELU layers
model.add(Flatten())
model.add(Dense(500))
model.add(Activation("relu"))
# a softmax classifier
model.add(Dense(classes))
model.add(Activation("softmax"))
return model
```

Congratulations, You have just defined the first deep learning network! Let's see how it looks visually:

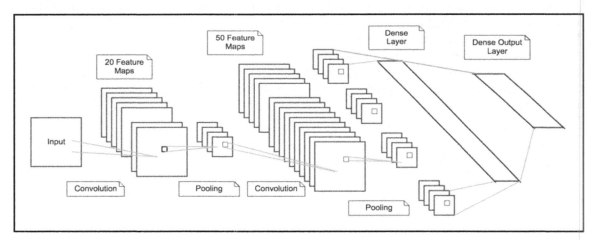

Now we need some additional code for training the network, but this is very similar to what we have already described in Chapter 1, *Neural Network Foundations*. This time, we also show the code for printing the loss:

```
# network and training
NB_EPOCH = 20
BATCH_SIZE = 128
VERBOSE = 1
OPTIMIZER = Adam()
VALIDATION_SPLIT=0.2
IMG_ROWS, IMG_COLS = 28, 28 # input image dimensions
NB_CLASSES = 10 # number of outputs = number of digits
INPUT_SHAPE = (1, IMG_ROWS, IMG_COLS)
# data: shuffled and split between train and test sets
(X_train, y_train), (X_test, y_test) = mnist.load_data()
k.set_image_dim_ordering("th")
# consider them as float and normalize
X_train = X_train.astype('float32')
X_test = X_test.astype('float32')
X_train /= 255
X_test /= 255
# we need a 60K x [1 x 28 x 28] shape as input to the CONVNET
X_train = X_train[:, np.newaxis, :, :]
X_test = X_test[:, np.newaxis, :, :]
print(X_train.shape[0], 'train samples')
print(X_test.shape[0], 'test samples')
# convert class vectors to binary class matrices
y_train = np_utils.to_categorical(y_train, NB_CLASSES)
y_test = np_utils.to_categorical(y_test, NB_CLASSES)
# initialize the optimizer and model
model = LeNet.build(input_shape=INPUT_SHAPE, classes=NB_CLASSES)
model.compile(loss="categorical_crossentropy", optimizer=OPTIMIZER,
metrics=["accuracy"])
history = model.fit(X_train, y_train,
batch_size=BATCH_SIZE, epochs=NB_EPOCH,
verbose=VERBOSE, validation_split=VALIDATION_SPLIT)
score = model.evaluate(X_test, y_test, verbose=VERBOSE)
print("Test score:", score[0])
print('Test accuracy:', score[1])
# list all data in history
print(history.history.keys())
# summarize history for accuracy
plt.plot(history.history['acc'])
plt.plot(history.history['val_acc'])
plt.title('model accuracy')
plt.ylabel('accuracy')
plt.xlabel('epoch')
plt.legend(['train', 'test'], loc='upper left')
```

```
plt.show()
# summarize history for loss
plt.plot(history.history['loss'])
plt.plot(history.history['val_loss'])
plt.title('model loss')
plt.ylabel('loss')
plt.xlabel('epoch')
plt.legend(['train', 'test'], loc='upper left')
plt.show()
```

Now let's run the code. As you can see, the time had a significant increase and each iteration in our deep net now takes ~134 seconds against ~1-2 seconds for the net defined in Chapter 1, *Neural Network Foundations*. However, the accuracy has reached a new peak at 99.06%:

```
gulli-macbookpro:code gulli$ python keras_LeNet.py
Using TensorFlow backend.
(60000, 'train samples')
(10000, 'test samples')
Train on 48000 samples, validate on 12000 samples
Epoch 1/20
48000/48000 [==============================] - 124s - loss: 0.1766 - acc: 0.9445 - val_loss: 0.0568 - val_acc: 0.9826
Epoch 2/20
48000/48000 [==============================] - 123s - loss: 0.0465 - acc: 0.9847 - val_loss: 0.0407 - val_acc: 0.9877
Epoch 3/20
48000/48000 [==============================] - 129s - loss: 0.0300 - acc: 0.9908 - val_loss: 0.0367 - val_acc: 0.9895
Epoch 4/20
48000/48000 [==============================] - 131s - loss: 0.0202 - acc: 0.9937 - val_loss: 0.0375 - val_acc: 0.9896
Epoch 5/20
48000/48000 [==============================] - 127s - loss: 0.0144 - acc: 0.9957 - val_loss: 0.0482 - val_acc: 0.9875
Epoch 6/20
48000/48000 [==============================] - 127s - loss: 0.0106 - acc: 0.9965 - val_loss: 0.0332 - val_acc: 0.9909
Epoch 7/20
48000/48000 [==============================] - 128s - loss: 0.0086 - acc: 0.9972 - val_loss: 0.0386 - val_acc: 0.9909
Epoch 8/20
48000/48000 [==============================] - 123s - loss: 0.0059 - acc: 0.9980 - val_loss: 0.0464 - val_acc: 0.9908
Epoch 9/20
48000/48000 [==============================] - 123s - loss: 0.0053 - acc: 0.9982 - val_loss: 0.0463 - val_acc: 0.9908
Epoch 10/20
48000/48000 [==============================] - 124s - loss: 0.0045 - acc: 0.9987 - val_loss: 0.0565 - val_acc: 0.9891
Epoch 11/20
48000/48000 [==============================] - 125s - loss: 0.0040 - acc: 0.9989 - val_loss: 0.0558 - val_acc: 0.9908
Epoch 12/20
48000/48000 [==============================] - 124s - loss: 0.0032 - acc: 0.9989 - val_loss: 0.0551 - val_acc: 0.9914
Epoch 13/20
48000/48000 [==============================] - 125s - loss: 0.0030 - acc: 0.9991 - val_loss: 0.0569 - val_acc: 0.9908
Epoch 14/20
48000/48000 [==============================] - 123s - loss: 0.0034 - acc: 0.9991 - val_loss: 0.0459 - val_acc: 0.9926
Epoch 15/20
48000/48000 [==============================] - 124s - loss: 0.0025 - acc: 0.9993 - val_loss: 0.0542 - val_acc: 0.9913
Epoch 16/20
48000/48000 [==============================] - 123s - loss: 0.0018 - acc: 0.9995 - val_loss: 0.0604 - val_acc: 0.9916
Epoch 17/20
48000/48000 [==============================] - 123s - loss: 0.0027 - acc: 0.9993 - val_loss: 0.0533 - val_acc: 0.9927
Epoch 18/20
48000/48000 [==============================] - 124s - loss: 0.0014 - acc: 0.9996 - val_loss: 0.0580 - val_acc: 0.9923
Epoch 19/20
48000/48000 [==============================] - 123s - loss: 0.0020 - acc: 0.9995 - val_loss: 0.0623 - val_acc: 0.9911
Epoch 20/20
48000/48000 [==============================] - 123s - loss: 0.0016 - acc: 0.9995 - val_loss: 0.0837 - val_acc: 0.9911
10000/10000 [==============================] - 11s
('\nTest score:', 0.072166633289733453)
('Test accuracy:', 0.99060000000000004)
['acc', 'loss', 'val_acc', 'val_loss']
```

Let's plot the model accuracy and the model loss, and we understand that we can train in only 4 - 5 iterations to achieve a similar accuracy of 99.2%:

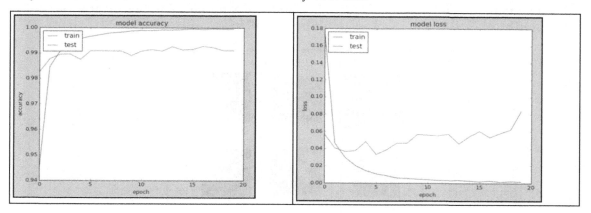

In the following screenshot, we show the final accuracy achieved by our model:

```
gulli-macbookpro:code gulli$ python keras_LeNet.py
Using TensorFlow backend.
(60000, 'train samples')
(10000, 'test samples')
Train on 48000 samples, validate on 12000 samples
Epoch 1/4
48000/48000 [==============================] - 139s - loss: 0.1758 - acc: 0.9450 - val_loss: 0.0618 - val_acc: 0.9806
Epoch 2/4
48000/48000 [==============================] - 136s - loss: 0.0461 - acc: 0.9849 - val_loss: 0.0408 - val_acc: 0.9878
Epoch 3/4
48000/48000 [==============================] - 130s - loss: 0.0294 - acc: 0.9905 - val_loss: 0.0413 - val_acc: 0.9889
Epoch 4/4
48000/48000 [==============================] - 129s - loss: 0.0199 - acc: 0.9936 - val_loss: 0.0373 - val_acc: 0.9900
10000/10000 [==============================] - 12s
('\nTest score:', 0.027107118735135736)
('Test accuracy:', 0.99209999999999998)
['acc', 'loss', 'val_acc', 'val_loss']
```

Let's see some of the MNIST images just to understand how good the number 99.2% is! For instance, there are many ways in which humans write a 9, one of them appearing in the following diagram. The same holds for 3, 7, 4, and 5. The number **1** in this diagram is so difficult to recognize that probably even a human will have issues with it:

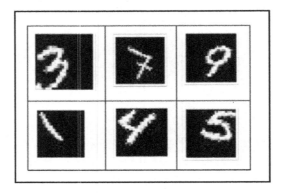

We can summarize all the progress made so far with our different models in the following graph. Our simple net started with an accuracy of **92.22%**, which means that about 8 handwritten characters out of 100 are not correctly recognized. Then, we gained 7% with the deep learning architecture by reaching an accuracy of **99.20%**, which means that about 1 handwritten character out of 100 is incorrectly recognized:

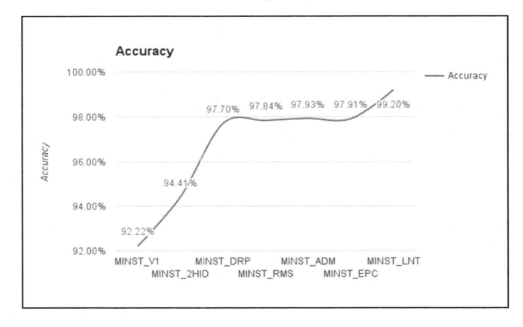

Understanding the power of deep learning

Another test that we can run to better understand the power of deep learning and ConvNet is to reduce the size of the training set and observe the consequent decay in performance. One way to do this is to split the training set of 50,000 examples into two different sets:

- The proper training set used for training our model will progressively reduce its size of (5,900, 3,000, 1,800, 600, and 300) examples
- The validation set used to estimate how well our model has been trained will consist of the remaining examples

Our test set is always fixed and it consists of 10,000 examples.

With this setup, we compare the just-defined deep learning ConvNet against the first example of neural network defined in Chapter 1, *Neural Network Foundations*. As we can see in the following graph, our deep network always outperforms the simple network and the gap is more and more evident when the number of examples provided for training is progressively reduced. With 5,900 training examples the deep learning net had an accuracy of 96.68% against an accuracy of 85.56% of the simple net. More important, with only 300 training examples our deep learning net still has an accuracy of 72.44% while the simple net shows a significant decay at 48.26%. All the experiments are run for only four training iterations. This confirms the breakthrough progress achieved with deep learning. At first glance this could be surprising from a mathematical point of view because the deep network has many more unknowns (the weights), so one would think we need many more data points.

However, preserving the spatial information, adding convolution, pooling, and feature maps is innovation with ConvNets, and this was optimized on millions of years (since this organization has been inspired by the visual cortex):

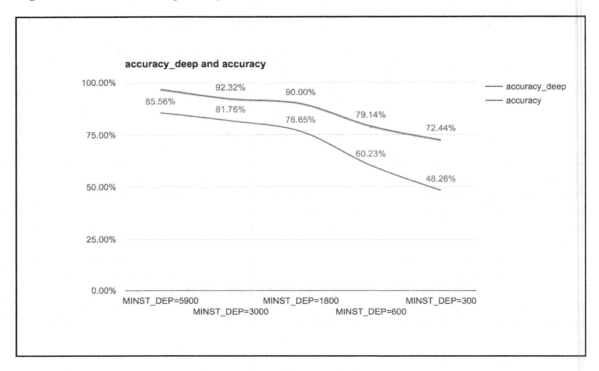

A list of state-of-the-art results for MNIST is available at: http://rodrigob.github.io/are _we_there_yet/build/classification_datasets_results.html. As of January, 2017, the best result has an error rate of 0.21%.

Recognizing CIFAR-10 images with deep learning

The CIFAR-10 dataset contains 60,000 color images of 32 x 32 pixels in 3 channels divided into 10 classes. Each class contains 6,000 images. The training set contains 50,000 images, while the test sets provides 10,000 images. This image taken from the CIFAR repository (htt ps://www.cs.toronto.edu/~kriz/cifar.html) describes a few random examples from the 10 classes:

The goal is to recognize previously unseen images and assign them to one of the 10 classes. Let us define a suitable deep net.

First of all we import a number of useful modules, define a few constants, and load the dataset:

```
from keras.datasets import cifar10
from keras.utils import np_utils
from keras.models import Sequential
from keras.layers.core import Dense, Dropout, Activation, Flatten
from keras.layers.convolutional import Conv2D, MaxPooling2D
from keras.optimizers import SGD, Adam, RMSprop
import matplotlib.pyplot as plt

# CIFAR_10 is a set of 60K images 32x32 pixels on 3 channels
IMG_CHANNELS = 3
```

```
IMG_ROWS = 32
IMG_COLS = 32

#constant
BATCH_SIZE = 128
NB_EPOCH = 20
NB_CLASSES = 10
VERBOSE = 1
VALIDATION_SPLIT = 0.2
OPTIM = RMSprop()

#load dataset
(X_train, y_train), (X_test, y_test) = cifar10.load_data()
print('X_train shape:', X_train.shape)
print(X_train.shape[0], 'train samples')
print(X_test.shape[0], 'test samples')
```

Now let's do a one-hot encoding and normalize the images:

```
# convert to categorical
Y_train = np_utils.to_categorical(y_train, NB_CLASSES)
Y_test = np_utils.to_categorical(y_test, NB_CLASSES)

# float and normalization
X_train = X_train.astype('float32')
X_test = X_test.astype('float32')
X_train /= 255
X_test /= 255
```

Our net will learn 32 convolutional filters, each of which with a 3 x 3 size. The output dimension is the same one of the input shape, so it will be 32 x 32 and activation is ReLU, which is a simple way of introducing non-linearity. After that we have a max-pooling operation with pool size 2 x 2 and a dropout at 25%:

```
# network
model = Sequential()
model.add(Conv2D(32, (3, 3), padding='same',
input_shape=(IMG_ROWS, IMG_COLS, IMG_CHANNELS)))
model.add(Activation('relu'))
model.add(MaxPooling2D(pool_size=(2, 2)))
model.add(Dropout(0.25))
```

The next stage in the deep pipeline is a dense network with 512 units and ReLU activation followed by a dropout at 50% and by a softmax layer with 10 classes as output, one for each category:

```
model.add(Flatten())
model.add(Dense(512))
model.add(Activation('relu'))
model.add(Dropout(0.5))
model.add(Dense(NB_CLASSES))
model.add(Activation('softmax'))
model.summary()
```

After defining the network, we can train the model. In this case, we split the data and compute a validation set in addition to the training and testing sets. The training is used to build our models, the validation is used to select the best performing approach, while the test set is to check the performance of our best models on fresh unseen data:

```
# train
model.compile(loss='categorical_crossentropy', optimizer=OPTIM,
metrics=['accuracy'])
model.fit(X_train, Y_train, batch_size=BATCH_SIZE,
epochs=NB_EPOCH, validation_split=VALIDATION_SPLIT,
verbose=VERBOSE)
score = model.evaluate(X_test, Y_test,
batch_size=BATCH_SIZE, verbose=VERBOSE)
print("Test score:", score[0])
print('Test accuracy:', score[1])
```

In this case we save the architecture of our deep network:

```
#save model
model_json = model.to_json()
open('cifar10_architecture.json', 'w').write(model_json)
And the weights learned by our deep network on the training set
model.save_weights('cifar10_weights.h5', overwrite=True)
```

Let us run the code. Our network reaches a test accuracy of 66.4% with 20 iterations. We also print the accuracy and loss plot, and dump the network with `model.summary()`:

```
● ● ●                      code — python keras_CIFAR10_simple.py — 121×77
gulli-macbookpro:code gulli$ python keras_CIFAR10_simple.py
Using TensorFlow backend.
('X_train shape:', (50000, 3, 32, 32))
(50000, 'train samples')
(10000, 'test samples')

Layer (type)                     Output Shape          Param #       Connected to
====================================================================================================
convolution2d_1 (Convolution2D)  (None, 32, 32, 32)    896           convolution2d_input_1[0][0]

activation_1 (Activation)        (None, 32, 32, 32)    0             convolution2d_1[0][0]

maxpooling2d_1 (MaxPooling2D)    (None, 32, 16, 16)    0             activation_1[0][0]

dropout_1 (Dropout)              (None, 32, 16, 16)    0             maxpooling2d_1[0][0]

flatten_1 (Flatten)              (None, 8192)          0             dropout_1[0][0]

dense_1 (Dense)                  (None, 512)           4194816       flatten_1[0][0]

activation_2 (Activation)        (None, 512)           0             dense_1[0][0]

dropout_2 (Dropout)              (None, 512)           0             activation_2[0][0]

dense_2 (Dense)                  (None, 10)            5130          dropout_2[0][0]

activation_3 (Activation)        (None, 10)            0             dense_2[0][0]
====================================================================================================
Total params: 4200842

Train on 40000 samples, validate on 10000 samples
Epoch 1/20
40000/40000 [==============================] - 114s - loss: 1.7380 - acc: 0.3855 - val_loss: 1.5353 - val_acc: 0.4376
Epoch 2/20
40000/40000 [==============================] - 114s - loss: 1.3847 - acc: 0.5081 - val_loss: 1.2392 - val_acc: 0.5629
Epoch 3/20
40000/40000 [==============================] - 116s - loss: 1.2481 - acc: 0.5566 - val_loss: 1.2737 - val_acc: 0.5446
Epoch 4/20
40000/40000 [==============================] - 114s - loss: 1.1590 - acc: 0.5913 - val_loss: 1.1919 - val_acc: 0.5722
Epoch 5/20
40000/40000 [==============================] - 116s - loss: 1.0904 - acc: 0.6138 - val_loss: 1.0860 - val_acc: 0.6257
Epoch 6/20
40000/40000 [==============================] - 115s - loss: 1.0282 - acc: 0.6391 - val_loss: 1.0771 - val_acc: 0.6245
Epoch 7/20
40000/40000 [==============================] - 115s - loss: 0.9828 - acc: 0.6523 - val_loss: 1.0491 - val_acc: 0.6375
Epoch 8/20
40000/40000 [==============================] - 114s - loss: 0.9328 - acc: 0.6739 - val_loss: 1.0344 - val_acc: 0.6453
Epoch 9/20
40000/40000 [==============================] - 114s - loss: 0.8978 - acc: 0.6858 - val_loss: 1.0789 - val_acc: 0.6384
Epoch 10/20
40000/40000 [==============================] - 115s - loss: 0.8556 - acc: 0.7004 - val_loss: 1.0072 - val_acc: 0.6538
Epoch 11/20
40000/40000 [==============================] - 114s - loss: 0.8215 - acc: 0.7142 - val_loss: 1.1334 - val_acc: 0.6450
Epoch 12/20
40000/40000 [==============================] - 115s - loss: 0.7938 - acc: 0.7256 - val_loss: 1.0761 - val_acc: 0.6464
Epoch 13/20
40000/40000 [==============================] - 118s - loss: 0.7631 - acc: 0.7337 - val_loss: 1.0204 - val_acc: 0.6587
Epoch 14/20
40000/40000 [==============================] - 121s - loss: 0.7381 - acc: 0.7433 - val_loss: 0.9647 - val_acc: 0.6853
Epoch 15/20
40000/40000 [==============================] - 114s - loss: 0.7094 - acc: 0.7529 - val_loss: 1.0852 - val_acc: 0.6604
Epoch 16/20
40000/40000 [==============================] - 114s - loss: 0.6872 - acc: 0.7608 - val_loss: 1.0144 - val_acc: 0.6680
Epoch 17/20
40000/40000 [==============================] - 115s - loss: 0.6642 - acc: 0.7682 - val_loss: 0.9787 - val_acc: 0.6781
Epoch 18/20
40000/40000 [==============================] - 114s - loss: 0.6524 - acc: 0.7758 - val_loss: 1.0035 - val_acc: 0.6803
Epoch 19/20
40000/40000 [==============================] - 114s - loss: 0.6302 - acc: 0.7834 - val_loss: 1.1080 - val_acc: 0.6571
Epoch 20/20
40000/40000 [==============================] - 113s - loss: 0.6081 - acc: 0.7902 - val_loss: 1.0744 - val_acc: 0.6672
Testing...
10000/10000 [==============================] - 13s
('\nTest score:', 1.0762448620796203)
('Test accuracy:', 0.66490000000000005)
['acc', 'loss', 'val_acc', 'val_loss']
```

In the following graph, we report the accuracy and the lost achieved by our net on both train and test datasets:

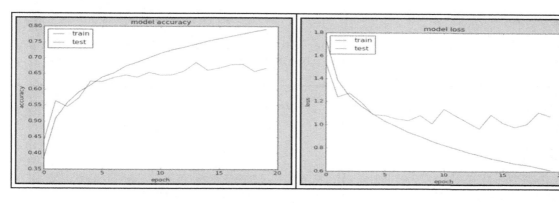

Improving the CIFAR-10 performance with deeper a network

One way to improve the performance is to define a deeper network with multiple convolutional operations. In this example, we have a sequence of modules:

conv+conv+maxpool+dropout+conv+conv+maxpool

Followed by a standard *dense+dropout+dense*. All the activation functions are ReLU.

Let us see the code for the new network:

```
model = Sequential()
model.add(Conv2D(32, (3, 3), padding='same',
input_shape=(IMG_ROWS, IMG_COLS, IMG_CHANNELS)))
model.add(Activation('relu'))
model.add(Conv2D(32, (3, 3), padding='same'))
model.add(Activation('relu'))
model.add(MaxPooling2D(pool_size=(2, 2)))
model.add(Dropout(0.25))
model.add(Conv2D(64, (3, 3), padding='same'))
model.add(Activation('relu'))
model.add(Conv2D(64, 3, 3))
model.add(Activation('relu'))
model.add(MaxPooling2D(pool_size=(2, 2)))
model.add(Dropout(0.25))
model.add(Flatten())
model.add(Dense(512))
```

```
model.add(Activation('relu'))
model.add(Dropout(0.5))
model.add(Dense(NB_CLASSES))
model.add(Activation('softmax'))
```

Congratulations! You have defined a deeper network. Let us run the code! First we dump the network, then we run for 40 iterations reaching an accuracy of 76.9%:

```
● ● ●                     code --- python keras_CIFAR10_V2.py — 121×77
      ~/Keras/codeBook/code — python keras_CIFAR10_V2.py          ~/Keras/codeBook/code — -bash          +

gulli-macbookpro:code gulli$ python keras_CIFAR10_V1.py
Using TensorFlow backend.
('X_train shape:', (50000, 3, 32, 32))
(50000, 'train samples')
(10000, 'test samples')

Layer (type)                    Output Shape          Param #      Connected to
====================================================================================================
convolution2d_1 (Convolution2D) (None, 32, 32, 32)    896          convolution2d_input_1[0][0]

activation_1 (Activation)       (None, 32, 32, 32)    0            convolution2d_1[0][0]

convolution2d_2 (Convolution2D) (None, 32, 32, 32)    9248         activation_1[0][0]

activation_2 (Activation)       (None, 32, 32, 32)    0            convolution2d_2[0][0]

maxpooling2d_1 (MaxPooling2D)   (None, 32, 16, 16)    0            activation_2[0][0]

dropout_1 (Dropout)             (None, 32, 16, 16)    0            maxpooling2d_1[0][0]

convolution2d_3 (Convolution2D) (None, 64, 16, 16)    18496        dropout_1[0][0]

activation_3 (Activation)       (None, 64, 16, 16)    0            convolution2d_3[0][0]

convolution2d_4 (Convolution2D) (None, 64, 14, 14)    36928        activation_3[0][0]

activation_4 (Activation)       (None, 64, 14, 14)    0            convolution2d_4[0][0]

maxpooling2d_2 (MaxPooling2D)   (None, 64, 7, 7)      0            activation_4[0][0]

dropout_2 (Dropout)             (None, 64, 7, 7)      0            maxpooling2d_2[0][0]

flatten_1 (Flatten)             (None, 3136)          0            dropout_2[0][0]

dense_1 (Dense)                 (None, 512)           1606144      flatten_1[0][0]

activation_5 (Activation)       (None, 512)           0            dense_1[0][0]

dropout_3 (Dropout)             (None, 512)           0            activation_5[0][0]

dense_2 (Dense)                 (None, 10)            5130         dropout_3[0][0]

activation_6 (Activation)       (None, 10)            0            dense_2[0][0]
====================================================================================================
Total params: 1676842

Train on 40000 samples, validate on 10000 samples
Epoch 1/40
40000/40000 [==============================] - 430s - loss: 1.8179 - acc: 0.3443 - val_loss: 1.5250 - val_acc: 0.4551
Epoch 2/40
40000/40000 [==============================] - 382s - loss: 1.3506 - acc: 0.5182 - val_loss: 1.1998 - val_acc: 0.5714
```

In the following screenshot, we will see the accuracy reached after 40 iterations:

```
Epoch 39/40
40000/40000 [==============================] - 348s - loss: 0.5497 - acc: 0.8246 - val_loss: 0.8669 - val_acc: 0.7811
Epoch 40/40
40000/40000 [==============================] - 346s - loss: 0.5447 - acc: 0.8280 - val_loss: 0.7910 - val_acc: 0.7816
Testing...
10000/10000 [==============================] - 41s
('\nTest score:', 0.79934534568786619)
('Test accuracy:', 0.76929999999999998)
['acc', 'loss', 'val_acc', 'val_loss']
```

So we have an improvement of 10.5% with respect to the previous simpler deeper network. For the sake of completeness, let us also report the accuracy and loss during training, shown as follows:

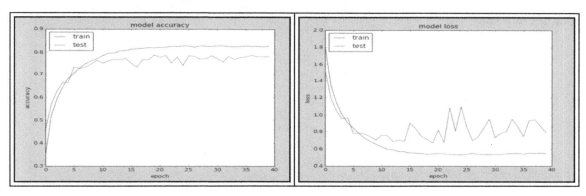

Improving the CIFAR-10 performance with data augmentation

Another way to improve the performance is to generate more images for our training. The key intuition is that we can take the standard CIFAR training set and augment this set with multiple types of transformations including rotation, rescaling, horizontal/vertical flip, zooming, channel shift, and many more. Let us see the code:

```
from keras.preprocessing.image import ImageDataGenerator
from keras.datasets import cifar10
import numpy as np
NUM_TO_AUGMENT=5

#load dataset
(X_train, y_train), (X_test, y_test) = cifar10.load_data()

# augmenting
print("Augmenting training set images...")
```

```
datagen = ImageDataGenerator(
rotation_range=40,
width_shift_range=0.2,
height_shift_range=0.2,
zoom_range=0.2,
horizontal_flip=True,
fill_mode='nearest')
```

The `rotation_range` is a value in degrees (0 - 180) for randomly rotating pictures. `width_shift` and `height_shift` are ranges for randomly translating pictures vertically or horizontally. `zoom_range` is for randomly zooming pictures. `horizontal_flip` is for randomly flipping half of the images horizontally. `fill_mode` is the strategy used for filling in new pixels that can appear after a rotation or a shift:

```
xtas, ytas = [], []
for i in range(X_train.shape[0]):
num_aug = 0
x = X_train[i] # (3, 32, 32)
x = x.reshape((1,) + x.shape) # (1, 3, 32, 32)
for x_aug in datagen.flow(x, batch_size=1,
save_to_dir='preview', save_prefix='cifar', save_format='jpeg'):
if num_aug >= NUM_TO_AUGMENT:
break
xtas.append(x_aug[0])
num_aug += 1
```

After augmentation, we will have generated many more training images starting from the standard CIFAR-10 set:

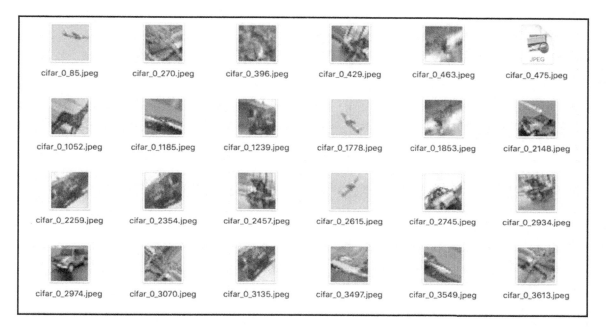

Now we can apply this intuition directly for training. Using the same ConvNet defined previously we simply generate more augmented images and then we train. For efficiency, the generator runs in parallel to the model. This allows an image augmentation on the CPU and in parallel to training on the GPU. Here is the code:

```
#fit the dataget
datagen.fit(X_train)

# train
history = model.fit_generator(datagen.flow(X_train, Y_train,
batch_size=BATCH_SIZE), samples_per_epoch=X_train.shape[0],
epochs=NB_EPOCH, verbose=VERBOSE)
score = model.evaluate(X_test, Y_test,
batch_size=BATCH_SIZE, verbose=VERBOSE)
print("Test score:", score[0])
print('Test accuracy:', score[1])
```

Each iteration is now more expensive because we have more training data. So let us run for 50 iterations only and see that we reach an accuracy of 78.3%:

```
Epoch 46/50
50000/50000 [==============================] - 405s - loss: 0.8288 - acc: 0.7297
Epoch 47/50
50000/50000 [==============================] - 424s - loss: 0.8349 - acc: 0.7303
Epoch 48/50
50000/50000 [==============================] - 408s - loss: 0.8319 - acc: 0.7295
Epoch 49/50
50000/50000 [==============================] - 403s - loss: 0.8386 - acc: 0.7281
Epoch 50/50
50000/50000 [==============================] - 398s - loss: 0.8394 - acc: 0.7267
Testing...
10000/10000 [==============================] - 42s
('\nTest score:', 0.73110332846641546)
('Test accuracy:', 0.78369999999999995)
['acc', 'loss']
```

The results obtained during our experiments are summarized in the following graph:

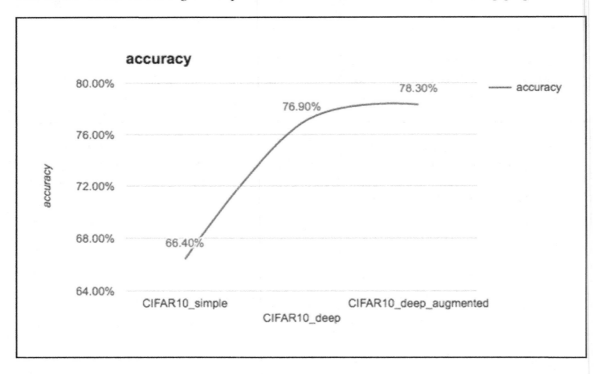

A list of state-of-the-art results for CIFAR-10 is available at: `http://rodrigob.github.io/a re_we_there_yet/build/classification_datasets_results.html`. As of January, 2017, the best result has an accuracy of 96.53%.

Predicting with CIFAR-10

Now let us suppose that we want to use the deep learning model we just trained for CIFAR-10 for a bulk evaluation of images. Since we saved the model and the weights, we do not need to train every time:

```
import numpy as np
import scipy.misc
from keras.models import model_from_json
from keras.optimizers import SGD

#load model
model_architecture = 'cifar10_architecture.json'
model_weights = 'cifar10_weights.h5'
model = model_from_json(open(model_architecture).read())
model.load_weights(model_weights)

#load images
img_names = ['cat-standing.jpg', 'dog.jpg']
imgs = [np.transpose(scipy.misc.imresize(scipy.misc.imread(img_name), (32,
32)),
(1, 0, 2)).astype('float32')
for img_name in img_names]
imgs = np.array(imgs) / 255

# train
optim = SGD()
model.compile(loss='categorical_crossentropy', optimizer=optim,
metrics=['accuracy'])

# predict
predictions = model.predict_classes(imgs)
print(predictions)
```

Now let us get the prediction for a and for a .

We get categories 3 (cat) and 5 (dog) as output, as expected:

```
gulli-macbookpro:code gulli$ python keras_EvaluateCIFAR10.py
Using TensorFlow backend.
2/2 [==============================] - 0s
[3 5]
gulli-macbookpro:code gulli$
```

Very deep convolutional networks for large-scale image recognition

In 2014, an interesting contribution for image recognition was presented (for more information refer to: *Very Deep Convolutional Networks for Large-Scale Image Recognition*, by K. Simonyan and A. Zisserman, 2014). The paper shows that, *a significant improvement on the prior-art configurations can be achieved by pushing the depth to 16-19 weight layers*. One model in the paper denoted as *D* or VGG-16 has 16 deep layers. An implementation in Java Caffe (http://caffe.berkeleyvision.org/) has been used for training the model on the ImageNet ILSVRC-2012 (http://image-net.org/challenges/LSVRC/2012/) dataset, which includes images of 1,000 classes and is split into three sets: training (1.3 million images), validation (50,000 images), and testing (100,000 images). Each image is (224 x 224) on three channels. The model achieves 7.5% top 5 error on ILSVRC-2012-val and 7.4% top 5 error on ILSVRC-2012-test.

According to the ImageNet site:

The goal of this competition is to estimate the content of photographs for the purpose of retrieval and automatic annotation using a subset of the large hand-labeled ImageNet dataset (10 million labeled images depicting 10,000 + object categories) as training. Test images will be presented with no initial annotation—no segmentation or labels—and algorithms will have to produce labelings specifying what objects are present in the images.

The weights learned by the model implemented in Caffe have been directly converted in Keras (for more information refer to: https://gist.github.com/baraldilorenzo/07d 7802847aaad0a35d3) and can be used for preloading into the Keras model, which is implemented next as described in the paper:

```
from keras.models import Sequential
from keras.layers.core import Flatten, Dense, Dropout
from keras.layers.convolutional import Conv2D, MaxPooling2D, ZeroPadding2D
from keras.optimizers import SGD
import cv2, numpy as np

# define a VGG16 network
def VGG_16(weights_path=None):
model = Sequential()
model.add(ZeroPadding2D((1,1),input_shape=(3,224,224)))
model.add(Conv2D(64, (3, 3), activation='relu'))
model.add(ZeroPadding2D((1,1)))
model.add(Conv2D(64, (3, 3), activation='relu'))
model.add(MaxPooling2D((2,2), strides=(2,2)))
model.add(ZeroPadding2D((1,1)))
```

```
model.add(Conv2D(128, (3, 3), activation='relu'))
model.add(ZeroPadding2D((1,1)))
model.add(Conv2D(128, (3, 3), activation='relu'))
model.add(MaxPooling2D((2,2), strides=(2,2)))
model.add(ZeroPadding2D((1,1)))
model.add(Conv2D(256, (3, 3), activation='relu'))
model.add(ZeroPadding2D((1,1)))
model.add(Conv2D(256, (3, 3), activation='relu'))
model.add(ZeroPadding2D((1,1)))
model.add(Conv2D(256, (3, 3), activation='relu'))
model.add(MaxPooling2D((2,2), strides=(2,2)))
model.add(ZeroPadding2D((1,1)))
model.add(Conv2D(512, (3, 3), activation='relu'))
model.add(ZeroPadding2D((1,1)))
model.add(Conv2D(512, (3, 3), activation='relu'))
model.add(ZeroPadding2D((1,1)))
model.add(Conv2D(512, (3, 3), activation='relu'))
model.add(MaxPooling2D((2,2), strides=(2,2)))
model.add(ZeroPadding2D((1,1)))
model.add(Conv2D(512, (3, 3), activation='relu'))
model.add(ZeroPadding2D((1,1)))
model.add(Conv2D(512, (3, 3), activation='relu'))
model.add(ZeroPadding2D((1,1)))
model.add(Conv2D(512, (3, 3), activation='relu'))
model.add(MaxPooling2D((2,2), strides=(2,2)))
model.add(Flatten())
#top layer of the VGG net
model.add(Dense(4096, activation='relu'))
model.add(Dropout(0.5))
model.add(Dense(4096, activation='relu'))
model.add(Dropout(0.5))
model.add(Dense(1000, activation='softmax'))
if weights_path:
model.load_weights(weights_path)
return model
```

Recognizing cats with a VGG-16 net

Now let us test the image of a :

```
im = cv2.resize(cv2.imread('cat.jpg'), (224, 224)).astype(np.float32)
im = im.transpose((2,0,1))
im = np.expand_dims(im, axis=0)

# Test pretrained model
model = VGG_16('/Users/gulli/Keras/codeBook/code/data/vgg16_weights.h5')
```

```
optimizer = SGD()
model.compile(optimizer=optimizer, loss='categorical_crossentropy')
out = model.predict(im)
print np.argmax(out)
```

When the code is executed, the class 285 is returned, which corresponds (for more information refer to: https://gist.github.com/yrevar/942d3a0ac09ec9e5eb3a) to Egyptian cat:

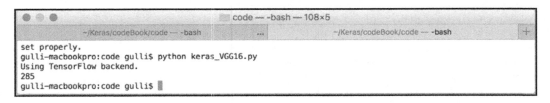

Utilizing Keras built-in VGG-16 net module

Keras applications are pre-built and pre-trained deep learning models. Weights are downloaded automatically when instantiating a model and stored at `~/.keras/models/`. Using built-in code is very easy:

```
from keras.models import Model
from keras.preprocessing import image
from keras.optimizers import SGD
from keras.applications.vgg16 import VGG16
import matplotlib.pyplot as plt
import numpy as np
import cv2

# prebuild model with pre-trained weights on imagenet
model = VGG16(weights='imagenet', include_top=True)
sgd = SGD(lr=0.1, decay=1e-6, momentum=0.9, nesterov=True)
model.compile(optimizer=sgd, loss='categorical_crossentropy')

# resize into VGG16 trained images' format
im = cv2.resize(cv2.imread('steam-locomotive.jpg'), (224, 224))
im = np.expand_dims(im, axis=0)

# predict
out = model.predict(im)
plt.plot(out.ravel())
plt.show()
print np.argmax(out)
#this should print 820 for steaming train
```

Now, let us consider a train:

It's like the ones my grandfather drove. If we run the code, we get result 820, which is the image net code for *steaming train*. Equally important is the fact that all the other classes have very weak support, as shown in the following graph:

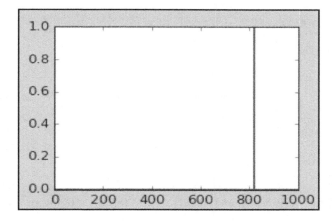

To conclude this section, note that VGG-16 is only one of the modules that are pre-built in Keras. A full list of pre-trained Keras models is available at: https://keras.io/applications/.

Recycling pre-built deep learning models for extracting features

One very simple idea is to use VGG-16 and, more generally, DCNN, for feature extraction. This code implements the idea by extracting features from a specific layer:

```
from keras.applications.vgg16 import VGG16
from keras.models import Model
from keras.preprocessing import image
from keras.applications.vgg16 import preprocess_input
import numpy as np

# pre-built and pre-trained deep learning VGG16 model
base_model = VGG16(weights='imagenet', include_top=True)
for i, layer in enumerate(base_model.layers):
    print (i, layer.name, layer.output_shape)

# extract features from block4_pool block
model =
Model(input=base_model.input,
output=base_model.get_layer('block4_pool').output)
img_path = 'cat.jpg'
img = image.load_img(img_path, target_size=(224, 224))
x = image.img_to_array(img)
x = np.expand_dims(x, axis=0)
x = preprocess_input(x)

# get the features from this block
features = model.predict(x)
```

Now you might wonder why we want to extract the features from an intermediate layer in a DCNN. The key intuition is that, as the network learns to classify images into categories, each layer learns to identify the features that are necessary to do the final classification. Lower layers identify lower order features such as color and edges, and higher layers compose these lower order feature into higher order features such as shapes or objects. Hence the intermediate layer has the capability to extract important features from an image, and these features are more likely to help in different kinds of classification. This has multiple advantages. First, we can rely on publicly available large-scale training and transfer this learning to novel domains. Second, we can save time for expensive large training. Third, we can provide reasonable solutions even when we don't have a large number of training examples for our domain. We also get a good starting network shape for the task at hand, instead of guessing it.

Very deep inception-v3 net used for transfer learning

Transfer learning is a very powerful deep learning technique which has more applications in different domains. The intuition is very simple and can be explained with an analogy. Suppose you want to learn a new language, say Spanish; then it could be useful to start from what you already know in a different language, say English.

Following this line of thinking, computer vision researchers now commonly use pre-trained CNNs to generate representations for novel tasks, where the dataset may not be large enough to train an entire CNN from scratch. Another common tactic is to take the pre-trained ImageNet network and then to fine-tune the entire network to the novel task.

Inception-v3 net is a very deep ConvNet developed by Google. Keras implements the full network described in the following diagram and it comes pre-trained on ImageNet. The default input size for this model is 299 x 299 on three channels:

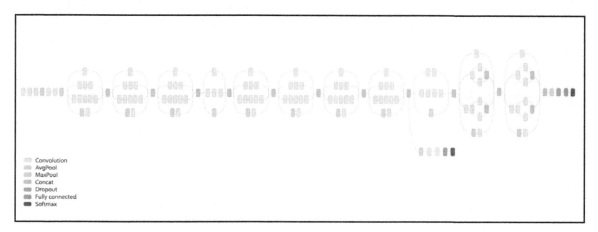

This skeleton example is inspired by a scheme available at: `https://keras.io/applicatio ns/`. We suppose to have a training dataset *D* in a domain, different from ImageNet. *D* has 1,024 features in input and 200 categories in output. Let us see a code fragment:

```
from keras.applications.inception_v3 import InceptionV3
from keras.preprocessing import image
from keras.models import Model
from keras.layers import Dense, GlobalAveragePooling2D
from keras import backend as K

# create the base pre-trained model
base_model = InceptionV3(weights='imagenet', include_top=False)
```

We use a trained inception-v3; we do not include the top model because we want to fine-tune on *D*. The top level is a dense layer with 1,024 inputs and where the last output level is a softmax dense layer with 200 classes of output. `x = GlobalAveragePooling2D()(x)` is used to convert the input to the correct shape for the dense layer to handle. In fact, `base_model.output` tensor has the shape *(samples, channels, rows, cols)* for `dim_ordering="th"` or *(samples, rows, cols, channels)* for `dim_ordering="tf"` but dense needs them as *(samples, channels)* and `GlobalAveragePooling2D` averages across *(rows, cols)*. So if you look at the last four layers (where `include_top=True`), you see these shapes:

```
# layer.name, layer.input_shape, layer.output_shape
('mixed10', [(None, 8, 8, 320), (None, 8, 8, 768), (None, 8, 8, 768),
(None, 8, 8, 192)], (None, 8, 8, 2048))
('avg_pool', (None, 8, 8, 2048), (None, 1, 1, 2048))
('flatten', (None, 1, 1, 2048), (None, 2048))
('predictions', (None, 2048), (None, 1000))
```

When you do `include_top=False`, you are removing the last three layers and exposing the `mixed10` layer, so the `GlobalAveragePooling2D` layer converts the *(None, 8, 8, 2048)* to *(None, 2048)*, where each element in the *(None, 2048)* tensor is the average value for each corresponding *(8, 8)* subtensor in the *(None, 8, 8, 2048)* tensor:

```
# add a global spatial average pooling layer
x = base_model.output
x = GlobalAveragePooling2D()(x) # let's add a fully-connected layer as first
layer
x = Dense(1024, activation='relu')(x) # and a logistic layer with 200
classes as last layer
predictions = Dense(200, activation='softmax')(x) # model to train
model = Model(input=base_model.input, output=predictions)
```

All the convolutional levels are pre-trained, so we freeze them during the training of the full model:

```
# that is, freeze all convolutional InceptionV3 layers
for layer in base_model.layers: layer.trainable = False
```

The model is then compiled and trained for a few epochs so that the top layers are trained:

```
# compile the model (should be done *after* setting layers to non-
trainable)
model.compile(optimizer='rmsprop', loss='categorical_crossentropy')

# train the model on the new data for a few epochs model.fit_generator(...)
```

Then we freeze the top layers in inception and fine-tune some inception layer. In this example, we decide to freeze the first 172 layers (an hyperparameter to tune):

```
# we chose to train the top 2 inception blocks, that is, we will freeze

# the first 172 layers and unfreeze the rest:
for layer in
model.layers[:172]: layer.trainable = False
for layer in
model.layers[172:]: layer.trainable = True
```

The model is then recompiled for fine-tune optimization. We need to recompile the model for these modifications to take effect:

```
# we use SGD with a low learning rate
from keras.optimizers
import SGD
model.compile(optimizer=SGD(lr=0.0001, momentum=0.9),
loss='categorical_crossentropy')

# we train our model again (this time fine-tuning the top 2 inception
blocks)
# alongside the top Dense layers
model.fit_generator(...)
```

Now we have a new deep network that reuses the standard Inception-v3 network, but it is trained on a new domain *D* via transfer learning. Of course, there are many parameters to fine-tune for achieving good accuracy. However, we are now reusing a very large pre-trained network as a starting point via transfer learning. In doing so, we can save the need to train on our machines by reusing what is already available in Keras.

Summary

In this chapter, we learned how to use Deep Learning ConvNets for recognizing MNIST handwritten characters with high accuracy. Then we used the CIFAR 10 dataset to build a deep learning classifier in 10 categories, and the ImageNet datasets to build an accurate classifier in 1,000 categories. In addition, we investigated how to use large deep learning networks such as VGG16 and very deep networks such as InceptionV3. The chapter concluded with a discussion on transfer learning in order to adapt pre-built models trained on large datasets so that they can work well on a new domain.

In the next chapter, we will introduce generative adversarial networks used to reproduce synthetic data that looks like data generated by humans; and we will present WaveNet, a deep neural network used for reproducing human voice and musical instruments with high quality.

4
Generative Adversarial Networks and WaveNet

In this chapter, we will discuss **generative adversarial networks** (**GANs**) and WaveNets. GANs have been defined as *the most interesting idea in the last 10 years in ML* (`https://www.quora.com/What-are-some-recent-and-potentially-upcoming-breakthroughs-in-deep-learning`) by Yann LeCun, one of the fathers of deep learning. GANs are able to learn how to reproduce synthetic data that looks real. For instance, computers can learn how to paint and create realistic images. The idea was originally proposed by Ian Goodfellow (for more information refer to: *NIPS 2016 Tutorial: Generative Adversarial Networks*, by I. Goodfellow, 2016); he was worked with the University of Montreal, Google Brain, and recently OpenAI (`https://openai.com/`). WaveNet is a deep generative network proposed by Google DeepMind to teach computers how to reproduce human voices and musical instruments, both with impressive quality.

In this chapter, we will cover cover the following topics:

- What is GAN?
- Deep convolutional GAN
- Applications of GAN

What is a GAN?

The key intuition of GAN can be easily considered as analogous to *art forgery*, which is the process of creating works of art (https://en.wikipedia.org/wiki/Art) that are falsely credited to other, usually more famous, artists. GANs train two neural nets simultaneously, as shown in the next diagram. The generator $G(Z)$ makes the forgery, and the discriminator $D(Y)$ can judge how realistic the reproductions based on its observations of authentic pieces of arts and copies are. $D(Y)$ takes an input, Y, (for instance, an image) and expresses a vote to judge how real the input is--in general, a value close to zero denotes *real* and a value close to one denotes *forgery*. $G(Z)$ takes an input from a random noise, Z, and trains itself to fool D into thinking that whatever $G(Z)$ produces is real. So, the goal of training the discriminator $D(Y)$ is to maximize $D(Y)$ for every image from the true data distribution, and to minimize $D(Y)$ for every image not from the true data distribution. So, G and D play an opposite game; hence the name *adversarial training*. Note that we train G and D in an alternating manner, where each of their objectives is expressed as a loss function optimized via a gradient descent. The generative model learns how to forge more successfully, and the discriminative model learns how to recognize forgery more successfully. The discriminator network (usually a standard convolutional neural network) tries to classify whether an input image is real or generated. The important new idea is to backpropagate through both the discriminator and the generator to adjust the generator's parameters in such a way that the generator can learn how to fool the the discriminator for an increasing number of situations. At the end, the generator will learn how to produce forged images that are indistinguishable from real ones:

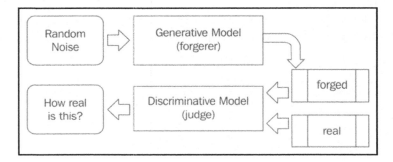

Of course, GANs require finding the equilibrium in a game with two players. For effective learning it is required that if a player successfully moves downhill in a round of updates, the same update must move the other player downhill too. Think about it! If the forger learns how to fool the judge on every occasion, then the forger himself has nothing more to learn. Sometimes the two players eventually reach an equilibrium, but this is not always guaranteed and the two players can continue playing for a long time. An example of learning from both sides has been provided in the following graph:

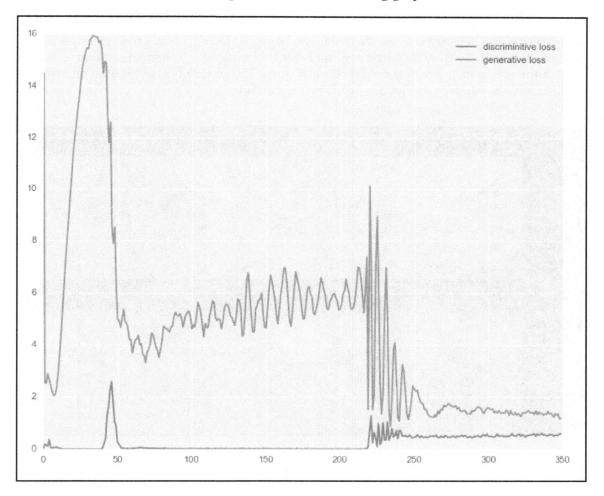

Some GAN applications

We have seen that the generator learns how to forge data. This means that it learns how to create new synthetic data, which is created by the network, that looks real and like it was created by humans. Before going into details of some GAN code, I'd like to share the results of a recent paper: *StackGAN: Text to Photo-Realistic Image Synthesis with Stacked Generative Adversarial Networks,* by Han Zhang, Tao Xu, Hongsheng Li, Shaoting Zhang, Xiaolei Huang, Xiaogang Wang, and Dimitris Metaxas (the code is available online at: `https://git hub.com/hanzhanggit/StackGAN`).

Here, a GAN has been used to synthesize forged images starting from a text description. The results are impressive. The first column is the real image in the test set, and the rest of the columns contain images generated from the same text description by **Stage-I** and **Stage-II** of StackGAN. More examples are available on YouTube (`https://www.youtube.com/wat ch?v=SuRyL5vhCIM&feature=youtu.be`):

Now let us see how a GAN can learn to *forge* the MNIST dataset. In this case, there is a combination of GAN and ConvNets (for more information refer to: *Unsupervised Representation Learning with Deep Convolutional Generative Adversarial Networks*, by A. Radford, L. Metz, and S. Chintala, arXiv: 1511.06434, 2015) used for the generator and the discriminator networks. At the beginning, the generator creates nothing understandable, but after a few iterations, synthetic forged numbers are progressively clearer and clearer. In the following image, the panels are ordered by increasing training epochs, and you can see the quality improving among panels:

The following image represents the forged handwritten numbers as the number of iterations increases:

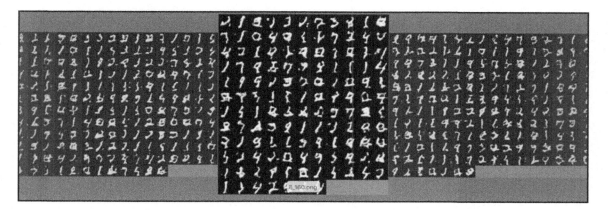

The following image represents the forged handwritten numbers at the hand of computation. The results are virtually indistinguishable from the original:

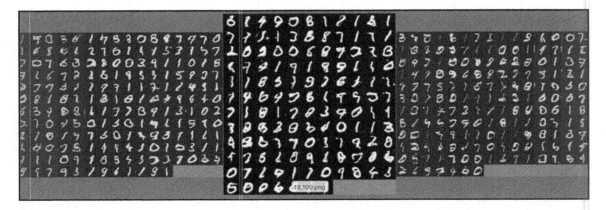

One of the coolest uses of GAN is arithmetic on faces in the generator's vector Z. In other words, if we stay in the space of synthetic forged images, it is possible to see things like this:

[smiling woman] - [neutral woman] + [neutral man] = [smiling man]

Or like this:

[man with glasses] - [man without glasses] + [woman without glasses] = [woman with glasses]

The next image is taken from the article, *Unsupervised Representation Learning with Deep Convolutional Generative Adversarial Networks*, by A. Radford, L. Metz, and S. Chintala, arXiv: 1511.06434, November, 2015:

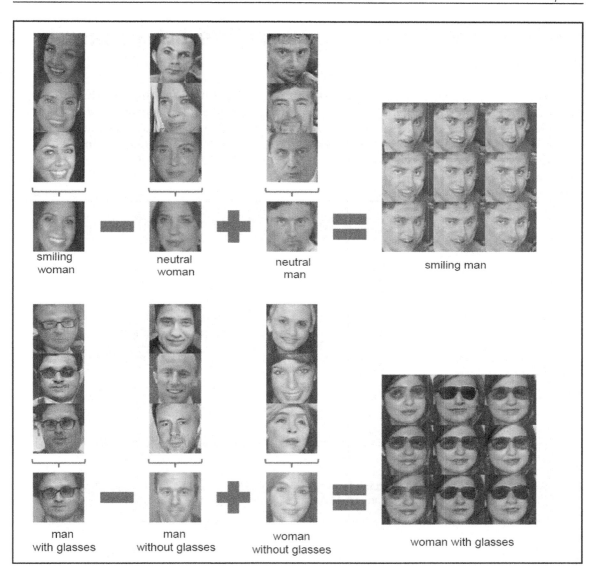

smiling woman − neutral woman + neutral man = smiling man

man with glasses − man without glasses + woman without glasses = woman with glasses

Deep convolutional generative adversarial networks

The **deep convolutional generative adversarial networks** (DCGAN) are introduced in the paper: *Unsupervised Representation Learning with Deep Convolutional Generative Adversarial Networks*, by A. Radford, L. Metz, and S. Chintala, arXiv: 1511.06434, 2015. The generator uses a 100-dimensional, uniform distribution space, Z, which is then projected into a smaller space by a series of vis-a-vis convolution operations. An example is shown in the following figure:

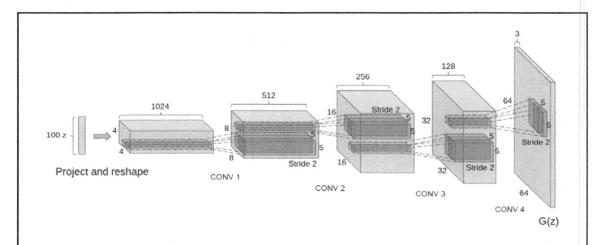

Figure 1: DCGAN generator used for LSUN scene modeling. A 100 dimensional uniform distribution Z is projected to a small spatial extent convolutional representation with many feature maps. A series of four fractionally-strided convolutions (in some recent papers, these are wrongly called deconvolutions) then convert this high level representation into a 64×64 pixel image. Notably, no fully connected or pooling layers are used.

A DCGAN generator can be described by the following Keras code; it is also described by one implementation, available at: https://github.com/jacobgil/keras-dcgan:

```
def generator_model():
    model = Sequential()
    model.add(Dense(input_dim=100, output_dim=1024))
    model.add(Activation('tanh'))
    model.add(Dense(128*7*7))
    model.add(BatchNormalization())
    model.add(Activation('tanh'))
    model.add(Reshape((128, 7, 7), input_shape=(128*7*7,)))
```

```
model.add(UpSampling2D(size=(2, 2)))
model.add(Convolution2D(64, 5, 5, border_mode='same'))
model.add(Activation('tanh'))
model.add(UpSampling2D(size=(2, 2)))
model.add(Convolution2D(1, 5, 5, border_mode='same'))
model.add(Activation('tanh'))
return model
```

Note that the code runs with Keras 1.x syntax. However, it is possible to run it with Keras 2.0 thanks to the Keras legacy interfaces. In this case a few warnings are reported as shown in the following figure:

```
keras-dcgan — python dcgan.py --mode train — 140×14
gulli-macbookpro:keras-dcgan gulli$ python dcgan.py --mode train
Using TensorFlow backend.
dcgan.py:40: UserWarning: Update your `Conv2D` call to the Keras 2 API: `Conv2D(64, (5, 5), padding="same", input_shape=(1, 28, 28...)`
  input_shape=(1, 28, 28)))
dcgan.py:43: UserWarning: Update your `Conv2D` call to the Keras 2 API: `Conv2D(128, (5, 5))`
  model.add(Convolution2D(128, 5, 5))
dcgan.py:20: UserWarning: Update your `Dense` call to the Keras 2 API: `Dense(units=1024, input_dim=100)`
  model.add(Dense(input_dim=100, output_dim=1024))
dcgan.py:27: UserWarning: Update your `Conv2D` call to the Keras 2 API: `Conv2D(64, (5, 5), padding="same")`
  model.add(Convolution2D(64, 5, 5, border_mode='same'))
dcgan.py:30: UserWarning: Update your `Conv2D` call to the Keras 2 API: `Conv2D(1, (5, 5), padding="same")`
  model.add(Convolution2D(1, 5, 5, border_mode='same'))
('Epoch is', 0)
('Number of batches', 468)
```

Now let's see the code. The first dense layer takes a vector of 100 dimensions as input and it produces 1,024 dimensions with the activation function `tanh` as the output. We assume that the input is sampled from a uniform distribution in *[-1, 1]*. The next dense layer produces data of 128 x 7 x 7 in the output using batch normalization (for more information refer to *Batch Normalization: Accelerating Deep Network Training by Reducing Internal Covariate Shift*, by S. Ioffe and C. Szegedy, arXiv: 1502.03167, 2014), a technique that can help stabilize learning by normalizing the input to each unit to zero mean and unit variance. Batch normalization has been empirically proven to accelerate the training in many situations, reduce the problems of poor initialization, and more generally produce more accurate results. There is also a `Reshape()` module that produces data of 127 x 7 x 7 (127 channels, 7 width, and 7 height), `dim_ordering` to `tf`, and a `UpSampling()` module that produces a repetition of each one into a 2 x 2 square. After that, we have a convolutional layer producing 64 filters on 5 x 5 convolutional kernels with the activation `tanh`, followed by a new `UpSampling()` and a final convolution with one filter, and on 5 x 5 convolutional kernels with the activation `tanh`. Notice that this ConvNet has no pooling operations. The discriminator can be described with the following code:

```
def discriminator_model():
    model = Sequential()
    model.add(Convolution2D(64, 5, 5, border_mode='same',
    input_shape=(1, 28, 28)))
    model.add(Activation('tanh'))
```

```
model.add(MaxPooling2D(pool_size=(2, 2)))
model.add(Convolution2D(128, 5, 5))
model.add(Activation('tanh'))
model.add(MaxPooling2D(pool_size=(2, 2)))
model.add(Flatten())
model.add(Dense(1024))
model.add(Activation('tanh'))
model.add(Dense(1))
model.add(Activation('sigmoid'))
return model
```

The code takes a standard MNIST image with the shape (1, 28, 28) and applies a convolution with 64 filters of size 5 x 5 with `tanh` as the activation function. This is followed by a max-pooling operation of size 2 x 2 and by a further convolution max-pooling operation. The last two stages are dense, with the final one being the prediction for forgery, which consists of only one neuron with a `sigmoid` activation function. For a chosen number of epochs, the generator and discriminator are in turn trained by using `binary_crossentropy` as loss function. At each epoch, the generator makes a number of predictions (for example, it creates forged MNIST images) and the discriminator tries to learn after mixing the prediction with real MNIST images. After 32 epochs, the generator learns to forge this set of handwritten numbers. No one has programmed the machine to write but it has learned how to write numbers that are indistinguishable from the ones written by humans. Note that training GANs could be very difficult because it is necessary to find the equilibrium between two players. If you are interested in this topic, I'd advise you to have a look at a series of tricks collected by practitioners (https://github.com/soumith/ganhacks):

Keras adversarial GANs for forging MNIST

Keras adversarial (https://github.com/bstriner/keras-adversarial) is an open source Python package for building GANs developed by Ben Striner (https://github.com/bstriner and https://github.com/bstriner/keras-adversarial/blob/master/LICENSE.txt). Since Keras just recently moved to 2.0, I suggest downloading latest Keras adversarial package:

```
git clone --depth=50 --branch=master
https://github.com/bstriner/keras-adversarial.git
```

And install setup.py:

```
python setup.py install
```

Note that compatibility with Keras 2.0 is tracked in this issue https://github.com/bstriner/keras-adversarial/issues/11.

 If the generator G and the discriminator D are based on the same model, M, then they can be combined into an adversarial model; it uses the same input, M, but separates targets and metrics for G and D. The library has the following API call:

```
adversarial_model = AdversarialModel(base_model=M,
    player_params=[generator.trainable_weights,
discriminator.trainable_weights],
    player_names=["generator", "discriminator"])
```

If the generator G and the discriminator D are based on the two different models, then it is possible to use this API call:

```
adversarial_model = AdversarialModel(player_models=[gan_g, gan_d],
    player_params=[generator.trainable_weights,
discriminator.trainable_weights],
    player_names=["generator", "discriminator"])
```

Let's see an example of a computation with MNIST:

```
import matplotlib as mpl
# This line allows mpl to run with no DISPLAY defined
mpl.use('Agg')
```

Let us see the open source code (`https://github.com/bstriner/keras-adversarial/blo b/master/examples/example_gan_convolutional.py`). Note that the code uses the syntax of Keras 1.x, but it also runs on the top of Keras 2.x thanks to a convenient set of utility functions contained in `legacy.py`. The code for `legacy.py` is reported in `Appendix`, *Conclusion*, and is available at `https://github.com/bstriner/keras-adversarial/blob /master/keras_adversarial/legacy.py`.

First, the open source example imports a number of modules. We have seen all of them previously, with the exception of LeakyReLU, a special version of ReLU that allows a small gradient when the unit is not active. Experimentally, it has been shown that LeakyReLU can improve the performance of GANs (for more information refer to: *Empirical Evaluation of Rectified Activations in Convolutional Network*, by B. Xu, N. Wang, T. Chen, and M. Li, arXiv:1505.00853, 2014) in a number of situations:

```
from keras.layers import Dense, Reshape, Flatten, Dropout, LeakyReLU,
    Input, Activation, BatchNormalization
from keras.models import Sequential, Model
from keras.layers.convolutional import Convolution2D, UpSampling2D
from keras.optimizers import Adam
from keras.regularizers import l1, l1l2
from keras.datasets import mnist

import pandas as pd
import numpy as np
```

Then, specific modules for GANs are imported:

```
from keras_adversarial import AdversarialModel, ImageGridCallback,
    simple_gan, gan_targets
from keras_adversarial import AdversarialOptimizerSimultaneous,
    normal_latent_sampling, AdversarialOptimizerAlternating
from image_utils import dim_ordering_fix, dim_ordering_input,
    dim_ordering_reshape, dim_ordering_unfix
```

Adversarial models train for multiplayer games. Given a base model with *n* targets and *k* players, create a model with *n*k* targets, where each player optimizes loss on that player's targets. In addition, `simple_gan` generates a GAN with the given `gan_targets`. Note that in the library, the labels for generator and discriminator are opposite; intuitively, this is a standard practice for GANs:

```
def gan_targets(n):
    """
    Standard training targets [generator_fake, generator_real,
discriminator_fake,
    discriminator_real] = [1, 0, 0, 1]
    :param n: number of samples
```

```
    :return: array of targets
    """
    generator_fake = np.ones((n, 1))
    generator_real = np.zeros((n, 1))
    discriminator_fake = np.zeros((n, 1))
    discriminator_real = np.ones((n, 1))
    return [generator_fake, generator_real, discriminator_fake,
discriminator_real]
```

The example defines the generator in a similar way to what we have seen previously. However, in this case, we use the functional syntax—each module in our pipeline is simply passed as input to the following module. So, the first module is dense, initialized by using `glorot_normal`. This initialization uses Gaussian noise scaled by the sum of the inputs plus outputs from the node. The same kind of initialization is used for all of the other modules. The `mode=2` parameter in `BatchNormlization` function produces feature-wise normalization based on per-batch statistics. Experimentally, this produces better results:

```
def model_generator():
    nch = 256
    g_input = Input(shape=[100])
    H = Dense(nch * 14 * 14, init='glorot_normal')(g_input)
    H = BatchNormalization(mode=2)(H)
    H = Activation('relu')(H)
    H = dim_ordering_reshape(nch, 14)(H)
    H = UpSampling2D(size=(2, 2))(H)
    H = Convolution2D(int(nch / 2), 3, 3, border_mode='same',
        init='glorot_uniform')(H)
    H = BatchNormalization(mode=2, axis=1)(H)
    H = Activation('relu')(H)
    H = Convolution2D(int(nch / 4), 3, 3, border_mode='same',
        init='glorot_uniform')(H)
    H = BatchNormalization(mode=2, axis=1)(H)
    H = Activation('relu')(H)
    H = Convolution2D(1, 1, 1, border_mode='same',
init='glorot_uniform')(H)
    g_V = Activation('sigmoid')(H)
    return Model(g_input, g_V)
```

The discriminator is very similar to the one defined previously in this chapter. The only major difference is the adoption of `LeakyReLU`:

```
def model_discriminator(input_shape=(1, 28, 28), dropout_rate=0.5):
    d_input = dim_ordering_input(input_shape, name="input_x")
    nch = 512
    H = Convolution2D(int(nch / 2), 5, 5, subsample=(2, 2),
        border_mode='same', activation='relu')(d_input)
    H = LeakyReLU(0.2)(H)
```

```
H = Dropout(dropout_rate)(H)
H = Convolution2D(nch, 5, 5, subsample=(2, 2),
    border_mode='same', activation='relu')(H)
H = LeakyReLU(0.2)(H)
H = Dropout(dropout_rate)(H)
H = Flatten()(H)
H = Dense(int(nch / 2))(H)
H = LeakyReLU(0.2)(H)
H = Dropout(dropout_rate)(H)
d_V = Dense(1, activation='sigmoid')(H)
return Model(d_input, d_V)
```

Then, two simple functions for loading and normalizing MNIST data are defined:

```
def mnist_process(x):
    x = x.astype(np.float32) / 255.0
    return x

def mnist_data():
    (xtrain, ytrain), (xtest, ytest) = mnist.load_data()
    return mnist_process(xtrain), mnist_process(xtest)
```

As a next step, the GAN is defined as a combination of generator and discriminator in a joint GAN model. Note that the weights are initialized with `normal_latent_sampling`, which samples from a normal Gaussian distribution:

```
if __name__ == "__main__":
    # z in R^100
    latent_dim = 100
    # x in R^{28x28}
    input_shape = (1, 28, 28)
    # generator (z -> x)
    generator = model_generator()
    # discriminator (x -> y)
    discriminator = model_discriminator(input_shape=input_shape)
    # gan (x - > yfake, yreal), z generated on GPU
    gan = simple_gan(generator, discriminator,
normal_latent_sampling((latent_dim,)))
    # print summary of models
    generator.summary()
    discriminator.summary()
    gan.summary()
```

After this, the example creates our GAN and it compiles the model trained using the Adam optimizer, with `binary_crossentropy` used as a loss function:

```
# build adversarial model
model = AdversarialModel(base_model=gan,
    player_params=[generator.trainable_weights,
discriminator.trainable_weights],
    player_names=["generator", "discriminator"])
model.adversarial_compile(adversarial_optimizer=AdversarialOptimizerSimulta
neous(),
    player_optimizers=[Adam(1e-4, decay=1e-4), Adam(1e-3, decay=1e-4)],
    loss='binary_crossentropy')
```

The generator for creating new images that look like real ones is defined. Each epoch will generate a new forged image during training that looks like the original:

```
def generator_sampler():
    zsamples = np.random.normal(size=(10 * 10, latent_dim))
    gen = dim_ordering_unfix(generator.predict(zsamples))
    return gen.reshape((10, 10, 28, 28))

generator_cb = ImageGridCallback(
    "output/gan_convolutional/epoch-{:03d}.png",generator_sampler)
xtrain, xtest = mnist_data()
xtrain = dim_ordering_fix(xtrain.reshape((-1, 1, 28, 28)))
xtest = dim_ordering_fix(xtest.reshape((-1, 1, 28, 28)))
y = gan_targets(xtrain.shape[0])
ytest = gan_targets(xtest.shape[0])
history = model.fit(x=xtrain, y=y,
validation_data=(xtest, ytest), callbacks=[generator_cb], nb_epoch=100,
    batch_size=32)
df = pd.DataFrame(history.history)
df.to_csv("output/gan_convolutional/history.csv")
generator.save("output/gan_convolutional/generator.h5")
discriminator.save("output/gan_convolutional/discriminator.h5")
```

Note that `dim_ordering_unfix` is utility function for supporting different image ordering defined in `image_utils.py`, as follows:

```
def dim_ordering_fix(x):
    if K.image_dim_ordering() == 'th':
        return x
    else:
        return np.transpose(x, (0, 2, 3, 1))
```

Now let's run the code and see the loss for the generator and discriminator. In the following screenshot, we see a dump of the networks for the discriminator and the generator:

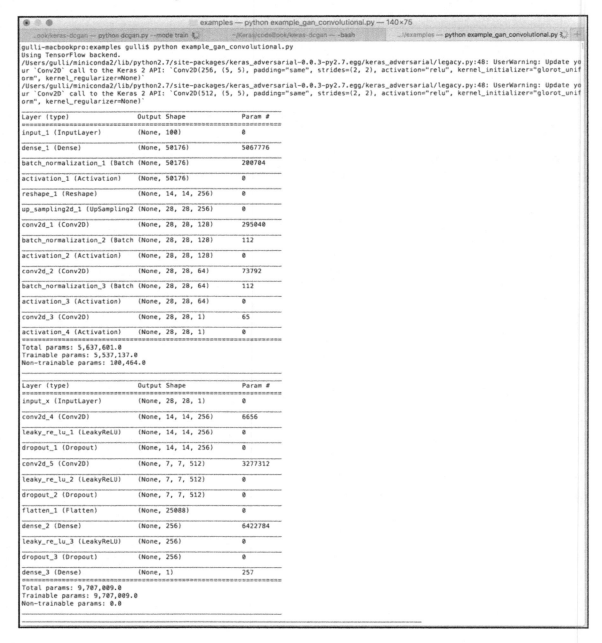

The following screenshot, shows the number of sample used for training and for validation:

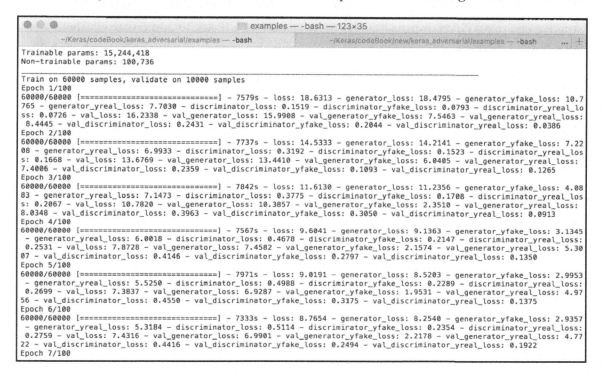

After 5-6 iterations, we already have acceptable artificial images generated and the computer has learned how to reproduce handwritten characters, as shown in the following image:

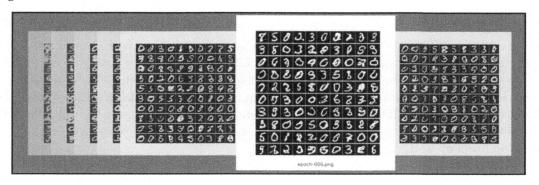

Keras adversarial GANs for forging CIFAR

Now we can use a GAN approach to learn how to forge CIFAR-10 and create synthetic images that look real. Let's see the open source code (https://github.com/bstriner/keras-adversarial/blob/master/examples/example_gan_cifar10.py). Again, note that it uses the syntax of Keras 1.x, but it also runs on the top of Keras 2.x thanks to a convenient set of utility functions contained in legacy.py (https://github.com/bstriner/keras-adversarial/blob/master/keras_adversarial/legacy.py). First, the open source example imports a number of packages:

```
import matplotlib as mpl
# This line allows mpl to run with no DISPLAY defined
mpl.use('Agg')
import pandas as pd
import numpy as np
import os
from keras.layers import Dense, Reshape, Flatten, Dropout, LeakyReLU,
    Activation, BatchNormalization, SpatialDropout2D
from keras.layers.convolutional import Convolution2D, UpSampling2D,
    MaxPooling2D, AveragePooling2D
from keras.models import Sequential, Model
from keras.optimizers import Adam
from keras.callbacks import TensorBoard
from keras.regularizers import l1l2
from keras_adversarial import AdversarialModel, ImageGridCallback,
    simple_gan, gan_targets
from keras_adversarial import AdversarialOptimizerSimultaneous,
    normal_latent_sampling, fix_names
import keras.backend as K
from cifar10_utils import cifar10_data
from image_utils import dim_ordering_fix, dim_ordering_unfix,
    dim_ordering_shape
```

Next, it defines a generator that uses a combination of convolutions with l1 and l2 regularization, batch normalization, and upsampling. Note that axis=1 says to normalize the dimension of the tensor first and mode=0 says to adopt a feature-wise normalization. This particular net is the result of many fine-tuning experiments, but it is still essentially a sequence of convolution 2D and upsampling operations, which uses a Dense module at the beginning and a sigmoid at the end. In addition, each convolution uses a LeakyReLU activation function and BatchNormalization:

```
def model_generator():
    model = Sequential()
    nch = 256
    reg = lambda: l1l2(l1=1e-7, l2=1e-7)
```

```
    h = 5
    model.add(Dense(input_dim=100, output_dim=nch * 4 * 4,
W_regularizer=reg()))
    model.add(BatchNormalization(mode=0))
    model.add(Reshape(dim_ordering_shape((nch, 4, 4))))
    model.add(Convolution2D(nch/2, h, h, border_mode='same',
W_regularizer=reg()))
    model.add(BatchNormalization(mode=0, axis=1))
    model.add(LeakyReLU(0.2))
    model.add(UpSampling2D(size=(2, 2)))
    model.add(Convolution2D(nch / 2, h, h, border_mode='same',
W_regularizer=reg()))
    model.add(BatchNormalization(mode=0, axis=1))
    model.add(LeakyReLU(0.2))
    model.add(UpSampling2D(size=(2, 2)))
    model.add(Convolution2D(nch / 4, h, h, border_mode='same',
W_regularizer=reg()))
    model.add(BatchNormalization(mode=0, axis=1))
    model.add(LeakyReLU(0.2))
    model.add(UpSampling2D(size=(2, 2)))
    model.add(Convolution2D(3, h, h, border_mode='same',
W_regularizer=reg()))
    model.add(Activation('sigmoid'))
    return model
```

Then, a discriminator is defined. Again, we have a sequence of convolution 2D operations, and in this case we adopt `SpatialDropout2D`, which drops entire 2D feature maps instead of individual elements. We also use `MaxPooling2D` and `AveragePooling2D` for similar reasons:

```
def model_discriminator():
    nch = 256
    h = 5
    reg = lambda: l1l2(l1=1e-7, l2=1e-7)
    c1 = Convolution2D(nch / 4, h, h, border_mode='same',
W_regularizer=reg(),
    input_shape=dim_ordering_shape((3, 32, 32)))
    c2 = Convolution2D(nch / 2, h, h, border_mode='same',
W_regularizer=reg())
    c3 = Convolution2D(nch, h, h, border_mode='same', W_regularizer=reg())
    c4 = Convolution2D(1, h, h, border_mode='same', W_regularizer=reg())
    def m(dropout):
        model = Sequential()
        model.add(c1)
        model.add(SpatialDropout2D(dropout))
        model.add(MaxPooling2D(pool_size=(2, 2)))
        model.add(LeakyReLU(0.2))
        model.add(c2)
```

```
        model.add(SpatialDropout2D(dropout))
        model.add(MaxPooling2D(pool_size=(2, 2)))
        model.add(LeakyReLU(0.2))
        model.add(c3)
        model.add(SpatialDropout2D(dropout))
        model.add(MaxPooling2D(pool_size=(2, 2)))
        model.add(LeakyReLU(0.2))
        model.add(c4)
        model.add(AveragePooling2D(pool_size=(4, 4), border_mode='valid'))
        model.add(Flatten())
        model.add(Activation('sigmoid'))
        return model
    return m
```

It is now possible to generate proper GANs. The following function takes multiple inputs, including a generator, a discriminator, the number of latent dimensions, and the GAN targets:

```
def example_gan(adversarial_optimizer, path, opt_g, opt_d, nb_epoch,
generator,
        discriminator, latent_dim, targets=gan_targets,
loss='binary_crossentropy'):
    csvpath = os.path.join(path, "history.csv")
    if os.path.exists(csvpath):
        print("Already exists: {}".format(csvpath))
    return
```

Then two GANs are created, one with dropout and the other without dropout for the discriminator:

```
print("Training: {}".format(csvpath))
# gan (x - > yfake, yreal), z is gaussian generated on GPU
# can also experiment with uniform_latent_sampling
d_g = discriminator(0)
d_d = discriminator(0.5)
generator.summary()
d_d.summary()
gan_g = simple_gan(generator, d_g, None)
gan_d = simple_gan(generator, d_d, None)
x = gan_g.inputs[1]
z = normal_latent_sampling((latent_dim,))(x)
# eliminate z from inputs
gan_g = Model([x], fix_names(gan_g([z, x]), gan_g.output_names))
gan_d = Model([x], fix_names(gan_d([z, x]), gan_d.output_names))
```

The two GANs are now combined into an adversarial model with separate weights, and the model is then compiled:

```
# build adversarial model
model = AdversarialModel(player_models=[gan_g, gan_d],
    player_params=[generator.trainable_weights, d_d.trainable_weights],
    player_names=["generator", "discriminator"])
model.adversarial_compile(adversarial_optimizer=adversarial_optimizer,
    player_optimizers=[opt_g, opt_d], loss=loss)
```

Next, there is a simple callback to sample images and a print on the file where the method `ImageGridCallback` is defined:

```
# create callback to generate images
zsamples = np.random.normal(size=(10 * 10, latent_dim))
def generator_sampler():
    xpred = dim_ordering_unfix(generator.predict(zsamples)).transpose((0,
2, 3, 1))
    return xpred.reshape((10, 10) + xpred.shape[1:])
generator_cb =
    ImageGridCallback(os.path.join(path, "epoch-{:03d}.png"),
    generator_sampler, cmap=None)
```

Now, the CIFAR-10 data is loaded and the model is fit. If the backend is TensorFlow, then the loss information is saved into a TensorBoard to check how the loss decreases over time. The history is also conveniently saved into a CVS format, and the models' weights are also stored in an `h5` format:

```
# train model
xtrain, xtest = cifar10_data()
y = targets(xtrain.shape[0])
ytest = targets(xtest.shape[0])
callbacks = [generator_cb]
if K.backend() == "tensorflow":
    callbacks.append(TensorBoard(log_dir=os.path.join(path, 'logs'),
        histogram_freq=0, write_graph=True, write_images=True))
history = model.fit(x=dim_ordering_fix(xtrain),y=y,
    validation_data=(dim_ordering_fix(xtest), ytest),
    callbacks=callbacks, nb_epoch=nb_epoch,
    batch_size=32)
# save history to CSV
df = pd.DataFrame(history.history)
df.to_csv(csvpath)
# save models
generator.save(os.path.join(path, "generator.h5"))
d_d.save(os.path.join(path, "discriminator.h5"))
```

Finally, the whole GANs can be run. The generator samples from a space with 100 latent dimensions, and we've used `Adam` as optimizer for both GANs:

```
def main():
    # z in R^100
    latent_dim = 100
    # x in R^{28x28}
    # generator (z -> x)
    generator = model_generator()
    # discriminator (x -> y)
    discriminator = model_discriminator()
    example_gan(AdversarialOptimizerSimultaneous(), "output/gan-cifar10",
        opt_g=Adam(1e-4, decay=1e-5),
        opt_d=Adam(1e-3, decay=1e-5),
        nb_epoch=100, generator=generator, discriminator=discriminator,
        latent_dim=latent_dim)
if __name__ == "__main__":
main()
```

In order to have a complete view on the open source code, we need to include a few simple utility functions for storing the grid of images:

```
from matplotlib import pyplot as plt, gridspec
import os

def write_image_grid(filepath, imgs, figsize=None, cmap='gray'):
    directory = os.path.dirname(filepath)
    if not os.path.exists(directory):
        os.makedirs(directory)
    fig = create_image_grid(imgs, figsize, cmap=cmap)
    fig.savefig(filepath)
    plt.close(fig)

def create_image_grid(imgs, figsize=None, cmap='gray'):
    n = imgs.shape[0]
    m = imgs.shape[1]
    if figsize is None:
        figsize=(n,m)
    fig = plt.figure(figsize=figsize)
    gs1 = gridspec.GridSpec(n, m)
    gs1.update(wspace=0.025, hspace=0.025) # set the spacing between axes.
    for i in range(n):
        for j in range(m):
            ax = plt.subplot(gs1[i, j])
            img = imgs[i, j, :]
    ax.imshow(img, cmap=cmap)
    ax.axis('off')
    return fig
```

In addition, we need some utility methods for dealing with different image ordering (for example, Theano or TensorFlow):

```python
import keras.backend as K
import numpy as np
from keras.layers import Input, Reshape

def dim_ordering_fix(x):
    if K.image_dim_ordering() == 'th':
        return x
    else:
        return np.transpose(x, (0, 2, 3, 1))

def dim_ordering_unfix(x):
    if K.image_dim_ordering() == 'th':
        return x
    else:
        return np.transpose(x, (0, 3, 1, 2))

def dim_ordering_shape(input_shape):
    if K.image_dim_ordering() == 'th':
        return input_shape
    else:
        return (input_shape[1], input_shape[2], input_shape[0])

def dim_ordering_input(input_shape, name):
    if K.image_dim_ordering() == 'th':
        return Input(input_shape, name=name)
    else:
        return Input((input_shape[1], input_shape[2], input_shape[0]),
name=name)

def dim_ordering_reshape(k, w, **kwargs):
    if K.image_dim_ordering() == 'th':
        return Reshape((k, w, w), **kwargs)
    else:
        return Reshape((w, w, k), **kwargs)

# One more utility function is used to fix names
def fix_names(outputs, names):
    if not isinstance(outputs, list):
        outputs = [outputs]
    if not isinstance(names, list):
        names = [names]
    return [Activation('linear', name=name)(output)
        for output, name in zip(outputs, names)]
```

The following screenshot, shows a dump of the defined networks:

```
●  ●  ●                              examples — python example_gan_cifar10.py — 140×78
...ook/keras-dcgan — python dcgan.py --mode train        ~/Keras/codeBook/keras-dcgan — -bash        ...rsarial/examples — python example_gan_cifar10.py
gulli-macbookpro:examples gulli$ python example_gan_cifar10.py
Using TensorFlow backend.
Training: output/gan-cifar10/history.csv

Layer (type)                    Output Shape              Param #
=================================================================
dense_1 (Dense)                 (None, 4096)              413696

batch_normalization_1 (Batch    (None, 4096)              16384

reshape_1 (Reshape)             (None, 256, 4, 4)         0

conv2d_1 (Conv2D)               (None, 128, 4, 4)         819328

batch_normalization_2 (Batch    (None, 128, 4, 4)         512

leaky_re_lu_1 (LeakyReLU)       (None, 128, 4, 4)         0

up_sampling2d_1 (UpSampling2    (None, 128, 8, 8)         0

conv2d_2 (Conv2D)               (None, 128, 8, 8)         409728

batch_normalization_3 (Batch    (None, 128, 8, 8)         512

leaky_re_lu_2 (LeakyReLU)       (None, 128, 8, 8)         0

up_sampling2d_2 (UpSampling2    (None, 128, 16, 16)       0

conv2d_3 (Conv2D)               (None, 64, 16, 16)        204864

batch_normalization_4 (Batch    (None, 64, 16, 16)        256

leaky_re_lu_3 (LeakyReLU)       (None, 64, 16, 16)        0

up_sampling2d_3 (UpSampling2    (None, 64, 32, 32)        0

conv2d_4 (Conv2D)               (None, 3, 32, 32)         4803

activation_1 (Activation)       (None, 3, 32, 32)         0
=================================================================
Total params: 1,870,083.0
Trainable params: 1,861,251.0
Non-trainable params: 8,832.0
_____

Layer (type)                    Output Shape              Param #
=================================================================
conv2d_5 (Conv2D)               (None, 64, 32, 32)        4864

max_pooling2d_1 (MaxPooling2    (None, 64, 16, 16)        0

leaky_re_lu_4 (LeakyReLU)       (None, 64, 16, 16)        0

conv2d_6 (Conv2D)               (None, 128, 16, 16)       204928

max_pooling2d_2 (MaxPooling2    (None, 128, 8, 8)         0

leaky_re_lu_5 (LeakyReLU)       (None, 128, 8, 8)         0

conv2d_7 (Conv2D)               (None, 256, 8, 8)         819456

max_pooling2d_3 (MaxPooling2    (None, 256, 4, 4)         0

leaky_re_lu_6 (LeakyReLU)       (None, 256, 4, 4)         0

conv2d_8 (Conv2D)               (None, 1, 4, 4)           6401

average_pooling2d_1 (Average    (None, 1, 1, 1)           0

flatten_1 (Flatten)             (None, 1)                 0

activation_2 (Activation)       (None, 1)                 0
=================================================================
Total params: 1,035,649.0
Trainable params: 1,035,649.0
Non-trainable params: 0.0
_____
Train on 50000 samples, validate on 10000 samples
```

If we run the open source code, the very first iteration will generate unrealistic images. However, after 99 iterations, the network will learn to forge images that look like real CIFAR-10 images, as shown here:

In the following images, we see the real CIFAR-10 image on the right and the forged one on the left:

Forged images	Real CIFAR-10 images
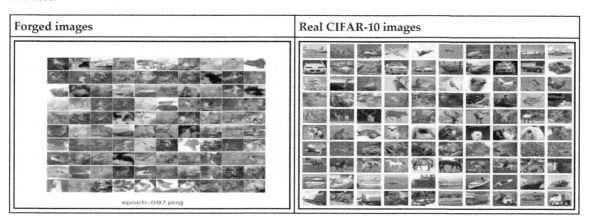	

WaveNet — a generative model for learning how to produce audio

WaveNet is a deep generative model for producing raw audio waveforms. This breakthrough technology was introduced (`https://deepmind.com/blog/wavenet-generat ive-model-raw-audio/`) by Google DeepMind (`https://deepmind.com/`) for teaching users how to speak to computers. The results are truly impressive, and you can find online examples of synthetic voices where the computer learns how to talk with the voices of celebrities such as Matt Damon. So, you might wonder why learning to synthesize audio is so difficult. Well, each digital sound we hear is based on 16,000 samples per second (sometimes, 48,000 or more), and building a predictive model where we learn to reproduce a sample based on all the previous ones is a very difficult challenge. Nevertheless, there are experiments showing that WaveNet has improved current state-of-the-art **text-to-speech (TTS)** systems, reducing the difference with human voices by 50% for both US English and Mandarin Chinese. What is even cooler is that DeepMind proved that WaveNet can also be used to teach computers how to generate the sound of musical instruments such as piano music. Now it's time for some definitions. TTS systems are typically divided into two different classes:

- **Concatenative TTS**: This is where single speech voice fragments are first memorized and then recombined when the voice has to be reproduced. However, this approach does not scale because it is only possible to reproduce the memorized voice fragments, and it is not possible to reproduce new speakers or different types of audio without memorizing the fragments from the beginning.
- **Parametric TTS**: This is where a model is created for storing all the characteristic features of the audio to be synthesized. Before WaveNet, the audio generated with parametric TTS was less natural than concatenative TTS. WaveNet improved the state-of-the-art by modeling directly the production of audio sounds, instead of using intermediate signal processing algorithms that have been used in the past.

In principle, WaveNet can be seen as a stack of 1D convolutional layers (we have seen 2D convolution for images in `Chapter 3`, *Deep Learning with ConvNets*), with a constant stride of one and with no pooling layers. Note that the input and the output have by construction the same dimension, so ConvNet is well-suited to model sequential data such as audio. However, it has been shown that in order to reach a large size for the receptive field (remember that the receptive field of a neuron in a layer is the cross section of the previous layer from which neurons provide inputs) in the output neuron it is necessary to either use a massive number of large filters or prohibitively increase the the depth of the network. For this reason, pure ConvNets are not so effective in learning how to synthesize audio. The key intuition beyond WaveNet is the dilated causal convolutions (for more information refer to the article: *Multi-Scale Context Aggregation by Dilated Convolutions*, by Fisher Yu, Vladlen Koltun, 2016, available at: `https://www.semanticscholar.org/paper/Multi-Scale-Context-Aggregation-by-Dilated-Yu-Koltun/420c46d7cafcb841309f02ad04cf51cb1f190a48`) or sometime atrous convolution (*atrous* is the *bastardization* of the French expression *à trous*, meaning *with holes*, so an atrous convolution is a convolution with holes), which simply means that some input values are skipped when the filter of a convolutional layer is applied. As an example, in one dimension, a filter, *w*, of size 3 with dilatation 1 would compute the following sum:

$$w\left[0\right]x\left[0\right] + w\left[1\right]x\left[2\right] + w\left[3\right]x\left[4\right]$$

Thanks to this simple idea of introducing *holes*, it is possible to stack multiple dilated convolutional layers with exponentially increasing filters, and learn long range input dependencies without having an excessively deep network. A WaveNet is therefore a ConvNet where the convolutional layers have various dilation factors, allowing the receptive field to grow exponentially with depth and therefore efficiently cover thousands of audio time-steps. When we train, the input are sounds recorded from human speakers. The waveforms are quantized to a fixed integer range. A WaveNet defines an initial convolutional layer accessing only the current and previous input. Then, there is a stack of dilated ConvNet layers, still accessing only current and previous inputs. At the end, there is a series of dense layers that combine previous results, followed by a softmax activation function for categorical outputs. At each step, a value is predicted from the network and fed back into the input. At the same time, a new prediction for the next step is computed. The loss function is the cross-entropy between the output for the current step and the input at the next step .One Keras implementation developed by Bas Veeling is available at: `https://github.com/basveeling/wavenet` and can be easily installed via `git`:

```
pip install virtualenv
mkdir ~/virtualenvs && cd ~/virtualenvs
virtualenv wavenet
source wavenet/bin/activate
cd ~
```

```
git clone https://github.com/basveeling/wavenet.git
cd wavenet
pip install -r requirements.txt
```

Note that this code is compatible with Keras 1.x and please check the issue at `https://gith ub.com/basveeling/wavenet/issues/29`, to understand what is the progress for porting it on the top of Keras 2.x. Training is very simple but requires a significant amount of computational power (so make sure that you have good GPU support):

```
$ python wavenet.py with 'data_dir=your_data_dir_name'
```

Sampling the network after training is equally very easy:

```
python wavenet.py predict with 'models/[run_folder]/config.json
predict_seconds=1'
```

You can find a large number of hyperparameters online, which can be used for fine-tuning our training process. The network is really deep, as explained by this dump of internal layers. Note that the input waveform are divided into (`fragment_length = 1152` and `nb_output_bins = 256`), which is the tensor propagating into WaveNet. WaveNet is organized in repeated blocks called residuals, each consisting of a multiplied merge of two dilated convolutional modules (one with `sigmoid` and the other with `tanh` activation), followed by a sum merged convolutional. Note that each dilated convolution has holes of growing exponential size (`2 ** i`) from 1 to 512, as defined in this piece of text:

```
def residual_block(x):
    original_x = x
    tanh_out = CausalAtrousConvolution1D(nb_filters, 2, atrous_rate=2 ** i,
        border_mode='valid', causal=True, bias=use_bias,
        name='dilated_conv_%d_tanh_s%d' % (2 ** i, s), activation='tanh',
        W_regularizer=l2(res_l2))(x)
    sigm_out = CausalAtrousConvolution1D(nb_filters, 2, atrous_rate=2 ** i,
        border_mode='valid', causal=True, bias=use_bias,
        name='dilated_conv_%d_sigm_s%d' % (2 ** i, s),
activation='sigmoid',
        W_regularizer=l2(res_l2))(x)
    x = layers.Merge(mode='mul',
        name='gated_activation_%d_s%d' % (i, s))([tanh_out, sigm_out])
    res_x = layers.Convolution1D(nb_filters, 1, border_mode='same',
bias=use_bias,
        W_regularizer=l2(res_l2))(x)
    skip_x = layers.Convolution1D(nb_filters, 1, border_mode='same',
bias=use_bias,
        W_regularizer=l2(res_l2))(x)
    res_x = layers.Merge(mode='sum')([original_x, res_x])
    return res_x, skip_x
```

After the residual dilated block, there is a sequence of merged convolutional modules, followed by two convolutional modules, followed by a `softmax` activation function in `nb_output_bins` categories. The full network structure is here:

```
Layer (type) Output Shape Param # Connected to
==========================================================================
=========================
input_part (InputLayer) (None, 1152, 256) 0


initial_causal_conv (CausalAtrou (None, 1152, 256) 131328 input_part[0][0]


dilated_conv_1_tanh_s0 (CausalAt (None, 1152, 256) 131072
initial_causal_conv[0][0]


dilated_conv_1_sigm_s0 (CausalAt (None, 1152, 256) 131072
initial_causal_conv[0][0]


gated_activation_0_s0 (Merge) (None, 1152, 256) 0
dilated_conv_1_tanh_s0[0][0]
dilated_conv_1_sigm_s0[0][0]


convolution1d_1 (Convolution1D) (None, 1152, 256) 65536
gated_activation_0_s0[0][0]


merge_1 (Merge) (None, 1152, 256) 0 initial_causal_conv[0][0]
convolution1d_1[0][0]


dilated_conv_2_tanh_s0 (CausalAt (None, 1152, 256) 131072 merge_1[0][0]


dilated_conv_2_sigm_s0 (CausalAt (None, 1152, 256) 131072 merge_1[0][0]


gated_activation_1_s0 (Merge) (None, 1152, 256) 0
dilated_conv_2_tanh_s0[0][0]
dilated_conv_2_sigm_s0[0][0]


convolution1d_3 (Convolution1D) (None, 1152, 256) 65536
gated_activation_1_s0[0][0]
```

```
merge_2 (Merge)              (None, 1152, 256)  0    merge_1[0][0]
convolution1d_3[0][0]
```

```
dilated_conv_4_tanh_s0 (CausalAt (None, 1152, 256)  131072 merge_2[0][0]
```

```
dilated_conv_4_sigm_s0 (CausalAt (None, 1152, 256)  131072 merge_2[0][0]
```

```
gated_activation_2_s0 (Merge)  (None, 1152, 256)  0
dilated_conv_4_tanh_s0[0][0]
dilated_conv_4_sigm_s0[0][0]
```

```
convolution1d_5 (Convolution1D) (None, 1152, 256)  65536
gated_activation_2_s0[0][0]
```

```
merge_3 (Merge)              (None, 1152, 256)  0    merge_2[0][0]
convolution1d_5[0][0]
```

```
dilated_conv_8_tanh_s0 (CausalAt (None, 1152, 256)  131072 merge_3[0][0]
```

```
dilated_conv_8_sigm_s0 (CausalAt (None, 1152, 256)  131072 merge_3[0][0]
```

```
gated_activation_3_s0 (Merge)  (None, 1152, 256)  0
dilated_conv_8_tanh_s0[0][0]
dilated_conv_8_sigm_s0[0][0]
```

```
convolution1d_7 (Convolution1D) (None, 1152, 256)  65536
gated_activation_3_s0[0][0]
```

```
merge_4 (Merge)              (None, 1152, 256)  0    merge_3[0][0]
convolution1d_7[0][0]
```

```
dilated_conv_16_tanh_s0 (CausalA (None, 1152, 256)  131072 merge_4[0][0]
```

```
dilated_conv_16_sigm_s0 (CausalA (None, 1152, 256)  131072 merge_4[0][0]
```

```
gated_activation_4_s0 (Merge) (None, 1152, 256) 0
dilated_conv_16_tanh_s0[0][0]
dilated_conv_16_sigm_s0[0][0]


convolution1d_9 (Convolution1D) (None, 1152, 256) 65536
gated_activation_4_s0[0][0]


merge_5 (Merge) (None, 1152, 256) 0 merge_4[0][0]
convolution1d_9[0][0]


dilated_conv_32_tanh_s0 (CausalA (None, 1152, 256) 131072 merge_5[0][0]


dilated_conv_32_sigm_s0 (CausalA (None, 1152, 256) 131072 merge_5[0][0]


gated_activation_5_s0 (Merge) (None, 1152, 256) 0
dilated_conv_32_tanh_s0[0][0]
dilated_conv_32_sigm_s0[0][0]


convolution1d_11 (Convolution1D) (None, 1152, 256) 65536
gated_activation_5_s0[0][0]


merge_6 (Merge) (None, 1152, 256) 0 merge_5[0][0]
convolution1d_11[0][0]


dilated_conv_64_tanh_s0 (CausalA (None, 1152, 256) 131072 merge_6[0][0]


dilated_conv_64_sigm_s0 (CausalA (None, 1152, 256) 131072 merge_6[0][0]


gated_activation_6_s0 (Merge) (None, 1152, 256) 0
dilated_conv_64_tanh_s0[0][0]
dilated_conv_64_sigm_s0[0][0]


convolution1d_13 (Convolution1D) (None, 1152, 256) 65536
gated_activation_6_s0[0][0]
```

```
merge_7 (Merge) (None, 1152, 256) 0 merge_6[0][0]
convolution1d_13[0][0]


dilated_conv_128_tanh_s0 (Causal (None, 1152, 256) 131072 merge_7[0][0]


dilated_conv_128_sigm_s0 (Causal (None, 1152, 256) 131072 merge_7[0][0]


gated_activation_7_s0 (Merge) (None, 1152, 256) 0
dilated_conv_128_tanh_s0[0][0]
dilated_conv_128_sigm_s0[0][0]


convolution1d_15 (Convolution1D) (None, 1152, 256) 65536
gated_activation_7_s0[0][0]


merge_8 (Merge) (None, 1152, 256) 0 merge_7[0][0]
convolution1d_15[0][0]


dilated_conv_256_tanh_s0 (Causal (None, 1152, 256) 131072 merge_8[0][0]


dilated_conv_256_sigm_s0 (Causal (None, 1152, 256) 131072 merge_8[0][0]


gated_activation_8_s0 (Merge) (None, 1152, 256) 0
dilated_conv_256_tanh_s0[0][0]
dilated_conv_256_sigm_s0[0][0]


convolution1d_17 (Convolution1D) (None, 1152, 256) 65536
gated_activation_8_s0[0][0]


merge_9 (Merge) (None, 1152, 256) 0 merge_8[0][0]
convolution1d_17[0][0]


dilated_conv_512_tanh_s0 (Causal (None, 1152, 256) 131072 merge_9[0][0]


dilated_conv_512_sigm_s0 (Causal (None, 1152, 256) 131072 merge_9[0][0]
```

```
gated_activation_9_s0 (Merge) (None, 1152, 256) 0
dilated_conv_512_tanh_s0[0][0]
dilated_conv_512_sigm_s0[0][0]
```

```
convolution1d_2 (Convolution1D) (None, 1152, 256) 65536
gated_activation_0_s0[0][0]
```

```
convolution1d_4 (Convolution1D) (None, 1152, 256) 65536
gated_activation_1_s0[0][0]
```

```
convolution1d_6 (Convolution1D) (None, 1152, 256) 65536
gated_activation_2_s0[0][0]
```

```
convolution1d_8 (Convolution1D) (None, 1152, 256) 65536
gated_activation_3_s0[0][0]
```

```
convolution1d_10 (Convolution1D) (None, 1152, 256) 65536
gated_activation_4_s0[0][0]
```

```
convolution1d_12 (Convolution1D) (None, 1152, 256) 65536
gated_activation_5_s0[0][0]
```

```
convolution1d_14 (Convolution1D) (None, 1152, 256) 65536
gated_activation_6_s0[0][0]
```

```
convolution1d_16 (Convolution1D) (None, 1152, 256) 65536
gated_activation_7_s0[0][0]
```

```
convolution1d_18 (Convolution1D) (None, 1152, 256) 65536
gated_activation_8_s0[0][0]
```

```
convolution1d_20 (Convolution1D) (None, 1152, 256) 65536
gated_activation_9_s0[0][0]
```

```
merge_11 (Merge) (None, 1152, 256) 0 convolution1d_2[0][0]
convolution1d_4[0][0]
convolution1d_6[0][0]
```

```
convolution1d_8[0][0]
convolution1d_10[0][0]
convolution1d_12[0][0]
convolution1d_14[0][0]
convolution1d_16[0][0]
convolution1d_18[0][0]
convolution1d_20[0][0]


activation_1 (Activation)      (None, 1152, 256) 0 merge_11[0][0]


convolution1d_21 (Convolution1D) (None, 1152, 256) 65792 activation_1[0][0]


activation_2 (Activation)      (None, 1152, 256) 0 convolution1d_21[0][0]


convolution1d_22 (Convolution1D) (None, 1152, 256) 65792 activation_2[0][0]


output_softmax (Activation)    (None, 1152, 256) 0 convolution1d_22[0][0]
========================================================================
========================
Total params: 4,129,536
Trainable params: 4,129,536
Non-trainable params: 0
```

DeepMind tried to train with data sets including multiple speakers, and this significantly improved the capacity to learn a shared representation of languages and tones and thus receive results close to natural speech. You'll find an amazing collection of examples of synthesized voice online (`https://deepmind.com/blog/wavenet-generative -model-raw-audio/`), and it is interesting to note that the quality of audio improves when WaveNet is conditioned on additional text that is transformed into a sequence of linguistic and phonetic features in addition to audio waveforms. My favorite examples are the ones where the same sentence is pronounced by the net with different tones of voice. Of course, it is also fascinating to hear WaveNet create piano music by itself. Check it out online!

Summary

In this chapter, we discussed GANs. A GAN typically consists of two networks; one is trained to forge synthetic data that looks authentic, and the second is trained to discriminate authentic data against forged data. The two networks continuously compete, and in doing so, they keep improving each other. We reviewed an open source code, learning to forge MNIST and CIFAR-10 images that look authentic. In addition, we discussed WaveNet, a deep generative network proposed by Google DeepMind for teaching computers how to reproduce human voices and musical instruments with impressive quality. WaveNet directly generates raw audio with a parametric text-to-speech approach based on dilated convolutional networks. Dilated convolutional networks are a special kind of ConvNets where convolution filters have holes, allowing the receptive field to grow exponentially in depth and therefore efficiently cover thousands of audio time-steps. DeepMind showed how it is possible to use WaveNet to synthesize human voice and musical instruments, and improved previous state-of-the-art. In the next chapter, we will discuss word embeddings—a set of deep learning methodologies for detecting relations among words and grouping together similar words.

5
Word Embeddings

Wikipedia defines word embedding as the collective name for a set of language modeling and feature learning techniques in **natural language processing** (**NLP**) where words or phrases from the vocabulary are mapped to vectors of real numbers.

Word embeddings are a way to transform words in text to numerical vectors so that they can be analyzed by standard machine learning algorithms that require vectors as numerical input.

You have already learned about one type of word embedding called **one-hot encoding**, in `Chapter 1`, *Neural Networks Foundations*. One-hot encoding is the most basic embedding approach. To recap, one-hot encoding represents a word in the text by a vector of the size of the vocabulary, where only the entry corresponding to the word is a one and all the other entries are zero.

A major problem with one-hot encoding is that there is no way to represent the similarity between words. In any given corpus, you would expect words such as (*cat*, *dog*), (*knife*, *spoon*), and so on to have some similarity. Similarity between vectors is computed using the dot product, which is the sum of element-wise multiplication between vector elements. In the case of one-hot encoded vectors, the dot product between any two words in a corpus is always zero.

To overcome the limitations of one-hot encoding, the NLP community has borrowed techniques from **information retrieval** (**IR**) to vectorize text using the document as the context. Notable techniques are TF-IDF (`https://en.wikipedia.org/wiki/Tf%E2%80%93id f`), **latent semantic analysis** (**LSA**) (`https://en.wikipedia.org/wiki/Latent_semantic_a nalysis`), and topic modeling (`https://en.wikipedia.org/wiki/Topic_model`). However, these representations capture a slightly different document-centric idea of semantic similarity.

Development of word embedding techniques began in earnest in 2000. Word embedding differs from previous IR-based techniques in that they use words as their context, which leads to a more natural form of semantic similarity from a human understanding perspective. Today, word embedding is the technique of choice for vectorizing text for all kinds of NLP tasks, such as text classification, document clustering, part of speech tagging, named entity recognition, sentiment analysis, and so on.

In this chapter, we will learn about two specific forms of word embedding, GloVe and word2vec, collectively known as distributed representations of words. These embeddings have proven more effective and have been widely adopted in the deep learning and NLP communities.

We will also learn different ways in which you can generate your own embeddings in your Keras code, as well as how to use and fine-tune pre-trained word2vec and GloVe models.

In this chapter, we will cover the following topics:

- Building various distributional representations of words in context
- Building models for leveraging embeddings to perform NLP tasks such as sentence parsing and sentiment analysis

Distributed representations

Distributed representations attempt to capture the meaning of a word by considering its relations with other words in its context. The idea is captured in this quote from J. R. Firth (for more information refer to the article: *Document Embedding with Paragraph Vectors*, by Andrew M. Dai, Christopher Olah, and Quoc V. Le, arXiv:1507.07998, 2015), a linguist who first proposed this idea:

You shall know a word by the company it keeps.

Consider the following pair of sentences:

Paris is the capital of France.
Berlin is the capital of Germany.

Even assuming you have no knowledge of world geography (or English for that matter), you would still conclude without too much effort that the word pairs (*Paris, Berlin*) and (*France, Germany*) were related in some way, and that corresponding words in each pair were related in the same way to each other, that is:

Paris : France :: Berlin : Germany

Thus, the aim of distributed representations is to find a general transformation function ϕ to convert each word to its associated vector such that relations of the following form hold true:

$$\varphi\left(\text{"Paris"}\right) - \varphi\left(\text{"France"}\right) \approx \varphi\left(\text{"Berlin"}\right) - \varphi\left(\text{"Germany"}\right)$$

In other words, distributed representation aims to convert words to vectors where the similarity between the vectors correlate with the semantic similarity between the words.

The most well-known word embeddings are word2vec and GloVe, which we cover in more detail in subsequent sections.

word2vec

The word2vec group of models was created in 2013 by a team of researchers at Google led by Tomas Mikolov. The models are unsupervised, taking as input a large corpus of text and producing a vector space of words. The dimensionality of the word2vec embedding space is usually lower than the dimensionality of the one-hot embedding space, which is the size of the vocabulary. The embedding space is also more dense compared to the sparse embedding of the one-hot embedding space.

The two architectures for word2vec are as follows:

- **Continuous Bag Of Words (CBOW)**
- **Skip-gram**

In the CBOW architecture, the model predicts the current word given a window of surrounding words. In addition, the order of the context words does not influence the prediction (that is, the bag of words assumption). In the case of skip-gram architecture, the model predicts the surrounding words given the center word. According to the authors, CBOW is faster but skip-gram does a better job at predicting infrequent words.

An interesting thing to note is that even though word2vec creates embeddings that are used in deep learning NLP models, both flavors of word2vec that we will discuss, which also happens to be the most successful and acknowledged recent models, are shallow neural networks.

The skip-gram word2vec model

The skip-gram model is trained to predict the surrounding words given the current word. To understand how the skip-gram word2vec model works, consider the following example sentence:

I love green eggs and ham.

Assuming a window size of three, this sentence can be broken down into the following sets of (context, word) pairs:

([I, green], love)
([love, eggs], green)
([green, and], eggs)
...

Since the skip-gram model predicts a context word given the center word, we can convert the preceding dataset to one of (input, output) pairs. That is, given an input word, we expect the skip-gram model to predict the output word:

(love, I), (love, green), (green, love), (green, eggs), (eggs, green), (eggs, and), ...

We can also generate additional negative samples by pairing each input word with some random word in the vocabulary. For example:

(love, Sam), (love, zebra), (green, thing), ...

Finally, we generate positive and negative examples for our classifier:

((love, I), 1), ((love, green), 1), ..., ((love, Sam), 0), ((love, zebra), 0), ...

We can now train a classifier that takes in a word vector and a context vector and learns to predict one or zero depending on whether it sees a positive or negative sample. The deliverables from this trained network are the weights of the word embedding layer (the gray box in the following figure):

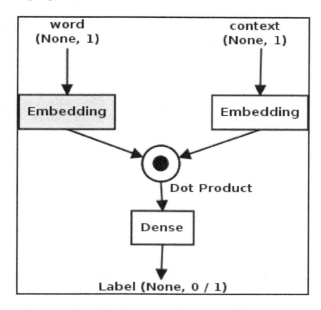

The skip-gram model can be built in Keras as follows. Assume that the vocabulary size is set at 5000, the output embedding size is 300, and the window size is 1. A window size of one means that the context for a word is the words immediately to the left and right. We first take care of the imports and set our variables to their initial values:

```
from keras.layers import Merge
from keras.layers.core import Dense, Reshape
from keras.layers.embeddings import Embedding
from keras.models import Sequential

vocab_size = 5000
embed_size = 300
```

We then create a sequential model for the word. The input to this model is the word ID in the vocabulary. The embedding weights are initially set to small random values. During training, the model will update these weights using backpropagation. The next layer reshapes the input to the embedding size:

```
word_model = Sequential()
word_model.add(Embedding(vocab_size, embed_size,
                    embeddings_initializer="glorot_uniform",
                    input_length=1))
word_model.add(Reshape((embed_size, )))
```

The other model that we need is a sequential model for the context words. For each of our skip-gram pairs, we have a single context word corresponding to the target word, so this model is identical to the word model:

```
context_model = Sequential()
context_model.add(Embedding(vocab_size, embed_size,
                    embeddings_initializer="glorot_uniform",
                    input_length=1))
context_model.add(Reshape((embed_size,)))
```

The outputs of the two models are each a vector of size (`embed_size`). These outputs are merged into one using a dot product and fed into a dense layer, which has a single output wrapped in a sigmoid activation layer. You have seen the sigmoid activation function in `Chapter 1`, *Neural Network Foundations*. As you will recall, it modulates the output so numbers higher than 0.5 tend rapidly to 1 and flatten out, and numbers lower than 0.5 tend rapidly to 0 and also flatten out:

```
model = Sequential()
model.add(Merge([word_model, context_model], mode="dot"))
model.add(Dense(1, init="glorot_uniform", activation="sigmoid"))
model.compile(loss="mean_squared_error", optimizer="adam")
```

The loss function used is the `mean_squared_error`; the idea is to minimize the dot product for positive examples and maximize it for negative examples. If you recall, the dot product multiplies corresponding elements of two vectors and sums up the result—this causes similar vectors to have higher dot products than dissimilar vectors, since the former has more overlapping elements.

Keras provides a convenience function to extract skip-grams for a text that has been converted to a list of word indices. Here is an example of using this function to extract the first 10 of 56 skip-grams generated (both positive and negative).

We first declare the necessary imports and the text to be analyzed:

```
from keras.preprocessing.text import *
from keras.preprocessing.sequence import skipgrams

text = "I love green eggs and ham ."
```

The next step is to declare the `tokenizer` and run the text against it. This will produce a list of word tokens:

```
tokenizer = Tokenizer()
tokenizer.fit_on_texts([text])
```

The `tokenizer` creates a dictionary mapping each unique word to an integer ID and makes it available in the `word_index` attribute. We extract this and create a two-way lookup table:

```
word2id = tokenizer.word_index
id2word = {v:k for k, v in word2id.items()}
```

Finally, we convert our input list of words to a list of IDs and pass it to the `skipgrams` function. We then print the first 10 of the 56 (pair, label) skip-gram tuples generated:

```
wids = [word2id[w] for w in text_to_word_sequence(text)]
pairs, labels = skipgrams(wids, len(word2id))
print(len(pairs), len(labels))
for i in range(10):
    print("({:s} ({:d}), {:s} ({:d})) -> {:d}".format(
            id2word[pairs[i][0]], pairs[i][0],
            id2word[pairs[i][1]], pairs[i][1],
            labels[i]))
```

The results from the code is shown below. Note that your results may be different since the skip-gram method randomly samples the results from the pool of possibilities for the positive examples. Additionally, the process of negative sampling, used for generating the negative examples, consists of randomly pairing up arbitrary tokens from the text. As the size of the input text increases, this is more likely to pick up unrelated word pairs. In our example, since our text is very short, there is a chance that it can end up generating positive examples as well.

```
(and (1), ham (3)) -> 0
(green (6), i (4)) -> 0
(love (2), i (4)) -> 1
(and (1), love (2)) -> 0
(love (2), eggs (5)) -> 0
(ham (3), ham (3)) -> 0
(green (6), and (1)) -> 1
(eggs (5), love (2)) -> 1
(i (4), ham (3)) -> 0
(and (1), green (6)) -> 1
```

The code for this example can be found in `skipgram_example.py` in the source code download for the chapter.

The CBOW word2vec model

Let us now look at the CBOW word2vec model. Recall that the CBOW model predicts the center word given the context words. Thus, in the first tuple in the following example, the CBOW model needs to predict the output word *love*, given the context words *I* and *green*:

([I, green], love) ([love, eggs], green) ([green, and], eggs) ...

Like the skip-gram model, the CBOW model is also a classifier that takes the context words as input and predicts the target word. The architecture is somewhat more straightforward than the skip-gram model. The input to the model is the word IDs for the context words. These word IDs are fed into a common embedding layer that is initialized with small random weights. Each word ID is transformed into a vector of size (`embed_size`) by the embedding layer. Thus, each row of the input context is transformed into a matrix of size (`2*window_size`, `embed_size`) by this layer. This is then fed into a lambda layer, which computes an average of all the embeddings. This average is then fed to a dense layer, which creates a dense vector of size (`vocab_size`) for each row. The activation function on the dense layer is a softmax, which reports the maximum value on the output vector as a probability. The ID with the maximum probability corresponds to the target word.

The deliverable for the CBOW model is the weights from the embedding layer shown in gray in the following figure:

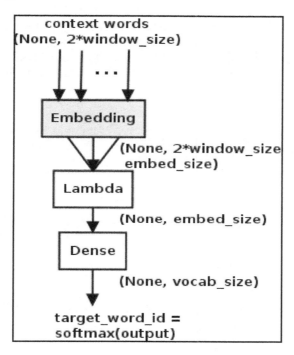

The corresponding Keras code for the model is shown as follows. Once again, assume a vocabulary size of 5000, an embedding size of 300, and a context window size of 1. Our first step is to set up all our imports and these values:

```
from keras.models import Sequential
from keras.layers.core import Dense, Lambda
from keras.layers.embeddings import Embedding
import keras.backend as K

vocab_size = 5000
embed_size = 300
window_size = 1
```

We then construct a sequential model, to which we add an embedding layer whose weights are initialized with small random values. Note that the `input_length` of this embedding layer is equal to the number of context words. So each context word is fed into this layer and will update the weights jointly during backpropagation. The output of this layer is a matrix of context word embeddings, which are averaged into a single vector (per row of input) by the lambda layer. Finally, the dense layer will convert each row into a dense vector of size (`vocab_size`). The target word is the one whose ID has the maximum value in the dense output vector:

```
model = Sequential()
model.add(Embedding(input_dim=vocab_size, output_dim=embed_size,
                    embeddings_initializer='glorot_uniform',
                    input_length=window_size*2))
model.add(Lambda(lambda x: K.mean(x, axis=1), output_shape=
(embed_size,)))
model.add(Dense(vocab_size, kernel_initializer='glorot_uniform',
activation='softmax'))

model.compile(loss='categorical_crossentropy', optimizer="adam")
```

The loss function used here is `categorical_crossentropy`, which is a common choice for cases where there are two or more (in our case, `vocab_size`) categories.

The source code for the example can be found in the `keras_cbow.py` file in the source code download for the chapter.

Extracting word2vec embeddings from the model

As noted previously, even though both word2vec models can be reduced to a classification problem, we are not really interested in the classification problem itself. Rather, we are interested in the side effect of this classification process, that is, the weight matrix that transforms a word from the vocabulary to its dense, low-dimensional distributed representation.

There are many examples of how these distributed representations exhibit often surprising syntactic and semantic information. For example, as shown in the following figure from Tomas Mikolov's presentation at NIPS 2013 (for more information refer to the article: *Learning Representations of Text using Neural Networks*, by T. Mikolov, I. Sutskever, K. Chen, G. S. Corrado, J. Dean, Q. Le, and T. Strohmann, NIPS 2013), vectors connecting words that have similar meanings but opposite genders are approximately parallel in the reduced 2D space, and we can often get very intuitive results by doing arithmetic with the word vectors. The presentation provides many other examples.

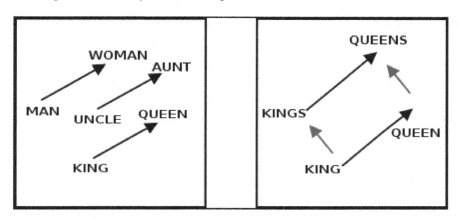

Intuitively, the training process imparts enough information to the internal encoding to predict an output word that occurs in the context of an input word. So points representing words shift in this space to be nearer to words with which it co-occurs. This causes similar words to clump together. Words that co-occur with these similar words also clump together in a similar way. As a result, vectors connecting points representing semantically related points tend to exhibit these regularities in the distributed representation.

Keras provides a way to extract weights from trained models. For the skip-gram example, the embedding weights can be extracted as follows:

```
merge_layer = model.layers[0]
word_model = merge_layer.layers[0]
word_embed_layer = word_model.layers[0]
weights = word_embed_layer.get_weights()[0]
```

Similarly, the embedding weights for the CBOW example can be extracted using the following one-liner:

```
weights = model.layers[0].get_weights()[0]
```

In both cases, the shape of the weights matrix is `vocab_size` and `embed_size`. In order to compute the distributed representation for a word in the vocabulary, you will need to construct a one-hot vector by setting the position of the word index to one in a zero vector of size (`vocab_size`) and multiply it with the matrix to get the embedding vector of size (`embed_size`).

A visualization of word embeddings from work done by Christopher Olah (for more information refer to the article: *Document Embedding with Paragraph Vectors*, by Andrew M. Dai, Christopher Olah, and Quoc V. Le, arXiv:1507.07998, 2015) is shown as follows. This is a visualization of word embeddings reduced to two dimensions and visualized with T-SNE. The words forming entity types were chosen using WordNet synset clusters. As you can see, points corresponding to similar entity types tend to cluster together:

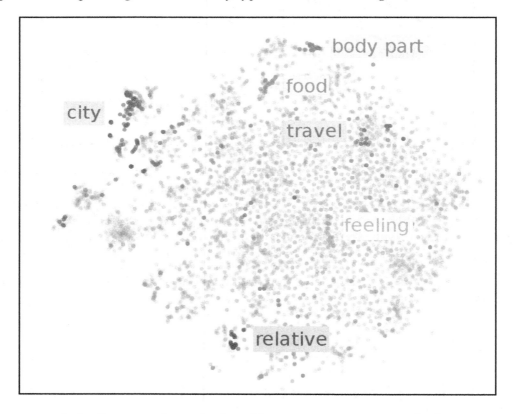

The source code for the example can be found in `keras_skipgram.py` in the source code download.

Using third-party implementations of word2vec

We have covered word2vec extensively over the past few sections. At this point, you understand how the skip-gram and CBOW models work and how to build your own implementation of these models using Keras. However, third-party implementations of word2vec are readily available, and unless your use case is very complex or different, it makes sense to just use one such implementation instead of rolling your own.

The gensim library provides an implementation of word2vec. Even though this is a book about Keras and not gensim, we include a discussion on this because Keras does not provide any support for word2vec, and integrating the gensim implementation into Keras code is very common practice.

 Installation of gensim is fairly simple and described in detail on the gensim installation page (`https://radimrehurek.com/gensim/install.h tml`).

The following code shows how to build a word2vec model using gensim and train it with the text from the text8 corpus, available for download at: `http://mattmahoney.net/dc/tex t8.zip`. The text8 corpus is a file containing about 17 million words derived from Wikipedia text. Wikipedia text was cleaned to remove markup, punctuation, and non-ASCII text, and the first 100 million characters of this cleaned text became the text8 corpus. This corpus is commonly used as an example for word2vec because it is quick to train and produces good results. First we set up the imports as usual:

```
from gensim.models import KeyedVectors
import logging
import os
```

We then read in the words from the text8 corpus, and split up the words into sentences of 50 words each. The gensim library provides a built-in text8 handler that does something similar. Since we want to illustrate how to generate a model with any (preferably large) corpus that may or may not fit into memory, we will show you how to generate these sentences using a Python generator.

The `Text8Sentences` class will generate sentences of `maxlen` words each from the text8 file. In this case, we do ingest the entire file into memory, but when traversing through directories of files, generators allows us to load parts of the data into memory at a time, process them, and yield them to the caller:

```
class Text8Sentences(object):
    def __init__(self, fname, maxlen):
        self.fname = fname
        self.maxlen = maxlen

    def __iter__(self):
        with open(os.path.join(DATA_DIR, "text8"), "rb") as ftext:
            text = ftext.read().split(" ")
            sentences, words = [], []
            for word in text:
                if len(words) >= self.maxlen:
                    yield words
                    words = []
                words.append(word)
            yield words
```

We then set up the caller code. The gensim word2vec uses Python logging to report on progress, so we first enable it. The next line declares an instance of the `Text8Sentences` class, and the line after that trains the model with the sentences from the dataset. We have chosen the size of the embedding vectors to be 300, and we only consider words that appear a minimum of 30 times in the corpus. The default window size is 5, so we will consider the words w_{i-5}, w_{i-4}, w_{i-3}, w_{i-2}, w_{i-1}, w_{i+1}, w_{i+2}, w_{i+3}, w_{i+4}, and w_{i+5} as the context for word w_i. By default, the word2vec model created is CBOW, but you can change that by setting `sg=1` in the parameters:

```
logging.basicConfig(format='%(asctime)s : %(levelname)s : %(message)s',
level=logging.INFO)

DATA_DIR = "../data/"
sentences = Text8Sentences(os.path.join(DATA_DIR, "text8"), 50)
model = word2vec.Word2Vec(sentences, size=300, min_count=30)
```

The word2vec implementation will make two passes over the data, first to generate a vocabulary and then to build the actual model. You can see its progress on the console as it runs:

```
2017-01-30 16:16:27,786 : INFO : PROGRESS: at 76.44% examples, 691859 words/s, in_qsize 0, out_qsize 0
2017-01-30 16:16:28,801 : INFO : PROGRESS: at 77.74% examples, 693040 words/s, in_qsize 0, out_qsize 0
2017-01-30 16:16:29,807 : INFO : PROGRESS: at 79.00% examples, 693746 words/s, in_qsize 2, out_qsize 0
2017-01-30 16:16:30,815 : INFO : PROGRESS: at 79.99% examples, 692107 words/s, in_qsize 0, out_qsize 0
2017-01-30 16:16:31,819 : INFO : PROGRESS: at 80.03% examples, 682583 words/s, in_qsize 0, out_qsize 0
2017-01-30 16:16:32,842 : INFO : PROGRESS: at 81.15% examples, 682090 words/s, in_qsize 1, out_qsize 0
2017-01-30 16:16:33,869 : INFO : PROGRESS: at 82.46% examples, 683117 words/s, in_qsize 0, out_qsize 1
2017-01-30 16:16:34,873 : INFO : PROGRESS: at 83.77% examples, 684403 words/s, in_qsize 0, out_qsize 0
2017-01-30 16:16:35,882 : INFO : PROGRESS: at 85.02% examples, 685224 words/s, in_qsize 5, out_qsize 0
2017-01-30 16:16:36,884 : INFO : PROGRESS: at 86.36% examples, 686831 words/s, in_qsize 0, out_qsize 1
2017-01-30 16:16:37,925 : INFO : PROGRESS: at 87.51% examples, 686556 words/s, in_qsize 2, out_qsize 0
2017-01-30 16:16:38,925 : INFO : PROGRESS: at 88.55% examples, 685873 words/s, in_qsize 0, out_qsize 0
2017-01-30 16:16:39,933 : INFO : PROGRESS: at 89.84% examples, 686756 words/s, in_qsize 0, out_qsize 0
2017-01-30 16:16:40,936 : INFO : PROGRESS: at 91.17% examples, 688126 words/s, in_qsize 0, out_qsize 0
2017-01-30 16:16:41,939 : INFO : PROGRESS: at 92.43% examples, 688894 words/s, in_qsize 0, out_qsize 1
2017-01-30 16:16:42,946 : INFO : PROGRESS: at 93.69% examples, 689612 words/s, in_qsize 1, out_qsize 0
2017-01-30 16:16:43,960 : INFO : PROGRESS: at 94.97% examples, 690484 words/s, in_qsize 1, out_qsize 0
2017-01-30 16:16:44,978 : INFO : PROGRESS: at 96.30% examples, 691348 words/s, in_qsize 0, out_qsize 0
2017-01-30 16:16:45,982 : INFO : PROGRESS: at 97.58% examples, 692158 words/s, in_qsize 0, out_qsize 0
2017-01-30 16:16:46,980 : INFO : PROGRESS: at 98.83% examples, 692731 words/s, in_qsize 2, out_qsize 0
2017-01-30 16:16:48,092 : INFO : PROGRESS: at 99.92% examples, 691317 words/s, in_qsize 4, out_qsize 1
2017-01-30 16:16:48,124 : INFO : worker thread finished; awaiting finish of 2 more threads
2017-01-30 16:16:48,125 : INFO : worker thread finished; awaiting finish of 1 more threads
2017-01-30 16:16:48,128 : INFO : worker thread finished; awaiting finish of 0 more threads
2017-01-30 16:16:48,129 : INFO : training on 85026040 raw words (59645573 effective words) took 86.2s, 691572 effective words/s
2017-01-30 16:16:48,129 : INFO : precomputing L2-norms of word weight vectors
```

Once the model is created, we should normalize the resulting vectors. According to the documentation, this saves lots of memory. Once the model is trained, we can optionally save it to disk:

```
model.init_sims(replace=True)
model.save("word2vec_gensim.bin")
```

The saved model can be brought back into memory using the following call:

```
model = Word2Vec.load("word2vec_gensim.bin")
```

We can now query the model to find all the words it knows about:

```
>>> model.vocab.keys()[0:10]
['homomorphism',
'woods',
'spiders',
'hanging',
```

```
'woody',
'localized',
'sprague',
'originality',
'alphabetic',
'hermann']
```

We can find the actual vector embedding for a given word:

```
>>> model["woman"]
array([ -3.13099056e-01, -1.85702944e+00, 1.18816841e+00,
-1.86561719e-01, -2.23673001e-01, 1.06527400e+00,
&mldr;
4.31755871e-01, -2.90115297e-01, 1.00955181e-01,
-5.17173052e-01, 7.22485244e-01, -1.30940580e+00], dtype="float32")
```

We can also find words that are most similar to a certain word:

```
>>> model.most_similar("woman")
[('child', 0.7057571411132812),
('girl', 0.702182412147522),
('man', 0.6846336126327515),
('herself', 0.6292711496353149),
('lady', 0.6229539513587952),
('person', 0.6190367937088013),
('lover', 0.6062309741973877),
('baby', 0.5993420481681824),
('mother', 0.5954475402832031),
('daughter', 0.5871444940567017)]
```

We can provide hints for finding word similarity. For example, the following command returns the top 10 words that are like woman and king but unlike man:

```
>>> model.most_similar(positive=['woman', 'king'], negative=['man'],
topn=10)
[('queen', 0.6237582564353943),
('prince', 0.5638638734817505),
('elizabeth', 0.5557916164398193),
('princess', 0.5456407070159912),
('throne', 0.5439794063568115),
('daughter', 0.5364126563072205),
('empress', 0.5354889631271362),
('isabella', 0.5233952403068542),
('regent', 0.520746111869812),
('matilda', 0.5167444944381714)]
```

We can also find similarities between individual words. To give a feel of how the positions of the words in the embedding space correlates with their semantic meanings, let us look at the following word pairs:

```
>>> model.similarity("girl", "woman")
 0.702182479574
 >>> model.similarity("girl", "man")
 0.574259909834
 >>> model.similarity("girl", "car")
 0.289332921793
 >>> model.similarity("bus", "car")
 0.483853497748
```

As you can see, girl and woman are more similar than girl and man, and car and bus are more similar than girl and car. This agrees very nicely with our human intuition about these words.

The source code for the example can be found in word2vec_gensim.py in the source code download.

Exploring GloVe

The global vectors for word representation, or GloVe, embeddings was created by Jeffrey Pennington, Richard Socher, and Christopher Manning (for more information refer to the article: *GloVe: Global Vectors for Word Representation*, by J. Pennington, R. Socher, and C. Manning, Proceedings of the 2014 Conference on Empirical Methods in Natural Language Processing (EMNLP), Pp. 1532–1543, 2013). The authors describe GloVe as an unsupervised learning algorithm for obtaining vector representations for words. Training is performed on aggregated global word-word co-occurrence statistics from a corpus, and the resulting representations showcase interesting linear substructures of the word vector space.

GloVe differs from word2vec in that word2vec is a predictive model while GloVe is a count-based model. The first step is to construct a large matrix of (word, context) pairs that co-occur in the training corpus. Each element of this matrix represents how often a word represented by the row co-occurs in the context (usually a sequence of words) represented by the column, as shown in the following figure:

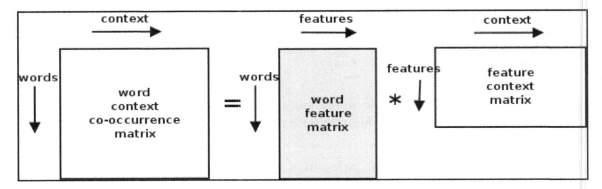

The GloVe process converts the co-occurrence matrix into a pair of (word, feature) and (feature, context) matrices. This process is known as **matrix factorization** and is done using **stochastic gradient descent** (**SGD**), an iterative numerical method. Rewriting in equation form:

$$\mathbf{R} = \mathbf{P} * \mathbf{Q} \approx \mathbf{R'}$$

Here, R is the original co-occurrence matrix. We first populate P and Q with random values and attempt to reconstruct a matrix R' by multiplying them. The difference between the reconstructed matrix R' and the original matrix R tells us how much we need to change the values of P and Q to move R' closer to R, to minimize the reconstruction error. This is repeated multiple times until the SGD converges and the reconstruction error is below a specified threshold. At that point, the (word, feature) matrix is the GloVe embedding. To speed up the process, SGD is often used in parallel mode, as outlined in the *HOGWILD!* paper.

One thing to note is that predictive neural network based models such as word2vec and count based models such as GloVe are very similar in intent. Both of them build a vector space where the position of a word is influenced by its neighboring words. Neural network models start with individual examples of word co-occurrences and count based models start with aggregate co-occurrence statistics between all words in the corpus. Several recent papers have demonstrated the correlation between these two types of model.

We will not cover generation of GloVe vectors in more detail in this book. Even though GloVe generally shows higher accuracy than word2vec and is faster to train if you use parallelization, Python tooling is not as mature as for word2vec. The only tool available to do this as of the time of writing is the GloVe-Python project (`https://github.com/maciejk ula/glove-python`), which provides a toy implementation for GloVe on Python.

Using pre-trained embeddings

In general, you will train your own word2vec or GloVe model from scratch only if you have a very large amount of very specialized text. By far the most common use case for Embeddings is to use pre-trained embeddings in some way in your network. The three main ways in which you would use embeddings in your network are as follows:

- Learn embeddings from scratch
- Fine-tune learned embeddings from pre-trained GloVe/word2vec models
- Look up embeddings from pre-trained GloVe/word2vec models

In the first option, the embedding weights are initialized to small random values and trained using backpropagation. You saw this in the examples for skip-gram and CBOW models in Keras. This is the default mode when you use a Keras Embedding layer in your network.

In the second option, you build a weight matrix from a pre-trained model and initialize the weights of your embedding layer with this weight matrix. The network will update these weights using backpropagation, but the model will converge faster because of good starting weights.

The third option is to look up word embeddings from a pre-trained model, and transform your input to embedded vectors. You can then train any machine learning model (that is, not necessarily even a deep learning network) on the transformed data. If the pre-trained model is trained on a similar domain as the target domain, this usually works very well and is the least expensive option.

For general use with English language text, you can use Google's word2vec model trained over 10 billion words from the Google news dataset. The vocabulary size is about 3 million words and the dimensionality of the embedding is 300. The Google news model (about 1.5 GB) can be downloaded from here: `https://drive.google.com/file/d/0B7XkCwpI5KDYN1 NUTT1SS21pQmM/edit?usp=sharing`.

Similarly, a pre-trained model trained on 6 billion tokens from English Wikipedia and the gigaword corpus can be downloaded from the GloVe site. The vocabulary size is about 400,000 words and the download provides vectors with dimensions 50, 100, 200, and 300. The model size is about 822 MB. Here is the direct download URL (`http://nlp.stanford.edu/data/glove.6B.zip`) for this model. Larger models based on the Common Crawl and Twitter are also available from the same location.

In the following sections, we will look at how to use these pre-trained models in the three ways listed.

Learn embeddings from scratch

In this example, we will train a one-dimensional **convolutional neural network** (**CNN**) to classify sentences as either positive or negative. You have already seen how to classify images using two-dimensional CNNs in `Chapter 3`, *Deep Learning with ConvNets*. Recall that CNNs exploit spatial structure in images by enforcing local connectivity between neurons of adjacent layers.

Words in sentences exhibit linear structure in the same way as images exhibit spatial structure. Traditional (non-deep learning) NLP approaches to language modeling involve creating word *n*-grams (`https://en.wikipedia.org/wiki/N-gram`) to exploit this linear structure inherent among words. One-dimensional CNNs do something similar, learning convolution filters that operate on sentences a few words at a time, and max pooling the results to create a vector that represents the most important ideas in the sentence.

There is another class of neural network, called **recurrent neural network** (**RNN**), which is specially designed to handle sequence data, including text, which is a sequence of words. The processing in RNNs is different from that in a CNN. We will learn about RNNs in a future chapter.

In our example network, the input text is converted to a sequence of word indices. Note that we have used the **natural language toolkit** (**NLTK**) to parse the text into sentences and words. We could also have used regular expressions to do this, but the statistical models supplied by NLTK are more powerful at parsing than regular expressions. If you are working with word embeddings, it is very likely that you are also working with NLP, in which case you would have NLTK installed already.

This link (`http://www.nltk.org/install.html`) has information to help you install NLTK on your machine. You will also need to install NLTK data, which is some trained corpora that comes standard with NLTK. Installation instructions for NLTK data are available here: `http://www.nl tk.org/data.html`.

The sequence of word indices is fed into an array of embedding layers of a set size (in our case, the number of words in the longest sentence). The embedding layer is initialized by default to random values. The output of the embedding layer is connected to a 1D convolutional layer that convolves (in our example) word trigrams in 256 different ways (essentially, it applies different learned linear combinations of weights on the word embeddings). These features are then pooled into a single pooled word by a global max pooling layer. This vector (256) is then input to a dense layer, which outputs a vector (2). A softmax activation will return a pair of probabilities, one corresponding to positive sentiment and another corresponding to negative sentiment. The network is shown in the following figure:

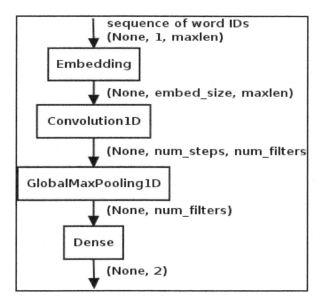

Let us look at how to code this up using Keras. First we declare our imports. Right after the constants, you will notice that I set the `random.seed` value to `42`. This is because we want consistent results between runs. Since the initializations of the weight matrices are random, differences in initialization can lead to differences in output, so this is a way to control that:

```
from keras.layers.core import Dense, Dropout, SpatialDropout1D
from keras.layers.convolutional import Conv1D
from keras.layers.embeddings import Embedding
from keras.layers.pooling import GlobalMaxPooling1D
from kera
s.models import Sequential
from keras.preprocessing.sequence import pad_sequences
from keras.utils import np_utils
from sklearn.model_selection import train_test_split
import collections
import matplotlib.pyplot as plt
import nltk
import numpy as np

np.random.seed(42)
```

We declare our constants. For all subsequent examples in this chapter, we will classify sentences from the UMICH SI650 sentiment classification competition on Kaggle. The dataset has around 7,000 sentences, and is labeled *1* for positive and *0* for negative. The `INPUT_FILE` defines the path to this file of sentences and labels. The format of the file is a sentiment label (*0* or *1*) followed by a tab, followed by a sentence.

The `VOCAB_SIZE` setting indicates that we will consider only the top 5,000 tokens in the text. The `EMBED_SIZE` setting is the size of the embedding that will be generated by the embedding layer in the network. `NUM_FILTERS` is the number of convolution filters we will train for our convolution layer, and `NUM_WORDS` is the size of each filter, that is, how many words we will convolve at a time. The `BATCH_SIZE` and `NUM_EPOCHS` is the number of records to feed the network each time and how many times we will run through the entire dataset during training:

```
INPUT_FILE = "../data/umich-sentiment-train.txt"
VOCAB_SIZE = 5000
EMBED_SIZE = 100
NUM_FILTERS = 256
NUM_WORDS = 3
BATCH_SIZE = 64
NUM_EPOCHS = 20
```

In the next block, we first read our input sentences and construct our vocabulary out of the most frequent words in the corpus. We then use this vocabulary to convert our input sentences into a list of word indices:

```
counter = collections.Counter()
fin = open(INPUT_FILE, "rb")
maxlen = 0
for line in fin:
    _, sent = line.strip().split("t")
    words = [x.lower() for x in  nltk.word_tokenize(sent)]
    if len(words) > maxlen:
        maxlen = len(words)
    for word in words:
        counter[word] += 1
fin.close()

word2index = collections.defaultdict(int)
for wid, word in enumerate(counter.most_common(VOCAB_SIZE)):
    word2index[word[0]] = wid + 1
vocab_size = len(word2index) + 1
index2word = {v:k for k, v in word2index.items()}
```

We pad each of our sentences to predetermined length `maxlen` (in this case the number of words in the longest sentence in the training set). We also convert our labels to categorical format using a Keras utility function. The last two steps are a standard workflow for handling text input that we will see again and again:

```
xs, ys = [], []
fin = open(INPUT_FILE, "rb")
for line in fin:
    label, sent = line.strip().split("t")
    ys.append(int(label))
    words = [x.lower() for x in nltk.word_tokenize(sent)]
    wids = [word2index[word] for word in words]
    xs.append(wids)
fin.close()
X = pad_sequences(xs, maxlen=maxlen)
Y = np_utils.to_categorical(ys)
```

Finally, we split up our data into a *70/30* training and test set. The data is now in a form ready to be fed into the network:

```
Xtrain, Xtest, Ytrain, Ytest = train_test_split(X, Y, test_size=0.3,
random_state=42)
```

We define the network that we described earlier in this section:

```
model = Sequential()
model.add(Embedding(vocab_size, EMBED_SIZE, input_length=maxlen)
model.add(SpatialDropout1D(Dropout(0.2)))
model.add(Conv1D(filters=NUM_FILTERS, kernel_size=NUM_WORDS,
activation="relu"))
model.add(GlobalMaxPooling1D())
model.add(Dense(2, activation="softmax"))
```

We then compile the model. Since our target is binary (positive or negative) we choose `categorical_crossentropy` as our loss function. For the optimizer, we choose `adam`. We then train the model using our training set, using a batch size of 64 and training for 20 epochs:

```
model.compile(loss="categorical_crossentropy", optimizer="adam",
                metrics=["accuracy"])
history = model.fit(Xtrain, Ytrain, batch_size=BATCH_SIZE,
                    epochs=NUM_EPOCHS,
                    validation_data=(Xtest, Ytest))
```

The output from the code looks as follows:

```
Epoch 9/20
4960/4960 [==============================] - 3s - loss: 0.0337 - acc: 0.9855 - val_loss: 0.0263 - val_acc: 0.9882
Epoch 10/20
4960/4960 [==============================] - 3s - loss: 0.0369 - acc: 0.9843 - val_loss: 0.0277 - val_acc: 0.9878
Epoch 11/20
4960/4960 [==============================] - 3s - loss: 0.0331 - acc: 0.9881 - val_loss: 0.0303 - val_acc: 0.9878
Epoch 12/20
4960/4960 [==============================] - 3s - loss: 0.0289 - acc: 0.9879 - val_loss: 0.0291 - val_acc: 0.9882
Epoch 13/20
4960/4960 [==============================] - 3s - loss: 0.0261 - acc: 0.9901 - val_loss: 0.0305 - val_acc: 0.9878
Epoch 14/20
4960/4960 [==============================] - 3s - loss: 0.0261 - acc: 0.9895 - val_loss: 0.0310 - val_acc: 0.9859
Epoch 15/20
4960/4960 [==============================] - 3s - loss: 0.0355 - acc: 0.9857 - val_loss: 0.0307 - val_acc: 0.9873
Epoch 16/20
4960/4960 [==============================] - 3s - loss: 0.0247 - acc: 0.9893 - val_loss: 0.0283 - val_acc: 0.9868
Epoch 17/20
4960/4960 [==============================] - 3s - loss: 0.0249 - acc: 0.9891 - val_loss: 0.0329 - val_acc: 0.9854
Epoch 18/20
4960/4960 [==============================] - 3s - loss: 0.0299 - acc: 0.9895 - val_loss: 0.0285 - val_acc: 0.9882
Epoch 19/20
4960/4960 [==============================] - 3s - loss: 0.0282 - acc: 0.9887 - val_loss: 0.0287 - val_acc: 0.9882
Epoch 20/20
4960/4960 [==============================] - 3s - loss: 0.0401 - acc: 0.9839 - val_loss: 0.0311 - val_acc: 0.9878

2126/2126 [==============================] - 0s
Test score: 0.031, accuracy: 0.986
```

As you can see, the network gives us 98.6% accuracy on the test set.

The source code for this example can be found in `learn_embedding_from_scratch.py` in the source code download for the chapter.

Fine-tuning learned embeddings from word2vec

In this example, we will use the same network as the one we used to learn our embeddings from scratch. In terms of code, the only major difference is an extra block of code to load the word2vec model and build up the weight matrix for the embedding layer.

As always, we start with the imports and set up a random seed for repeatability. In addition to the imports we have seen previously, there is an additional one to import the word2vec model from gensim:

```
from gensim.models import KeyedVectors
from keras.layers.core import Dense, Dropout, SpatialDropout1D
from keras.layers.convolutional import Conv1D
from keras.layers.embeddings import Embedding
from keras.layers.pooling import GlobalMaxPooling1D
from keras.models import Sequential
from keras.preprocessing.sequence import pad_sequences
from keras.utils import np_utils
from sklearn.model_selection import train_test_split
import collections
import matplotlib.pyplot as plt
import nltk
import numpy as np

np.random.seed(42)
```

Next up is setting up the constants. The only difference here is that we reduced the NUM_EPOCHS setting from 20 to 10. Recall that initializing the matrix with values from a pre-trained model tends to set them to good values that converge faster:

```
INPUT_FILE = "../data/umich-sentiment-train.txt"
WORD2VEC_MODEL = "../data/GoogleNews-vectors-negative300.bin.gz"
VOCAB_SIZE = 5000
EMBED_SIZE = 300
NUM_FILTERS = 256
NUM_WORDS = 3
BATCH_SIZE = 64
NUM_EPOCHS = 10
```

The next block extracts the words from the dataset and creates a vocabulary of the most frequent terms, then parses the dataset again to create a list of padded word lists. It also converts the labels to categorical format. Finally, it splits the data into a training and a test set. This block is identical to the previous example and has been explained in depth there:

```
counter = collections.Counter()
fin = open(INPUT_FILE, "rb")
maxlen = 0
for line in fin:
    _, sent = line.strip().split("t")
    words = [x.lower() for x in nltk.word_tokenize(sent)]
    if len(words) > maxlen:
        maxlen = len(words)
    for word in words:
        counter[word] += 1
fin.close()

word2index = collections.defaultdict(int)
for wid, word in enumerate(counter.most_common(VOCAB_SIZE)):
    word2index[word[0]] = wid + 1
vocab_sz = len(word2index) + 1
index2word = {v:k for k, v in word2index.items()}

xs, ys = [], []
fin = open(INPUT_FILE, "rb")
for line in fin:
    label, sent = line.strip().split("t")
    ys.append(int(label))
    words = [x.lower() for x in nltk.word_tokenize(sent)]
    wids = [word2index[word] for word in words]
    xs.append(wids)
fin.close()
X = pad_sequences(xs, maxlen=maxlen)
Y = np_utils.to_categorical(ys)

Xtrain, Xtest, Ytrain, Ytest = train_test_split(X, Y, test_size=0.3,
    random_state=42)
```

The next block loads up the word2vec model from a pre-trained model. This model is trained with about 10 billion words of Google News articles and has a vocabulary size of 3 million. We load it and look up embedding vectors from it for words in our vocabulary, and write out the embedding vector into our weight matrix embedding_weights. Rows of this weight matrix correspond to words in the vocabulary, and columns of each row constitute the embedding vector for the word.

The dimensions of the `embedding_weights` matrix is `vocab_sz` and `EMBED_SIZE`. The `vocab_sz` is one more than the maximum number of unique terms in the vocabulary, the additional pseudo-token _UNK_ representing words that are not seen in the vocabulary.

Note that it is possible that some words in our vocabulary may not be there in the Google News word2vec model, so when we encounter such words, the embedding vectors for them remain at the default value of all zeros:

```
# load word2vec model
word2vec = Word2Vec.load_word2vec_format(WORD2VEC_MODEL, binary=True)
embedding_weights = np.zeros((vocab_sz, EMBED_SIZE))
for word, index in word2index.items():
    try:
        embedding_weights[index, :] = word2vec[word]
    except KeyError:
        pass
```

We define our network. The difference in this block from our previous example is that we initialize the weights of the embedding layer with the `embedding_weights` matrix we built in the previous block:

```
model = Sequential()
model.add(Embedding(vocab_sz, EMBED_SIZE, input_length=maxlen,
            weights=[embedding_weights]))
model.add(SpatialDropout1D(Dropout(0.2)))
model.add(Conv1D(filters=NUM_FILTERS, kernel_size=NUM_WORDS,
                        activation="relu"))
model.add(GlobalMaxPooling1D())
model.add(Dense(2, activation="softmax"))
```

We then compile our model with the categorical cross-entropy loss function and the Adam optimizer, and train the network with batch size 64 and for 10 epochs, then evaluate the trained model:

```
model.compile(optimizer="adam", loss="categorical_crossentropy",
            metrics=["accuracy"])
history = model.fit(Xtrain, Ytrain, batch_size=BATCH_SIZE,
                epochs=NUM_EPOCHS,
                validation_data=(Xtest, Ytest))

score = model.evaluate(Xtest, Ytest, verbose=1)
print("Test score: {:.3f}, accuracy: {:.3f}".format(score[0], score[1]))
```

Output from running the code is shown as follows:

```
((4960, 42), (2126, 42), (4960, 2), (2126, 2))
Train on 4960 samples, validate on 2126 samples
Epoch 1/10
4960/4960 [==============================] - 7s - loss: 0.1766 - acc:
0.9369 - val_loss: 0.0397 - val_acc: 0.9854
Epoch 2/10
4960/4960 [==============================] - 7s - loss: 0.0725 - acc:
0.9706 - val_loss: 0.0346 - val_acc: 0.9887
Epoch 3/10
4960/4960 [==============================] - 7s - loss: 0.0553 - acc:
0.9784 - val_loss: 0.0210 - val_acc: 0.9915
Epoch 4/10
4960/4960 [==============================] - 7s - loss: 0.0519 - acc:
0.9790 - val_loss: 0.0241 - val_acc: 0.9934
Epoch 5/10
4960/4960 [==============================] - 7s - loss: 0.0576 - acc:
0.9746 - val_loss: 0.0219 - val_acc: 0.9929
Epoch 6/10
4960/4960 [==============================] - 7s - loss: 0.0515 - acc:
0.9764 - val_loss: 0.0185 - val_acc: 0.9929
Epoch 7/10
4960/4960 [==============================] - 7s - loss: 0.0528 - acc:
0.9790 - val_loss: 0.0204 - val_acc: 0.9920
Epoch 8/10
4960/4960 [==============================] - 7s - loss: 0.0373 - acc:
0.9849 - val_loss: 0.0221 - val_acc: 0.9934
Epoch 9/10
4960/4960 [==============================] - 7s - loss: 0.0360 - acc:
0.9845 - val_loss: 0.0194 - val_acc: 0.9929
Epoch 10/10
4960/4960 [==============================] - 7s - loss: 0.0389 - acc:
0.9853 - val_loss: 0.0254 - val_acc: 0.9915
2126/2126 [==============================] - 1s
Test score: 0.025, accuracy: 0.993
```

The model gives us an accuracy of 99.3% on the test set after 10 epochs of training. This is an improvement over the previous example, where we got an accuracy of 98.6% accuracy after 20 epochs.

The source code for this example can be found in `finetune_word2vec_embeddings.py` in the source code download for the chapter.

Fine-tune learned embeddings from GloVe

Fine tuning using pre-trained GloVe embeddings is very similar to fine tuning using pre-trained word2vec embeddings. In fact, all of the code, except for the block that builds the weight matrix for the embedding layer, is identical. Since we have already seen this code twice, I will just focus on the block of code that builds the weight matrix from the GloVe embeddings.

GloVe embeddings come in various flavors. We use the model pre-trained on 6 billion tokens from the English Wikipedia and the gigaword corpus. The vocabulary size for the model is about 400,000, and the download provides vectors of dimensions 50, 100, 200, and 300. We will use embeddings from the 300 dimensional model.

The only thing we need to change in the code for the previous example is to replace the block that instantiated a word2vec model and loaded the embedding matrix using the following block of code. If we use a model with vector size other than 300, then we also need to update `EMBED_SIZE`.

The vectors are provided in space-delimited text format, so the first step is to read the code into a dictionary, `word2emb`. This is analogous to the line instantiating the Word2Vec model in our previous example:

```
GLOVE_MODEL = "../data/glove.6B.300d.txt"
word2emb = {}
fglove = open(GLOVE_MODEL, "rb")
for line in fglove:
    cols = line.strip().split()
    word = cols[0]
    embedding = np.array(cols[1:], dtype="float32")
    word2emb[word] = embedding
fglove.close()
```

We then instantiate an embedding weight matrix of size (`vocab_sz` and `EMBED_SIZE`) and populate the vectors from the `word2emb` dictionary. Vectors for words that are found in the vocabulary but not in the GloVe model remain set to all zeros:

```
embedding_weights = np.zeros((vocab_sz, EMBED_SIZE))
for word, index in word2index.items():
    try:
        embedding_weights[index, :] = word2emb[word]
    except KeyError:
        pass
```

The full code for this program can be found in `finetune_glove_embeddings.py` in the book's code repository on GitHub. The output of the run is shown as follows:

```
((4960, 42), (2126, 42), (4960, 2), (2126, 2))
Train on 4960 samples, validate on 2126 samples
Epoch 1/10
4960/4960 [==============================] - 7s - loss: 0.1748 - acc: 0.9240 - val_loss: 0.0390 - val_acc: 0.9840
Epoch 2/10
4960/4960 [==============================] - 7s - loss: 0.0859 - acc: 0.9649 - val_loss: 0.0431 - val_acc: 0.9845
Epoch 3/10
4960/4960 [==============================] - 7s - loss: 0.0586 - acc: 0.9754 - val_loss: 0.0528 - val_acc: 0.9779
Epoch 4/10
4960/4960 [==============================] - 8s - loss: 0.0565 - acc: 0.9798 - val_loss: 0.0386 - val_acc: 0.9873
Epoch 5/10
4960/4960 [==============================] - 8s - loss: 0.0792 - acc: 0.9683 - val_loss: 0.0233 - val_acc: 0.9892
Epoch 6/10
4960/4960 [==============================] - 8s - loss: 0.0618 - acc: 0.9746 - val_loss: 0.0247 - val_acc: 0.9911
Epoch 7/10
4960/4960 [==============================] - 7s - loss: 0.0569 - acc: 0.9752 - val_loss: 0.0266 - val_acc: 0.9906
Epoch 8/10
4960/4960 [==============================] - 8s - loss: 0.0419 - acc: 0.9829 - val_loss: 0.0211 - val_acc: 0.9920
Epoch 9/10
4960/4960 [==============================] - 7s - loss: 0.0371 - acc: 0.9849 - val_loss: 0.0206 - val_acc: 0.9920
Epoch 10/10
4960/4960 [==============================] - 9s - loss: 0.0422 - acc: 0.9815 - val_loss: 0.0266 - val_acc: 0.9906
2126/2126 [==============================] - 1s
Test score: 0.027, accuracy: 0.991
```

This gives us 99.1% accuracy in 10 epochs, which is almost as good as the results we got from fine-tuning the network using word2vec `embedding_weights`.

The source code for this example can be found in `finetune_glove_embeddings.py` in the source code download for this chapter.

Look up embeddings

Our final strategy is to look up embeddings from pre-trained networks. The simplest way to do this with the current examples is to just set the `trainable` parameter of the embedding layer to `False`. This ensures that backpropagation will not update the weights on the embedding layer:

```
model.add(Embedding(vocab_sz, EMBED_SIZE, input_length=maxlen,
                    weights=[embedding_weights],
                    trainable=False))
model.add(SpatialDropout1D(Dropout(0.2)))
```

Setting this value with the word2vec and GloVe examples gave us accuracies of 98.7% and 98.9% respectively after 10 epochs of training.

However, in general, this is not how you would use pre-trained embeddings in your code. Typically, it involves preprocessing your dataset to create word vectors by looking up words in one of the pre-trained models, and then using this data to train some other model. The second model would not contain an Embedding layer, and may not even be a deep learning network.

The following example describes a dense network that takes as its input a vector of size 100, representing a sentence, and outputs a 1 or 0 for positive or negative sentiment. Our dataset is still the one from the UMICH S1650 sentiment classification competition with around 7,000 sentences.

As previously, large parts of the code are repeated, so we only explain the parts that are new or otherwise need explanation.
We begin with the imports, set the random seed for repeatability, and set some constant values. In order to create the 100-dimensional vectors for each sentence, we add up the GloVe 100-dimensional vectors for the words in the sentence, so we choose the glove.6B.100d.txt file:

```
from keras.layers.core import Dense, Dropout, SpatialDropout1D
from keras.models import Sequential
from keras.preprocessing.sequence import pad_sequences
from keras.utils import np_utils
from sklearn.model_selection import train_test_split
import collections
import matplotlib.pyplot as plt
import nltk
import numpy as np

np.random.seed(42)

INPUT_FILE = "../data/umich-sentiment-train.txt"
GLOVE_MODEL = "../data/glove.6B.100d.txt"
VOCAB_SIZE = 5000
EMBED_SIZE = 100
BATCH_SIZE = 64
NUM_EPOCHS = 10
```

The next block reads the sentences and creates a word frequency table. From this, the most common 5,000 tokens are selected and lookup tables (from word to word index and back) are created. In addition, we create a pseudo-token _UNK_ for tokens that do not exist in the vocabulary. Using these lookup tables, we convert each sentence to a sequence of word IDs, padding these sequences so that all sequences are of the same length (the maximum number of words in a sentence in the training set). We also convert the labels to categorical format:

```
counter = collections.Counter()
fin = open(INPUT_FILE, "rb")
maxlen = 0
for line in fin:
    _, sent = line.strip().split("t")
    words = [x.lower() for x in nltk.word_tokenize(sent)]
    if len(words) > maxlen:
        maxlen = len(words)
    for word in words:
        counter[word] += 1
fin.close()

word2index = collections.defaultdict(int)
for wid, word in enumerate(counter.most_common(VOCAB_SIZE)):
    word2index[word[0]] = wid + 1
vocab_sz = len(word2index) + 1
index2word = {v:k for k, v in word2index.items()}
index2word[0] = "_UNK_"

ws, ys = [], []
fin = open(INPUT_FILE, "rb")
for line in fin:
    label, sent = line.strip().split("t")
    ys.append(int(label))
    words = [x.lower() for x in nltk.word_tokenize(sent)]
    wids = [word2index[word] for word in words]
    ws.append(wids)
fin.close()
W = pad_sequences(ws, maxlen=maxlen)
Y = np_utils.to_categorical(ys)
```

We load the GloVe vectors into a dictionary. If we wanted to use word2vec here, all we have to do is replace this block with a gensim `Word2Vec.load_word2vec_format()` call and replace the following block to look up the word2vec model instead of the `word2emb` dictionary:

```
word2emb = collections.defaultdict(int)
fglove = open(GLOVE_MODEL, "rb")
for line in fglove:
```

```
        cols = line.strip().split()
        word = cols[0]
        embedding = np.array(cols[1:], dtype="float32")
        word2emb[word] = embedding
    fglove.close()
```

The next block looks up the words for each sentence from the word ID matrix W and populates a matrix E with the corresponding embedding vector. These embedding vectors are then added to create a sentence vector, which is written back into the X matrix. The output of this code block is the matrix X of size (num_records and EMBED_SIZE):

```
X = np.zeros((W.shape[0], EMBED_SIZE))
for i in range(W.shape[0]):
    E = np.zeros((EMBED_SIZE, maxlen))
    words = [index2word[wid] for wid in W[i].tolist()]
    for j in range(maxlen):
        E[:, j] = word2emb[words[j]]
    X[i, :] = np.sum(E, axis=1)
```

We have now preprocessed our data using the pre-trained model and are ready to use it to train and evaluate our final model. Let us split the data into *70/30* training/test as usual:

```
Xtrain, Xtest, Ytrain, Ytest = train_test_split(X, Y, test_size=0.3,
random_state=42)
```

The network we will train for doing the sentiment analysis task is a simple dense network. We compile it with a categorical cross-entropy loss function and the Adam optimizer, and train it with the sentence vectors that we built out of the pre-trained embeddings. Finally, we evaluate the model on the 30% test set:

```
model = Sequential()
model.add(Dense(32, input_dim=100, activation="relu"))
model.add(Dropout(0.2))
model.add(Dense(2, activation="softmax"))

model.compile(optimizer="adam", loss="categorical_crossentropy",
metrics=["accuracy"])
history = model.fit(Xtrain, Ytrain, batch_size=BATCH_SIZE,
                    epochs=NUM_EPOCHS,
                    validation_data=(Xtest, Ytest))

score = model.evaluate(Xtest, Ytest, verbose=1)
print("Test score: {:.3f}, accuracy: {:.3f}".format(score[0], score[1]))
```

The output for the code using GloVe embeddings is shown as follows:

```
((4960, 100), (2126, 100), (4960, 2), (2126, 2))
Train on 4960 samples, validate on 2126 samples
Epoch 1/10
4960/4960 [==============================] - 0s - loss: 1.9577 - acc: 0.5667 - val_loss: 0.4448 - val_acc: 0.8556
Epoch 2/10
4960/4960 [==============================] - 0s - loss: 0.5245 - acc: 0.7942 - val_loss: 0.3167 - val_acc: 0.9078
Epoch 3/10
4960/4960 [==============================] - 0s - loss: 0.3026 - acc: 0.9002 - val_loss: 0.2456 - val_acc: 0.9473
Epoch 4/10
4960/4960 [==============================] - 0s - loss: 0.2338 - acc: 0.9270 - val_loss: 0.2068 - val_acc: 0.9398
Epoch 5/10
4960/4960 [==============================] - 0s - loss: 0.1802 - acc: 0.9520 - val_loss: 0.1720 - val_acc: 0.9581
Epoch 6/10
4960/4960 [==============================] - 0s - loss: 0.1561 - acc: 0.9552 - val_loss: 0.1561 - val_acc: 0.9610
Epoch 7/10
4960/4960 [==============================] - 0s - loss: 0.1396 - acc: 0.9631 - val_loss: 0.1535 - val_acc: 0.9577
Epoch 8/10
4960/4960 [==============================] - 0s - loss: 0.1216 - acc: 0.9645 - val_loss: 0.1338 - val_acc: 0.9628
Epoch 9/10
4960/4960 [==============================] - 0s - loss: 0.1152 - acc: 0.9641 - val_loss: 0.1273 - val_acc: 0.9643
Epoch 10/10
4960/4960 [==============================] - 0s - loss: 0.1044 - acc: 0.9706 - val_loss: 0.1257 - val_acc: 0.9647

1888/2126 [=========================>....] - ETA: 0s
Test score: 0.126, accuracy: 0.965
```

The dense network gives us 96.5% accuracy on the test set after 10 epochs of training when preprocessed with the 100-dimensional GloVe embeddings. With preprocessed with the word2vec embeddings (300-dimensional fixed) the network gives us 98.5% on the test set.

The source code for this example can be found in `transfer_glove_embeddings.py` (for the GloVe example) and `transfer_word2vec_embeddings.py` (for the word2vec example) in the source code download for the chapter.

Summary

In this chapter, we learned how to transform words in text into vector embeddings that retain the distributional semantics of the word. We also now have an intuition of why word embeddings exhibit this kind of behavior and why word embeddings are useful for working with deep learning models for text data.

We then looked at two popular word embedding schemes, word2vec and GloVe, and understood how these models work. We also looked at using gensim to train our own word2vec model from data.

Finally, we learned about different ways of using embeddings in our network. The first was to learn embeddings from scratch as part of training our network. The second was to import embedding weights from pre-trained word2vec and GloVe models into our networks and fine-tune them as we train the network. The third was to use these pre-trained weights as is in our downstream applications.

In the next chapter, we will learn about recurrent neural networks, a class of network that is optimized for handling sequence data such as text.

6
Recurrent Neural Network — RNN

In Chapter 3, *Deep Learning with ConvNets*, we learned about **convolutional neural networks** (CNN) and saw how they exploit the spatial geometry of their input. For example, CNNs apply convolution and pooling operations in one dimension for audio and text data along the time dimension, in two dimensions for images along the (height x width) dimensions and in three dimensions, for videos along the (height x width x time) dimensions.

In this chapter, we will learn about **recurrent neural networks (RNN)**, a class of neural networks that exploit the sequential nature of their input. Such inputs could be text, speech, time series, and anything else where the occurrence of an element in the sequence is dependent on the elements that appeared before it. For example, the next word in the sentence *the dog...* is more likely to be *barks* than *car*, therefore, given such a sequence, an RNN is more likely to predict *barks* than *car*.

An RNN can be thought of as a graph of RNN cells, where each cell performs the same operation on every element in the sequence. RNNs are very flexible and have been used to solve problems such as speech recognition, language modeling, machine translation, sentiment analysis, and image captioning, to name a few. RNNs can be adapted to different types of problems by rearranging the way the cells are arranged in the graph. We will see some examples of these configurations and how they are used to solve specific problems.

We will also learn about a major limitation of the SimpleRNN cell, and how two variants of the SimpleRNN cell—**long short term memory (LSTM)** and **gated recurrent unit (GRU)**—overcome this limitation. Both LSTM and GRU are drop-in replacements for the SimpleRNN cell, so just replacing the RNN cell with one of these variants can often result in a major performance improvement in your network. While LSTM and GRU are not the only variants, it has been shown empirically (for more information refer to the articles: *An Empirical Exploration of Recurrent Network Architectures*, by R. Jozefowicz, W. Zaremba, and I. Sutskever, JMLR, 2015 and *LSTM: A Search Space Odyssey*, by K. Greff, arXiv:1503.04069, 2015) that they are the best choices for most sequence problems.

Finally, we will also learn about some tips to improve the performance of our RNNs and when and how to apply them.

In this chapter, we will cover the following topics:

- SimpleRNN cell
- Basic RNN implementation in Keras in generating text
- RNN topologies
- LSTM, GRU, and other RNN variants

SimpleRNN cells

Traditional multilayer perceptron neural networks make the assumption that all inputs are independent of each other. This assumption breaks down in the case of sequence data. You have already seen the example in the previous section where the first two words in the sentence affect the third. The same idea is true of speech—if we are having a conversation in a noisy room, I can make reasonable guesses about a word I may not have understood based on the words I have heard so far. Time series data, such as stock prices or weather, also exhibit a dependence on past data, called the secular trend.

RNN cells incorporate this dependence by having a hidden state, or memory, that holds the essence of what has been seen so far. The value of the hidden state at any point in time is a function of the value of the hidden state at the previous time step and the value of the input at the current time step, that is:

$$\mathbf{h_t} = \phi(\mathbf{h_{t-1}}, \mathbf{x_t})$$

h_t and h_{t-1} are the values of the hidden states at the time steps t and $t-1$ respectively, and x_t is the value of the input at time t. Notice that the equation is recursive, that is, h_{t-1} can be represented in terms of h_{t-2} and x_{t-1}, and so on, until the beginning of the sequence. This is how RNNs encode and incorporate information from arbitrarily long sequences.

We can also represent the RNN cell graphically as shown in the following diagram on the left. At time t, the cell has an input x_t and an output y_t. Part of the output y_t (the hidden state h_t) is fed back into the cell for use at a later time step $t+1$. Just as a traditional neural network's parameters are contained in its weight matrix, the RNN's parameters are defined by three weight matrices U, V, and W, corresponding to the input, output, and hidden state respectively:

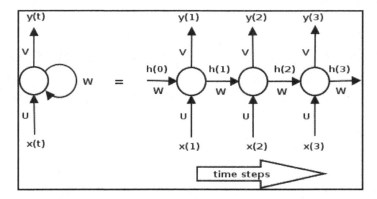

Another way to look at an RNN to *unroll* it, as shown in the preceding diagram on the right. Unrolling means that we draw the network out for the complete sequence. The network shown here is a three-layer RNN, suitable for processing three element sequences. Notice that the weight matrices U, V, and W are shared across the steps. This is because we are applying the same operation on different inputs at each time step. Being able to share these weight vectors across all the time steps greatly reduces the number of parameters that the RNN needs to learn.

We can also describe the computations within an RNN in terms of equations. The internal state of the RNN at a time t is given by the value of the hidden vector h_t, which is the sum of the product of the weight matrix W and the hidden state h_{t-1} at time $t-1$ and the product of the weight matrix U and the input x_t at time t, passed through the *tanh* nonlinearity. The choice of *tanh* over other nonlinearities has to do with its second derivative decaying very slowly to zero. This keeps the gradients in the linear region of the activation function and helps combat the vanishing gradient problem. We will learn more about the vanishing gradient problem later in this chapter.

The output vector y_t at time t is the product of the weight matrix V and the hidden state h_t, with *softmax* applied to the product so the resulting vector is a set of output probabilities:

$$\mathbf{h_t} = \tanh(\mathbf{Wh_{t-1}} + \mathbf{Ux_t})$$
$$\mathbf{y_t} = \mathbf{softmax}(\mathbf{Vh_t})$$

Keras provides the SimpleRNN (for more information refer to: `https://keras.io/layers/recurrent/`) recurrent layer that incorporates all the logic we have seen so far, as well as the more advanced variants such as LSTM and GRU that we will see later in this chapter, so it is not strictly necessary to understand how they work in order to start building with them. However, an understanding of the structure and equations is helpful when you need to compose your own RNN to solve a given problem.

SimpleRNN with Keras — generating text

RNNs have been used extensively by the **natural language processing** (**NLP**) community for various applications. One such application is building language models. A language model allows us to predict the probability of a word in a text given the previous words. Language models are important for various higher level tasks such as machine translation, spelling correction, and so on.

A side effect of the ability to predict the next word given previous words is a generative model that allows us to generate text by sampling from the output probabilities. In language modeling, our input is typically a sequence of words and the output is a sequence of predicted words. The training data used is existing unlabeled text, where we set the label y_t at time t to be the input x_{t+1} at time *t+1*.

For our first example of using Keras for building RNNs, we will train a character based language model on the text of *Alice in Wonderland* to predict the next character given 10 previous characters. We have chosen to build a character-based model here because it has a smaller vocabulary and trains quicker. The idea is the same as using a word-based language model, except we use characters instead of words. We will then use the trained model to generate some text in the same style.

First we import the necessary modules:

```
from __future__ import print_function
from keras.layers import Dense, Activation
from keras.layers.recurrent import SimpleRNN
from keras.models import Sequential
from keras.utils.visualize_util import plot
import numpy as np
```

We read our input text from the text of *Alice in Wonderland* on the Project Gutenberg website (`http://www.gutenberg.org/files/11/11-0.txt`). The file contains line breaks and non-ASCII characters, so we do some preliminary cleanup and write out the contents into a variable called `text`:

```
fin = open("../data/alice_in_wonderland.txt", 'rb')
lines = []
for line in fin:
    line = line.strip().lower()
    line = line.decode("ascii", "ignore")
    if len(line) == 0:
        continue
    lines.append(line)
fin.close()
text = " ".join(lines)
```

Since we are building a character-level RNN, our vocabulary is the set of characters that occur in the text. There are 42 of them in our case. Since we will be dealing with the indexes to these characters rather than the characters themselves, the following code snippet creates the necessary lookup tables:

```
chars = set([c for c in text])
nb_chars = len(chars)
char2index = dict((c, i) for i, c in enumerate(chars))
index2char = dict((i, c) for i, c in enumerate(chars))
```

The next step is to create the input and label texts. We do this by stepping through the text by a number of characters given by the `STEP` variable (1 in our case) and then extracting a span of text whose size is determined by the `SEQLEN` variable (10 in our case). The next character after the span is our label character:

```
SEQLEN = 10
STEP = 1

input_chars = []
label_chars = []
for i in range(0, len(text) - SEQLEN, STEP):
    input_chars.append(text[i:i + SEQLEN])
    label_chars.append(text[i + SEQLEN])
```

Using the preceding code, the input and label texts for the text `it turned into a pig` would look like this:

```
it turned -> i
 t turned i -> n
  turned in -> t
turned int -> o
```

```
urned into ->
rned into -> a
ned into a ->
ed into a -> p
d into a p -> i
 into a pi -> g
```

The next step is to vectorize these input and label texts. Each row of the input to the RNN corresponds to one of the input texts shown previously. There are SEQLEN characters in this input, and since our vocabulary size is given by nb_chars, we represent each input character as a one-hot encoded vector of size (nb_chars). Thus each input row is a tensor of size (SEQLEN and nb_chars). Our output label is a single character, so similar to the way we represent each character of our input, it is represented as a one-hot vector of size (nb_chars). Thus, the shape of each label is nb_chars:

```
X = np.zeros((len(input_chars), SEQLEN, nb_chars), dtype=np.bool)
y = np.zeros((len(input_chars), nb_chars), dtype=np.bool)
for i, input_char in enumerate(input_chars):
    for j, ch in enumerate(input_char):
        X[i, j, char2index[ch]] = 1
    y[i, char2index[label_chars[i]]] = 1
```

Finally, we are ready to build our model. We define the RNN's output dimension to have a size of 128. This is a hyper-parameter that needs to be determined by experimentation. In general, if we choose too small a size, then the model does not have sufficient capacity for generating good text, and you will see long runs of repeating characters or runs of repeating word groups. On the other hand, if the value chosen is too large, the model has too many parameters and needs a lot more data to train effectively. We want to return a single character as output, not a sequence of characters, so return_sequences=False. We have already seen that the input to the RNN is of shape (SEQLEN and nb_chars). In addition, we set unroll=True because it improves performance on the TensorFlow backend.

The RNN is connected to a dense (fully connected) layer. The dense layer has (nb_char) units, which emits scores for each of the characters in the vocabulary. The activation on the dense layer is a softmax, which normalizes the scores to probabilities. The character with the highest probability is chosen as the prediction. We compile the model with the categorical cross-entropy loss function, a good loss function for categorical outputs, and the RMSprop optimizer:

```
HIDDEN_SIZE = 128
BATCH_SIZE = 128
NUM_ITERATIONS = 25
NUM_EPOCHS_PER_ITERATION = 1
NUM_PREDS_PER_EPOCH = 100
```

```
model = Sequential()
model.add(SimpleRNN(HIDDEN_SIZE, return_sequences=False,
    input_shape=(SEQLEN, nb_chars),
    unroll=True))
model.add(Dense(nb_chars))
model.add(Activation("softmax"))

model.compile(loss="categorical_crossentropy", optimizer="rmsprop")
```

Our training approach is a little different from what we have seen so far. So far our approach has been to train a model for a fixed number of epochs, then evaluate it against a portion of held-out test data. Since we don't have any labeled data here, we train the model for an epoch (NUM_EPOCHS_PER_ITERATION=1) then test it. We continue training like this for 25 (NUM_ITERATIONS=25) iterations, stopping once we see intelligible output. So effectively, we are training for NUM_ITERATIONS epochs and testing the model after each epoch.

Our test consists of generating a character from the model given a random input, then dropping the first character from the input and appending the predicted character from our previous run, and generating another character from the model. We continue this 100 times (NUM_PREDS_PER_EPOCH=100) and generate and print the resulting string. The string gives us an indication of the quality of the model:

```
for iteration in range(NUM_ITERATIONS):
    print("=" * 50)
    print("Iteration #: %d" % (iteration))
    model.fit(X, y, batch_size=BATCH_SIZE, epochs=NUM_EPOCHS_PER_ITERATION)

    test_idx = np.random.randint(len(input_chars))
    test_chars = input_chars[test_idx]
    print("Generating from seed: %s" % (test_chars))
    print(test_chars, end="")
    for i in range(NUM_PREDS_PER_EPOCH):
        Xtest = np.zeros((1, SEQLEN, nb_chars))
        for i, ch in enumerate(test_chars):
            Xtest[0, i, char2index[ch]] = 1
        pred = model.predict(Xtest, verbose=0)[0]
        ypred = index2char[np.argmax(pred)]
        print(ypred, end="")
        # move forward with test_chars + ypred
        test_chars = test_chars[1:] + ypred
    print()
```

The output of this run is shown as follows. As you can see, the model starts out predicting gibberish, but by the end of the 25th epoch, it has learned to spell reasonably well, although it has trouble expressing coherent thoughts. The amazing thing about this model is that it is character-based and has no knowledge of words, yet it learns to spell words that look like they might have come from the original text:

```
===================================================
Iteration #: 21
Epoch 1/1
142544/142544 [==============================] - 10s - loss: 1.3916
Generating from seed: e with the
e with the white rabbit had no the that the mouse the mouse the mouse the mouse the mouse the mouse the mouse
===================================================
Iteration #: 22
Epoch 1/1
142544/142544 [==============================] - 10s - loss: 1.3831
Generating from seed: and an ol
and an ollar the caterpillar the seapped did not a moment the cook of the courter the caterpillar the seapped
===================================================
Iteration #: 23
Epoch 1/1
142544/142544 [==============================] - 10s - loss: 1.3757
Generating from seed: ' the mock
' the mock turtle said the dormouse some of the conce in the dormouse some of the conce in the dormouse some o
===================================================
Iteration #: 24
Epoch 1/1
142544/142544 [==============================] - 10s - loss: 1.3685
Generating from seed: raving mad
raving made to goon of the sord alice could got to the dormouse so they looked at the sord alice could got to
```

Generating the next character or next word of text is not the only thing you can do with this sort of model. This kind of model has been successfully used to make stock predictions (for more information refer to the article: *Financial Market Time Series Prediction with Recurrent Neural Networks*, by A. Bernal, S. Fok, and R. Pidaparthi, 2012) and generate classical music (for more information refer to the article: *DeepBach: A Steerable Model for Bach Chorales Generation*, by G. Hadjeres and F. Pachet, arXiv:1612.01010, 2016), to name a few interesting applications. Andrej Karpathy covers a few other fun examples, such as generating fake Wikipedia pages, algebraic geometry proofs, and Linux source code in his blog post at: *The Unreasonable Effectiveness of Recurrent Neural Networks* at `http://karpathy.github.io /2015/05/21/rnn-effectiveness/`.

The source code for this example is available in `alice_chargen_rnn.py` in the code download for the chapter. The data is available from Project Gutenberg.

RNN topologies

The APIs for MLP and CNN architectures are limited. Both architectures accept a fixed-size tensor as input and produce a fixed-size tensor as output; and they perform the transformation from input to output in a fixed number of steps given by the number of layers in the model. RNNs don't have this limitation—you can have sequences in the input, the output, or both. This means that RNNs can be arranged in many ways to solve specific problems.

As we have learned, RNNs combine the input vector with the previous state vector to produce a new state vector. This can be thought of as similar to running a program with some inputs and some internal variables. Thus RNNs can be thought of as essentially describing computer programs. In fact, it has been shown that RNNs are turing complete (for more information refer to the article: *On the Computational Power of Neural Nets*, by H. T. Siegelmann and E. D. Sontag, proceedings of the fifth annual workshop on computational learning theory, ACM, 1992.) in the sense that given the proper weights, they can simulate arbitrary programs.

This property of being able to work with sequences gives rise to a number of common topologies, some of which we'll discuss, as follows:

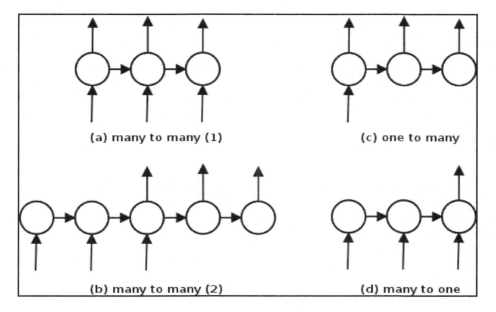

(a) many to many (1)

(c) one to many

(b) many to many (2)

(d) many to one

All these different topologies derive from the same basic structure shown in the preceding diagram. In this basic topology, all input sequences are of the same length and an output is produced at each time step. We have already seen an example of this with our character level RNN for generating words in *Alice in Wonderland*.

Another example of a many to many RNN could be a machine translation network shown as **(b)**, part of a general family of networks called sequence-to-sequence (for more information refer to: *Grammar as a Foreign Language*, by O. Vinyals, Advances in Neural Information Processing Systems, 2015). These take in a sequence and produces another sequence. In the case of machine translation, the input could be a sequence of English words in a sentence and the output could be the words in a translated Spanish sentence. In the case of a model that uses sequence-to-sequence to do **part-of-speech** (**POS**) tagging, the input could be the words in a sentence and the output could be the corresponding POS tags. It differs from the previous topology in that at certain time steps there is no input and at others there is no output. We will see an example of such a network later in this chapter.

Other variants are the one-to-many network shown as **(c)**, an example of which could be an image captioning network (for more information refer to the article: *Deep Visual-Semantic Alignments for Generating Image Descriptions*, by A. Karpathy, and F. Li, Proceedings of the IEEE Conference on Computer Vision and Pattern Recognition, 2015.), where the input is an image and the output a sequence of words.

Similarly, an example of a many-to-one network as shown in **(d)** could be a network that does sentiment analysis of sentences, where the input is a sequence of words and the output is a positive or negative sentiment (for more information refer to the article: *Recursive Deep Models for Semantic Compositionality over a Sentiment Treebank*, by R. Socher, Proceedings of the Conference on Empirical Methods in Natural Language Processing (EMNLP). Vol. 1631, 2013). We will see an (much simplified compared to the cited model) example of this topology as well later in the chapter.

Vanishing and exploding gradients

Just like traditional neural networks, training the RNN also involves backpropagation. The difference in this case is that since the parameters are shared by all time steps, the gradient at each output depends not only on the current time step, but also on the previous ones. This process is called **backpropagation through time** (**BPTT**) (for more information refer to the article: *Learning Internal Representations by Backpropagating errors*, by G. E. Hinton, D. E. Rumelhart, and R. J. Williams, Parallel Distributed Processing: Explorations in the Microstructure of Cognition 1, 1985):

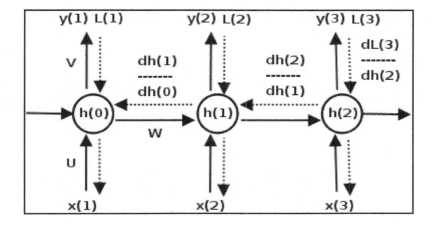

Consider the small three layer RNN shown in the preceding diagram. During the forward propagation (shown by the solid lines), the network produces predictions that are compared to the labels to compute a loss L_t at each time step. During backpropagation (shown by dotted lines), the gradients of the loss with respect to the parameters U, V, and W are computed at each time step and the parameters are updated with the sum of the gradients.

The following equation shows the gradient of the loss with respect to W, the matrix that encodes weights for the long term dependencies. We focus on this part of the update because it is the cause of the vanishing and exploding gradient problem. The other two gradients of the loss with respect to the matrices U and V are also summed up across all time steps in a similar way:

$$\frac{\partial L}{\partial W} = \sum_t \frac{\partial L_t}{\partial W}$$

Let us now look at what happens to the gradient of the loss at the last time step ($t=3$). As you can see, this gradient can be decomposed to a product of three sub gradients using the chain rule. The gradient of the hidden state $h2$ with respect to W can be further decomposed as the sum of the gradient of each hidden state with respect to the previous one. Finally, each gradient of the hidden state with respect to the previous one can be further decomposed as the product of gradients of the current hidden state against the previous one:

$$\frac{\partial L_3}{\partial W} = \frac{\partial L_3}{\partial y_3} \cdot \frac{\partial y_3}{\partial h_2} \cdot \frac{\partial h_2}{\partial W}$$

$$= \sum_{t=0}^{2} \frac{\partial L_3}{\partial y_3} \cdot \frac{\partial y_3}{\partial h_2} \cdot \frac{\partial h_2}{\partial h_t} \cdot \frac{\partial h_t}{\partial W}$$

$$= \sum_{t=0}^{2} \frac{\partial L_3}{\partial y_3} \cdot \frac{\partial y_3}{\partial h_2} \cdot \left(\prod_{j=t+1}^{2} \frac{\partial h_j}{\partial h_{j-1}} \right) \cdot \frac{\partial h_t}{\partial W}$$

Similar calculations are done to compute the gradient of losses L_1 and L_2 (at time steps 1 and 2) with respect to W and to sum them into the gradient update for W. We will not explore the math further in this book. If you want to do so on your own, this WILDML blog post (`http tps://goo.gl/l06lbX`) has a very good explanation of BPTT, including more detailed derivations of the mathematics behind the process.

For our purposes, the final form of the gradient in the equation above tells us why RNNs have the problem of vanishing and exploding gradients. Consider the case where the individual gradients of a hidden state with respect to the previous one is less than one. As we backpropagate across multiple time steps, the product of gradients get smaller and smaller, leading to the problem of vanishing gradients. Similarly, if the gradients are larger than one, the products get larger and larger, leading to the problem of exploding gradients.

The effect of vanishing gradients is that the gradients from steps that are far away do not contribute anything to the learning process, so the RNN ends up not learning long range dependencies. Vanishing gradients can happen for traditional neural networks as well, it is just more visible in case of RNNs, since RNNs tend to have many more layers (time steps) over which back propagation must occur.

Exploding gradients are more easily detectable, the gradients will become very large and then turn into **not a number** (**NaN**) and the training process will crash. Exploding gradients can be controlled by clipping them at a predefined threshold as discussed in the paper: *On the Difficulty of Training Recurrent Neural Networks*, by R. Pascanu, T. Mikolov, and Y. Bengio, ICML, Pp 1310-1318, 2013.

While there are a few approaches to minimize the problem of vanishing gradients, such as proper initialization of the *W* matrix, using a ReLU instead of *tanh* layers, and pre-training the layers using unsupervised methods, the most popular solution is to use the LSTM or GRU architectures. These architectures have been designed to deal with the vanishing gradient problem and learn long term dependencies more effectively. We will learn more about LSTM and GRU architectures later in this chapter.

Long short term memory — LSTM

The LSTM is a variant of RNN that is capable of learning long term dependencies. LSTMs were first proposed by Hochreiter and Schmidhuber and refined by many other researchers. They work well on a large variety of problems and are the most widely used type of RNN.

We have seen how the SimpleRNN uses the hidden state from the previous time step and the current input in a *tanh* layer to implement recurrence. LSTMs also implement recurrence in a similar way, but instead of a single *tanh* layer, there are four layers interacting in a very specific way. The following diagram illustrates the transformations that are applied to the hidden state at time step *t*:

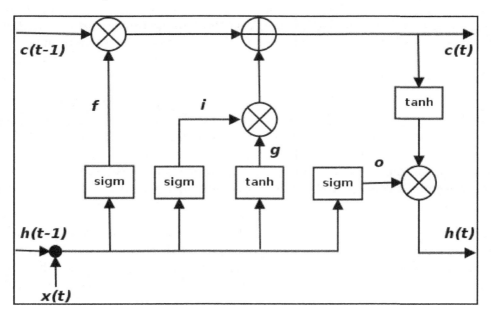

The diagram looks complicated, but let us look at it component by component. The line across the top of the diagram is the cell state c, and represents the internal memory of the unit. The line across the bottom is the hidden state, and the i, f, o, and g gates are the mechanism by which the LSTM works around the vanishing gradient problem. During training, the LSTM learns the parameters for these gates.

In order to gain a deeper understanding of how these gates modulate the LSTM's hidden state, let us consider the equations that show how it calculates the hidden state h_t at time t from the hidden state h_{t-1} at the previous time step:

$$i = \sigma(W_i h_{t-1} + U_i x_t)$$
$$f = \sigma(W_f h_{t-1} + U_f x_t)$$
$$o = \sigma(W_o h_{t-1} + U_o x_t)$$
$$g = tanh(W_g h_{t-1} + U_g x_t)$$
$$c_t = (c_{t-1} \otimes f) \oplus (g \otimes i)$$
$$h_t = tanh(c_t) \otimes o$$

Here i, f, and o are the input, forget, and output gates. They are computed using the same equations but with different parameter matrices. The sigmoid function modulates the output of these gates between zero and one, so the output vector produced can be multiplied element-wise with another vector to define how much of the second vector can pass through the first one.

The forget gate defines how much of the previous state h_{t-1} you want to allow to pass through. The input gate defines how much of the newly computed state for the current input x_t you want to let through, and the output gate defines how much of the internal state you want to expose to the next layer. The internal hidden state g is computed based on the current input x_t and the previous hidden state h_{t-1}. Notice that the equation for g is identical to that for the SimpleRNN cell, but in this case we will modulate the output by the output of the input gate i.

Given i, f, o, and g, we can now calculate the cell state c_t at time t in terms of c_{t-1} at time $(t-1)$ multiplied by the forget gate and the state g multiplied by the input gate i. So this is basically a way to combine the previous memory and the new input—setting the forget gate to 0 ignores the old memory and setting the input gate to 0 ignores the newly computed state.

Finally, the hidden state h_t at time t is computed by multiplying the memory c_t with the output gate.

One thing to realize is that an LSTM is a drop-in replacement for a SimpleRNN cell, the only difference is that LSTMs are resistant to the vanishing gradient problem. You can replace an RNN cell in a network with an LSTM without worrying about any side effects. You should generally see better results along with longer training times.

If you would like to know more, WILDML blog post has a very detailed explanation of these LSTM gates and how they work. For a more visual explanation, take a look at Christopher Olah's blog post: *Understanding LSTMs* (http://colah.github.io/posts/2015-08-Understanding-LSTMs/) where he walks you step by step through these computations, with illustrations at each step.

LSTM with Keras — sentiment analysis

Keras provides an LSTM layer that we will use here to construct and train a many-to-one RNN. Our network takes in a sentence (a sequence of words) and outputs a sentiment value (positive or negative). Our training set is a dataset of about 7,000 short sentences from UMICH SI650 sentiment classification competition on Kaggle (https://inclass.kaggle.com/c/si650winter11). Each sentence is labeled *1* or *0* for positive or negative sentiment respectively, which our network will learn to predict.

We start with the imports, as usual:

```
from keras.layers.core import Activation, Dense, Dropout, SpatialDropout1D
from keras.layers.embeddings import Embedding
from keras.layers.recurrent import LSTM
from keras.models import Sequential
from keras.preprocessing import sequence
from sklearn.model_selection import train_test_split
import collections
import matplotlib.pyplot as plt
import nltk
import numpy as np
import os
```

Before we start, we want to do a bit of exploratory analysis on the data. Specifically we need to know how many unique words there are in the corpus and how many words are there in each sentence:

```
maxlen = 0
word_freqs = collections.Counter()
num_recs = 0
```

```
ftrain = open(os.path.join(DATA_DIR, "umich-sentiment-train.txt"), 'rb')
for line in ftrain:
    label, sentence = line.strip().split("t")
    words = nltk.word_tokenize(sentence.decode("ascii", "ignore").lower())
    if len(words) > maxlen:
        maxlen = len(words)
    for word in words:
        word_freqs[word] += 1
    num_recs += 1
ftrain.close()
```

Using this, we get the following estimates for our corpus:

```
maxlen : 42
len(word_freqs) : 2313
```

Using the number of unique words `len(word_freqs)`, we set our vocabulary size to a fixed number and treat all the other words as **out of vocabulary (OOV)** words and replace them with the pseudo-word UNK (for unknown). At prediction time, this will allow us to handle previously unseen words as OOV words as well.

The number of words in the sentence (`maxlen`) allows us to set a fixed sequence length and zero pad shorter sentences and truncate longer sentences to that length as appropriate. Even though RNNs handle variable sequence length, this is usually achieved either by padding and truncating as above, or by grouping the inputs in different batches by sequence length. We will use the former approach here. For the latter approach, Keras recommends using batches of size one (for more information refer to: `https://github.com/fchollet/keras/issues/40`).

Based on the preceding estimates, we set our VOCABULARY_SIZE to 2002. This is 2,000 words from our vocabulary plus the UNK pseudo-word and the PAD pseudo word (used for padding sentences to a fixed number of words), in our case 40 given by MAX_SENTENCE_LENGTH:

```
DATA_DIR = "../data"

MAX_FEATURES = 2000
MAX_SENTENCE_LENGTH = 40
```

Next we need a pair of lookup tables. Each row of input to the RNN is a sequence of word indices, where the indices are ordered by most frequent to least frequent word in the training set. The two lookup tables allow us to lookup an index given the word and the word given the index. This includes the PAD and UNK pseudo-words as well:

```
vocab_size = min(MAX_FEATURES, len(word_freqs)) + 2
word2index = {x[0]: i+2 for i, x in
enumerate(word_freqs.most_common(MAX_FEATURES))}
word2index["PAD"] = 0
word2index["UNK"] = 1
index2word = {v:k for k, v in word2index.items()}
```

Next, we convert our input sentences to word index sequences, pad them to the MAX_SENTENCE_LENGTH words. Since our output label in this case is binary (positive or negative sentiment), we don't need to process the labels:

```
X = np.empty((num_recs, ), dtype=list)
y = np.zeros((num_recs, ))
i = 0
ftrain = open(os.path.join(DATA_DIR, "umich-sentiment-train.txt"), 'rb')
for line in ftrain:
    label, sentence = line.strip().split("t")
    words = nltk.word_tokenize(sentence.decode("ascii", "ignore").lower())
    seqs = []
    for word in words:
        if word2index.has_key(word):
            seqs.append(word2index[word])
        else:
            seqs.append(word2index["UNK"])
    X[i] = seqs
    y[i] = int(label)
    i += 1
ftrain.close()
X = sequence.pad_sequences(X, maxlen=MAX_SENTENCE_LENGTH)
```

Finally, we split the training set into a 80-20 training test split:

```
Xtrain, Xtest, ytrain, ytest = train_test_split(X, y, test_size=0.2,
random_state=42)
```

The following diagram shows the structure of our RNN:

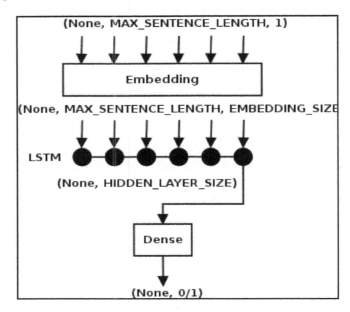

The input for each row is a sequence of word indices. The sequence length is given by MAX_SENTENCE_LENGTH. The first dimension of the tensor is set to None to indicate that the batch size (the number of records fed to the network each time) is currently unknown at definition time; it is specified during run time using the batch_size parameter. So assuming an as-yet undetermined batch size, the shape of the input tensor is (None, MAX_SENTENCE_LENGTH, 1). These tensors are fed into an embedding layer of size EMBEDDING_SIZE whose weights are initialized with small random values and learned during training. This layer will transform the tensor to a shape (None,MAX_SENTENCE_LENGTH, EMBEDDING_SIZE). The output of the embedding layer is fed into an LSTM with sequence length MAX_SENTENCE_LENGTH and output layer size HIDDEN_LAYER_SIZE, so the output of the LSTM is a tensor of shape (None, HIDDEN_LAYER_SIZE, MAX_SENTENCE_LENGTH). By default, the LSTM will output a single tensor of shape (None, HIDDEN_LAYER_SIZE) at its last sequence (return_sequences=False). This is fed to a dense layer with output size of 1 with a sigmoid activation function, so it will output either 0 (negative review) or 1 (positive review).

We compile the model using the binary cross-entropy loss function since it predicts a binary value, and the Adam optimizer, a good general purpose optimizer. Note that the hyperparameters EMBEDDING_SIZE, HIDDEN_LAYER_SIZE, BATCH_SIZE and NUM_EPOCHS (set as constants as follows) were tuned experimentally over several runs:

```
EMBEDDING_SIZE = 128
HIDDEN_LAYER_SIZE = 64
BATCH_SIZE = 32
NUM_EPOCHS = 10

model = Sequential()
model.add(Embedding(vocab_size, EMBEDDING_SIZE,
input_length=MAX_SENTENCE_LENGTH))
model.add(SpatialDropout1D(Dropout(0.2)))
model.add(LSTM(HIDDEN_LAYER_SIZE, dropout=0.2, recurrent_dropout=0.2))
model.add(Dense(1))
model.add(Activation("sigmoid"))

model.compile(loss="binary_crossentropy", optimizer="adam",
    metrics=["accuracy"])
```

We then train the network for 10 epochs (NUM_EPOCHS) and batch size of 32 (BATCH_SIZE). At each epoch we validate the model using the test data:

```
history = model.fit(Xtrain, ytrain, batch_size=BATCH_SIZE,
epochs=NUM_EPOCHS,
    validation_data=(Xtest, ytest))
```

The output of this step shows how the loss decreases and accuracy increases over multiple epochs:

```
Train on 5668 samples, validate on 1418 samples
Epoch 1/10
5668/5668 [==============================] - 20s - loss: 0.3316 - acc: 0.8626 - val_loss: 0.0799 - val_acc: 0.9746
Epoch 2/10
5668/5668 [==============================] - 19s - loss: 0.0911 - acc: 0.9626 - val_loss: 0.0512 - val_acc: 0.9810
Epoch 3/10
5668/5668 [==============================] - 18s - loss: 0.0649 - acc: 0.9730 - val_loss: 0.0553 - val_acc: 0.9859
Epoch 4/10
5668/5668 [==============================] - 19s - loss: 0.0642 - acc: 0.9746 - val_loss: 0.0596 - val_acc: 0.9845
Epoch 5/10
5668/5668 [==============================] - 20s - loss: 0.0531 - acc: 0.9787 - val_loss: 0.0434 - val_acc: 0.9845
Epoch 6/10
5668/5668 [==============================] - 19s - loss: 0.0575 - acc: 0.9762 - val_loss: 0.0396 - val_acc: 0.9852
Epoch 7/10
5668/5668 [==============================] - 19s - loss: 0.0494 - acc: 0.9797 - val_loss: 0.0374 - val_acc: 0.9873
Epoch 8/10
5668/5668 [==============================] - 19s - loss: 0.0467 - acc: 0.9809 - val_loss: 0.0374 - val_acc: 0.9859
Epoch 9/10
5668/5668 [==============================] - 18s - loss: 0.0440 - acc: 0.9811 - val_loss: 0.0425 - val_acc: 0.9852
Epoch 10/10
5668/5668 [==============================] - 18s - loss: 0.0464 - acc: 0.9795 - val_loss: 0.0378 - val_acc: 0.9873

1418/1418 [==============================] - 0s
```

We can also plot the loss and accuracy values over time using the following code:

```
plt.subplot(211)
plt.title("Accuracy")
plt.plot(history.history["acc"], color="g", label="Train")
plt.plot(history.history["val_acc"], color="b", label="Validation")
plt.legend(loc="best")

plt.subplot(212)
plt.title("Loss")
plt.plot(history.history["loss"], color="g", label="Train")
plt.plot(history.history["val_loss"], color="b", label="Validation")
plt.legend(loc="best")

plt.tight_layout()
plt.show()
```

The output of the preceding example is as follows:

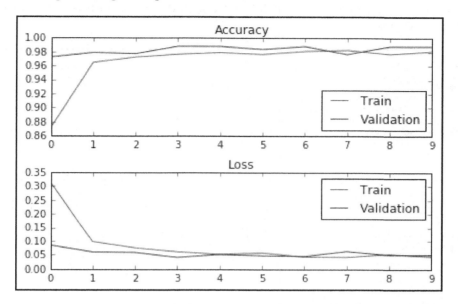

Finally, we evaluate our model against the full test set and print the score and accuracy. We also pick a few random sentences from our test set and print the RNN's prediction, the label and the actual sentence:

```
score, acc = model.evaluate(Xtest, ytest, batch_size=BATCH_SIZE)
print("Test score: %.3f, accuracy: %.3f" % (score, acc))

for i in range(5):
    idx = np.random.randint(len(Xtest))
    xtest = Xtest[idx].reshape(1,40)
    ylabel = ytest[idx]
    ypred = model.predict(xtest)[0][0]
    sent = " ".join([index2word[x] for x in xtest[0].tolist() if x != 0])
    print("%.0ft%dt%s" % (ypred, ylabel, sent))
```

As you can see from the results, we get back close to 99% accuracy. The predictions the model makes for this particular set match exactly with the labels, although this is not the case for all predictions:

```
Test score: 0.038, accuracy: 0.987

#pred label sentence
1     1     i like th mission impossible one ...
1     1     we 're gon na like watch mission impossible or hoot . (
1     1     the people who are worth it know how much i love the da vinci code .
0     0     ok brokeback mountain is such a horrible movie .
1     1     brokeback mountain is the most amazing / beautiful / romantic /
            Heartbraking movie i have ever or will ever see in my life
```

If you would like to run this code locally, you need to get the data from the Kaggle website.

The source code for this example is available in the file `umich_sentiment_lstm.py` in the code download for this chapter.

Gated recurrent unit — GRU

The GRU is a variant of the LSTM and was introduced by K. Cho (for more information refer to: *Learning Phrase Representations using RNN Encoder-Decoder for Statistical Machine Translation*, by K. Cho, arXiv:1406.1078, 2014). It retains the LSTM's resistance to the vanishing gradient problem, but its internal structure is simpler, and therefore is faster to train, since fewer computations are needed to make updates to its hidden state. The gates for a GRU cell are illustrated in the following diagram:

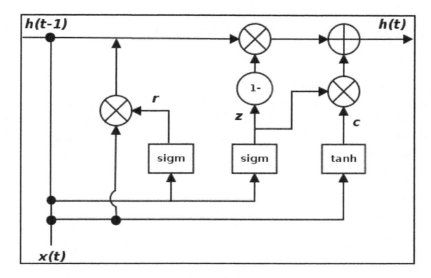

Instead of the input, forget, and output gates in the LSTM cell, the GRU cell has two gates, an update gate z, and a reset gate r. The update gate defines how much previous memory to keep around and the reset gate defines how to combine the new input with the previous memory. There is no persistent cell state distinct from the hidden state as in LSTM. The following equations define the gating mechanism in a GRU:

$$z = \sigma(W_z h_{t-1} + U_z x_t)$$
$$r = \sigma(W_r h_{t-1} + U_r x_t)$$
$$c = tanh(W_c(h_{t-1} \otimes r) + U_c x_t)$$
$$h_t = (z \otimes c) \oplus ((1 - z) \otimes h_{t-1})$$

According to several empirical evaluations (for more information refer to the articles: *An Empirical Exploration of Recurrent Network Architectures*, by R. Jozefowicz, W. Zaremba, and I. Sutskever, JMLR, 2015 and *Empirical Evaluation of Gated Recurrent Neural Networks on Sequence Modeling*, by J. Chung, arXiv:1412.3555. 2014), GRU and LSTM have comparable performance and there is no simple way to recommend one or the other for a specific task. While GRUs are faster to train and need less data to generalize, in situations where there is enough data, an LSTM's greater expressive power may lead to better results. Like LSTMs, GRUs are drop-in replacements for the SimpleRNN cell.

Keras provides built in implementations of both LSTM and GRU, as well as the SimpleRNN class we saw earlier.

GRU with Keras — POS tagging

Keras provides a GRU implementation, that we will use here to build a network that does POS tagging. A POS is a grammatical category of words that are used in the same way across multiple sentences. Examples of POS are nouns, verbs, adjectives, and so on. For example, nouns are typically used to identify things, verbs are typically used to identify what they do, and adjectives to describe some attribute of these things. POS tagging used to be done manually, but nowadays this is done automatically using statistical models. In recent years, deep learning has been applied to this problem as well (for more information refer to the article: *Natural Language Processing (almost) from Scratch*, by R. Collobert, Journal of Machine Learning Research, Pp. 2493-2537, 2011).

For our training data, we will need sentences tagged with part of speech tags. The Penn Treebank (`https://catalog.ldc.upenn.edu/ldc99t42`) is one such dataset, it is a human annotated corpus of about 4.5 million words of American English. However, it is a non-free resource. A 10% sample of the Penn Treebank is freely available as part of the NLTK (`http://www.nltk.org/`), which we will use to train our network.

Our model will take in a sequence of words in a sentence and output the corresponding POS tags for each word. Thus for an input sequence consisting of the words [*The, cat, sat, on, the, mat, .*], the output sequence emitted would be the POS symbols [*DT, NN, VB, IN, DT, NN*].

We start with the imports:

```
from keras.layers.core import Activation, Dense, Dropout, RepeatVector,
SpatialDropout1D
from keras.layers.embeddings import Embedding
from keras.layers.recurrent import GRU
from keras.layers.wrappers import TimeDistributed
from keras.models import Sequential
from keras.preprocessing import sequence
from keras.utils import np_utils
from sklearn.model_selection import train_test_split
import collections
import nltk
import numpy as np
import os
```

We then download the data from NLTK in a format suitable for our downstream code. Specifically, the data is available in parsed form as part of the NLTK Treebank corpus. We use the following Python code to download this data into two parallel files, one for the words in the sentences and one for the POS tags:

```
DATA_DIR = "../data"

fedata = open(os.path.join(DATA_DIR, "treebank_sents.txt"), "wb")
ffdata = open(os.path.join(DATA_DIR, "treebank_poss.txt"), "wb")

sents = nltk.corpus.treebank.tagged_sents()
for sent in sents:
    words, poss = [], []
    for word, pos in sent:
        if pos == "-NONE-":
            continue
        words.append(word)
        poss.append(pos)
    fedata.write("{:s}n".format(" ".join(words)))
    ffdata.write("{:s}n".format(" ".join(poss)))

fedata.close()
ffdata.close()
```

Once again, we want to explore the data a little to find out what vocabulary size to set. This time, we have to consider two different vocabularies, the source vocabulary for the words and the target vocabulary for the POS tags. We need to find the number of unique words in each vocabulary. We also need to find the maximum number of words in a sentence in our training corpus and the number of records. Because of the one-to-one nature of POS tagging, the last two values are identical for both vocabularies:

```
def parse_sentences(filename):
    word_freqs = collections.Counter()
    num_recs, maxlen = 0, 0
    fin = open(filename, "rb")
    for line in fin:
        words = line.strip().lower().split()
        for word in words:
            word_freqs[word] += 1
        if len(words) > maxlen:
            maxlen = len(words)
        num_recs += 1
    fin.close()
    return word_freqs, maxlen, num_recs

s_wordfreqs, s_maxlen, s_numrecs = parse_sentences(
    os.path.join(DATA_DIR, "treebank_sents.txt"))
```

```
        t_wordfreqs, t_maxlen, t_numrecs = parse_sentences(
        os.path.join(DATA_DIR, "treebank_poss.txt"))
print(len(s_wordfreqs), s_maxlen, s_numrecs, len(t_wordfreqs), t_maxlen,
t_numrecs)
```

Running this code tells us that there are 10,947 unique words and 45 unique POS tags. The maximum sentence size is 249, and the number of sentences in the 10% set is 3,914. Using this information, we decide to consider only the top 5,000 words for our source vocabulary. Our target vocabulary has 45 unique POS tags, we want to be able to predict all of them, so we will consider all of them in our vocabulary. Finally, we set 250 to be our maximum sequence length:

```
MAX_SEQLEN = 250
S_MAX_FEATURES = 5000
T_MAX_FEATURES = 45
```

Just like our sentiment analysis example, each row of the input will be represented as a sequence of word indices. The corresponding output will be a sequence of POS tag indices. So we need to build lookup tables to translate between the words/POS tags and their corresponding indices. Here is the code to do that. On the source side, we build a vocabulary index with two extra slots to hold the PAD and UNK pseudo-words. On the target side, we don't drop any words so there is no need for the UNK pseudo-word:

```
s_vocabsize = min(len(s_wordfreqs), S_MAX_FEATURES) + 2
s_word2index = {x[0]:i+2 for i, x in
enumerate(s_wordfreqs.most_common(S_MAX_FEATURES))}
s_word2index["PAD"] = 0
s_word2index["UNK"] = 1
s_index2word = {v:k for k, v in s_word2index.items()}

t_vocabsize = len(t_wordfreqs) + 1
t_word2index = {x[0]:i for i, x in
enumerate(t_wordfreqs.most_common(T_MAX_FEATURES))}
t_word2index["PAD"] = 0
t_index2word = {v:k for k, v in t_word2index.items()}
```

The next step is to build our datasets to feed into our network. We will use these lookup tables to convert our input sentences into a word ID sequence of length MAX_SEQLEN (250). The labels need to be structured as a sequence of one-hot vectors of size T_MAX_FEATURES + 1 (46), also of length MAX_SEQLEN (250). The build_tensor function reads the data from the two files and converts them to the input and output tensors. Additional default parameters are passed in to build the output tensor. This triggers the call to np_utils.to_categorical() to convert the output sequence of POS tag IDs to one-hot vector representation:

```
def build_tensor(filename, numrecs, word2index, maxlen,
        make_categorical=False, num_classes=0):
    data = np.empty((numrecs, ), dtype=list)
    fin = open(filename, "rb")
    i = 0
    for line in fin:
        wids = []
        for word in line.strip().lower().split():
            if word2index.has_key(word):
                wids.append(word2index[word])
            else:
                wids.append(word2index["UNK"])
        if make_categorical:
            data[i] = np_utils.to_categorical(wids,
                num_classes=num_classes)
        else:
            data[i] = wids
        i += 1
    fin.close()
    pdata = sequence.pad_sequences(data, maxlen=maxlen)
    return pdata

X = build_tensor(os.path.join(DATA_DIR, "treebank_sents.txt"),
    s_numrecs, s_word2index, MAX_SEQLEN)
Y = build_tensor(os.path.join(DATA_DIR, "treebank_poss.txt"),
    t_numrecs, t_word2index, MAX_SEQLEN, True, t_vocabsize)
```

We can then split the dataset into a 80-20 train-test split:

```
Xtrain, Xtest, Ytrain, Ytest = train_test_split(X, Y, test_size=0.2,
random_state=42)
```

The following figure shows the schematic of our network. It looks complicated, so let us deconstruct it:

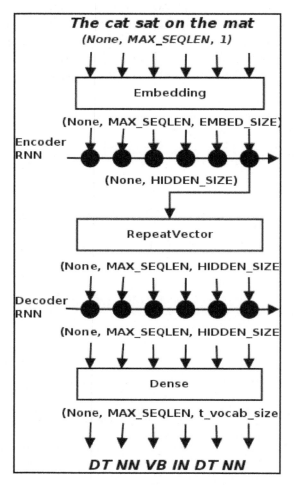

As previously, assuming that the batch size is as yet undetermined, the input to the network is a tensor of word IDs of shape (None, MAX_SEQLEN, 1). This is sent through an embedding layer, which converts each word into a dense vector of shape (EMBED_SIZE), so the output tensor from this layer has the shape (None, MAX_SEQLEN, EMBED_SIZE). This tensor is fed to the encoder GRU with an output size of HIDDEN_SIZE. The GRU is set to return a single context vector (return_sequences=False) after seeing a sequence of size MAX_SEQLEN, so the output tensor from the GRU layer has shape (None, HIDDEN_SIZE).

This context vector is then replicated using the RepeatVector layer into a tensor of shape (None, MAX_SEQLEN, HIDDEN_SIZE) and fed into the decoder GRU layer. This is then fed into a dense layer which produces an output tensor of shape (None, MAX_SEQLEN, t_vocab_size). The activation function on the dense layer is a softmax. The argmax of each column of this tensor is the index of the predicted POS tag for the word at that position.

The model definition is shown as follows: EMBED_SIZE, HIDDEN_SIZE, BATCH_SIZE, and NUM_EPOCHS are hyperparameters which have been assigned these values after experimenting with multiple different values. The model is compiled with the categorical_crossentropy loss function since we have multiple categories of labels, and the optimizer used is the popular adam optimizer:

```
EMBED_SIZE = 128
HIDDEN_SIZE = 64
BATCH_SIZE = 32
NUM_EPOCHS = 1

model = Sequential()
model.add(Embedding(s_vocabsize, EMBED_SIZE,
input_length=MAX_SEQLEN))
model.add(SpatialDropout1D(Dropout(0.2)))
model.add(GRU(HIDDEN_SIZE, dropout=0.2, recurrent_dropout=0.2))
model.add(RepeatVector(MAX_SEQLEN))
model.add(GRU(HIDDEN_SIZE, return_sequences=True))
model.add(TimeDistributed(Dense(t_vocabsize)))
model.add(Activation("softmax"))

model.compile(loss="categorical_crossentropy", optimizer="adam",
    metrics=["accuracy"])
```

We train this model for a single epoch. The model is very rich, with many parameters, and begins to overfit after the first epoch of training. When fed the same data multiple times in the next epochs, the model begins to overfit to the training data and does worse on the validation data:

```
model.fit(Xtrain, Ytrain, batch_size=BATCH_SIZE, epochs=NUM_EPOCHS,
    validation_data=[Xtest, Ytest])

score, acc = model.evaluate(Xtest, Ytest, batch_size=BATCH_SIZE)
print("Test score: %.3f, accuracy: %.3f" % (score, acc))
```

The output of the training and the evaluation is shown as follows. As you can see, the model does quite well after the first epoch of training:

```
Train on 3131 samples, validate on 783 samples
Epoch 1/1
3131/3131 [==============================] - 81s - loss: 0.3013 - acc: 0.8263 - val_loss: 0.2934 - val_acc: 0.9159

783/783 [==============================] - 3s
Test score: 0.293, accuracy: 0.916
```

Similar to actual RNNs, the three recurrent classes in Keras (`SimpleRNN`, `LSTM`, and `GRU`) are interchangeable. To demonstrate, we simply replace all occurrences of `GRU` in the previous program with `LSTM` and rerun the program. The model definition and the import statements are the only things that change:

```
from keras.layers.recurrent import GRU

model = Sequential()
model.add(Embedding(s_vocabsize, EMBED_SIZE,
input_length=MAX_SEQLEN))
model.add(SpatialDropout1D(Dropout(0.2)))
model.add(GRU(HIDDEN_SIZE, dropout=0.2, recurrent_dropout=0.2))
model.add(RepeatVector(MAX_SEQLEN))
model.add(GRU(HIDDEN_SIZE, return_sequences=True))
model.add(TimeDistributed(Dense(t_vocabsize)))
model.add(Activation("softmax"))
```

As you can see from the output, the results of the GRU-based network are quite comparable to our previous LSTM-based network.

Sequence-to-sequence models are a very powerful class of model. Its most canonical application is machine translation, but there are many others such as the previous example. Indeed, a lot of NLP tasks further up in the hierarchy, such as named entity recognition (for more information refer to the article: *Named Entity Recognition with Long Short Term Memory*, by J. Hammerton, Proceedings of the Seventh Conference on Natural Language Learning at HLT-NAACL, Association for Computational Linguistics, 2003) and sentence parsing (for more information refer to the article: *Grammar as a Foreign Language*, by O. Vinyals, Advances in Neural Information Processing Systems, 2015), as well as more complex networks such as those for image captioning (for more information refer to the article: *Deep Visual-Semantic Alignments for Generating Image Descriptions*, by A. Karpathy, and F. Li, Proceedings of the IEEE Conference on Computer Vision and Pattern Recognition, 2015.), are examples of the sequence-to-sequence compositional model.

The full code for this example can be found in the file `pos_tagging_gru.py` in the the code download for this chapter.

Bidirectional RNNs

At a given time step t, the output of the RNN is dependent on the outputs at all previous time steps. However, it is entirely possible that the output is also dependent on the future outputs as well. This is especially true for applications such as NLP, where the attributes of the word or phrase we are trying to predict may be dependent on the context given by the entire enclosing sentence, not just the words that came before it. Bidirectional RNNs also help a network architecture place equal emphasis on the beginning and end of the sequence, and increase the data available for training.

Bidirectional RNNs are two RNNs stacked on top of each other, reading the input in opposite directions. So in our example, one RNN will read the words left to right and the other RNN will read the words right to left. The output at each time step will be based on the hidden state of both RNNs.

Keras provides support for bidirectional RNNs through a bidirectional wrapper layer. For example, for our POS tagging example, we could make our LSTMs bidirectional simply by wrapping them with this Bidirectional wrapper, as shown in the model definition code as follows:

```
from keras.layers.wrappers import Bidirectional

model = Sequential()
model.add(Embedding(s_vocabsize, EMBED_SIZE,
input_length=MAX_SEQLEN))
model.add(SpatialDropout1D(Dropout(0.2)))
model.add(Bidirectional(LSTM(HIDDEN_SIZE, dropout=0.2,
recurrent_dropout=0.2)))
model.add(RepeatVector(MAX_SEQLEN))
model.add(Bidirectional(LSTM(HIDDEN_SIZE, return_sequences=True)))
model.add(TimeDistributed(Dense(t_vocabsize)))
model.add(Activation("softmax"))
```

This gives us performance comparable to the unidirectional LSTM example shown as follows:

```
Train on 3131 samples, validate on 783 samples
Epoch 1/1
3131/3131 [==============================] - 268s - loss: 0.2889 - acc: 0.8226 - val_loss: 0.2788 - val_acc: 0.9036

783/783 [==============================] - 12s
Test score: 0.279, accuracy: 0.904
```

Stateful RNNs

RNNs can be stateful, which means that they can maintain state across batches during training. That is, the hidden state computed for a batch of training data will be used as the initial hidden state for the next batch of training data. However, this needs to be explicitly set, since Keras RNNs are stateless by default and resets the state after each batch. Setting an RNN to be stateful means that it can build a state across its training sequence and even maintain that state when doing predictions.

The benefits of using stateful RNNs are smaller network sizes and/or lower training times. The disadvantage is that we are now responsible for training the network with a batch size that reflects the periodicity of the data, and resetting the state after each epoch. In addition, data should not be shuffled while training the network, since the order in which the data is presented is relevant for stateful networks.

Stateful LSTM with Keras — predicting electricity consumption

In this example, we predict electricity consumption for a consumer using a stateful and stateless LSTM network and compare their behaviors. As you will recall, RNNs in Keras are stateless by default. In case of stateful models, the internal states computed after processing a batch of input is reused as initial states for the next batch. In other words, the state computed from element i in a batch will be used as initial state for for the element i in the next batch.

The dataset we will use is the electricity load diagram dataset from the UCI Machine Learning Repository (https://archive.ics.uci.edu/ml/datasets/ElectricityLoadDiagrams20112014), and contains consumption information about 370 customers, taken at 15 minute intervals over a four year period from 2011 to 2014. We randomly choose customer number 250 for our example.

One thing to remember is that most problems can be solved with stateless RNNs, so if you do use a stateful RNN, make sure you need it. Typically, you would need it when the data has a periodic component. If you think a bit, you will realize that electricity consumption is periodic. Consumption tends to be higher during the day than at night. Let us extract the consumption data for customer number 250 and plot the first 10 days of data. Finally we also save it to a binary NumPy file for our next step:

```python
import numpy as np
import matplotlib.pyplot as plt
import os
import re

DATA_DIR = "../data"

fld = open(os.path.join(DATA_DIR, "LD2011_2014.txt"), "rb")
data = []
cid = 250
for line in fld:
    if line.startswith(""";"):
        continue
    cols = [float(re.sub(",", ".", x)) for x in
            line.strip().split(";")[1:]]
    data.append(cols[cid])
fld.close()

NUM_ENTRIES = 1000
plt.plot(range(NUM_ENTRIES), data[0:NUM_ENTRIES])
plt.ylabel("electricity consumption")
plt.xlabel("time (1pt = 15 mins)")
plt.show()

np.save(os.path.join(DATA_DIR, "LD_250.npy"), np.array(data))
```

The output of the preceding example is as follow:

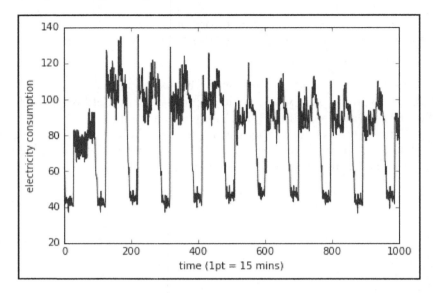

As you can see, there is clearly a daily periodic trend. So the problem is a good candidate for a stateful model. Also, based on our observation, a BATCH_SIZE of 96 (number of 15 minute readings over 24 hours) seems appropriate.

We will show the code for the stateless version of the model simultaneously with the one for the stateful version. Most of the code is identical for both versions, so we will look at both versions simultaneously. I will point out the differences in the code as they arise.

First, as usual, we import the necessary libraries and classes:

```
from keras.layers.core import Dense
from keras.layers.recurrent import LSTM
from keras.models import Sequential
from sklearn.preprocessing import MinMaxScaler
import numpy as np
import math
import os
```

Next we load the data for customer 250 into a long array of size (140256) from the saved NumPy binary file and rescale it to the range *(0, 1)*. Finally, we reshape the input to three dimensions as needed by our network:

```
DATA_DIR = "../data"

data = np.load(os.path.join(DATA_DIR, "LD_250.npy"))
data = data.reshape(-1, 1)
scaler = MinMaxScaler(feature_range=(0, 1), copy=False)
data = scaler.fit_transform(data)
```

Within each batch, the model will take a sequence of 15 minute readings and predict the next one. The length of the input sequence is given by the NUM_TIMESTEPS variable in the code. Based on some experimentation, we get a value of NUM_TIMESTEPS as 20, that is, each input row will be a sequence of length 20, and the output will have length 1. The next step rearranges the input array into X and Y tensors of shapes (None, 4) and (None, 1). Finally, we reshape the input tensor X to three dimensions as required by the network:

```
X = np.zeros((data.shape[0], NUM_TIMESTEPS))
Y = np.zeros((data.shape[0], 1))
for i in range(len(data) - NUM_TIMESTEPS - 1):
    X[i] = data[i:i + NUM_TIMESTEPS].T
    Y[i] = data[i + NUM_TIMESTEPS + 1]

# reshape X to three dimensions (samples, timesteps, features)
X = np.expand_dims(X, axis=2)
```

We then split our X and Y tensors into a 70-30 training test split. Since we are working with time series, we just choose a split point and cut the data into two parts, rather than using the train_test_split function, which also shuffles the data:

```
sp = int(0.7 * len(data))
Xtrain, Xtest, Ytrain, Ytest = X[0:sp], X[sp:], Y[0:sp], Y[sp:]
print(Xtrain.shape, Xtest.shape, Ytrain.shape, Ytest.shape)
```

First we define our stateless model. We also set the values of BATCH_SIZE and NUM_TIMESTEPS, as we discussed previously. Our LSTM output size is given by HIDDEN_SIZE, another hyperparameter that is usually arrived at through experimentation. Here, we just set it to 10 since our objective is to compare two networks:

```
NUM_TIMESTEPS = 20
HIDDEN_SIZE = 10
BATCH_SIZE = 96 # 24 hours (15 min intervals)

# stateless
model = Sequential()
model.add(LSTM(HIDDEN_SIZE, input_shape=(NUM_TIMESTEPS, 1),
    return_sequences=False))
model.add(Dense(1))
```

The corresponding definition for the stateful model is very similar, as you can see as follows. In the LSTM constructor, you need to set stateful=True, and instead of input_shape where the batch size is determined at runtime, you need to set batch_input_shape explicitly with the batch size. You also need to ensure that your training and test data sizes are perfect multiples of your batch size. We will see how to do that later when we look at the training code:

```
# stateful
model = Sequential()
model.add(LSTM(HIDDEN_SIZE, stateful=True,
    batch_input_shape=(BATCH_SIZE, NUM_TIMESTEPS, 1),
    return_sequences=False))
model.add(Dense(1))
```

Next we compile the model, which is the same for both stateless and stateful RNNs. Notice that our metric here is mean squared error instead of our usual accuracy. This is because this is really a regression problem; we are interested in knowing how far off our predictions are with respect to the labels rather than knowing whether our prediction matched the label. You can find a full list of Keras built-in metrics on the Keras metrics page:

```
model.compile(loss="mean_squared_error", optimizer="adam",
    metrics=["mean_squared_error"])
```

To train the stateless model, we can use the one liner that we have probably become very familiar with by now:

```
BATCH_SIZE = 96 # 24 hours (15 min intervals)

# stateless
model.fit(Xtrain, Ytrain, epochs=NUM_EPOCHS, batch_size=BATCH_SIZE,
    validation_data=(Xtest, Ytest),
    shuffle=False)
```

The corresponding code for the stateful model is shown as follows. There are three things to be aware of here.

First, you should select a batch size that reflects the periodicity of your data. This is because stateful RNNs align the states from each batch to the next, so selecting the right batch size allows the network to learn faster.

Once you set the batch size, the size of your training and test sets needs to be exact multiples of your batch size. We have ensured this below by truncating the last few records from both our training and test sets.

The second thing is that you need to fit the model manually, training the model in a loop for the required number of epochs. Each iteration trains the model for one epoch, and the state is retained across multiple batches. After each epoch, the state of the model needs to be reset manually.

The third thing is that the data should be fed in sequence. By default, Keras will shuffle the rows within each batch, which will destroy the alignment we need for the stateful RNN to learn effectively. This is done by setting shuffle=False in the call to model.fit():

```
BATCH_SIZE = 96 # 24 hours (15 min intervals)

# stateful
# need to make training and test data to multiple of BATCH_SIZE
train_size = (Xtrain.shape[0] // BATCH_SIZE) * BATCH_SIZE
test_size = (Xtest.shape[0] // BATCH_SIZE) * BATCH_SIZE
Xtrain, Ytrain = Xtrain[0:train_size], Ytrain[0:train_size]
Xtest, Ytest = Xtest[0:test_size], Ytest[0:test_size]
print(Xtrain.shape, Xtest.shape, Ytrain.shape, Ytest.shape)
for i in range(NUM_EPOCHS):
    print("Epoch {:d}/{:d}".format(i+1, NUM_EPOCHS))
    model.fit(Xtrain, Ytrain, batch_size=BATCH_SIZE, epochs=1,
        validation_data=(Xtest, Ytest),
        shuffle=False)
    model.reset_states()
```

Finally, we evaluate the model against the test data and print out the scores:

```
score, _ = model.evaluate(Xtest, Ytest, batch_size=BATCH_SIZE)
rmse = math.sqrt(score)
print("MSE: {:.3f}, RMSE: {:.3f}".format(score, rmse))
```

The output for the stateless model, run over five epochs, is as follows:

```
(98179, 20, 1) (42077, 20, 1) (98179, 1) (42077, 1)
Train on 98179 samples, validate on 42077 samples
Epoch 1/5
98179/98179 [==============================] - 41s - loss: 0.0086 - mean_squared_error: 0.0086 - val_loss: 0.0040 -
val_mean_squared_error: 0.0040
Epoch 2/5
98179/98179 [==============================] - 41s - loss: 0.0045 - mean_squared_error: 0.0045 - val_loss: 0.0039 -
val_mean_squared_error: 0.0039
Epoch 3/5
98179/98179 [==============================] - 43s - loss: 0.0041 - mean_squared_error: 0.0041 - val_loss: 0.0038 -
val_mean_squared_error: 0.0038
Epoch 4/5
98179/98179 [==============================] - 44s - loss: 0.0039 - mean_squared_error: 0.0039 - val_loss: 0.0040 -
val_mean_squared_error: 0.0040
Epoch 5/5
98179/98179 [==============================] - 44s - loss: 0.0038 - mean_squared_error: 0.0038 - val_loss: 0.0038 -
val_mean_squared_error: 0.0038

42077/42077 [==============================] - 2s

MSE: 0.004, RMSE: 0.062
```

The corresponding output for the stateful model, also run in a loop five times for one epoch each time, is as follows. Notice the result of the truncating operation in the second line:

```
Train on 98112 samples, validate on 42048 samples
Epoch 1/1
98112/98112 [==============================] - 37s - loss: 0.0056 - mean_squared_error: 0.0056 - val_loss: 0.0038 -
val_mean_squared_error: 0.0038
Epoch 2/5
Train on 98112 samples, validate on 42048 samples
Epoch 1/1
98812/98112 [==============================] - 36s - loss: 0.0044 - mean_squared_error: 0.0044 - val_loss: 0.0037 -
val_mean_squared_error: 0.0037
Epoch 3/5
Train on 98112 samples, validate on 42048 samples
Epoch 1/1
98112/98112 [==============================] - 38s - loss: 0.0043 - mean_squared_error: 0.0043 - val_loss: 0.0038 -
val_mean_squared_error: 0.0038
Epoch 4/5
Train on 98112 samples, validate on 42048 samples
Epoch 1/1
98112/98112 [==============================] - 37s - loss: 0.0042 - mean_squared_error: 0.0042 - val_loss: 0.0038 -
val_mean_squared_error: 0.0038
Epoch 5/5
Train on 98112 samples, validate on 42048 samples
Epoch 1/1
98112/98112 [==============================] - 37s - loss: 0.0040 - mean_squared_error: 0.0040 - val_loss: 0.0035 -
val_mean_squared_error: 0.0035
41952/42048 [==========================>.] - ETA: 0s

MSE: 0.003, RMSE: 0.059
```

As you can see, the stateful model produces results that are slightly better than the stateless model. In absolute terms, since we have scaled our data to the *(0, 1)* range, this means that the stateless model has about 6.2% error rate and the stateful model has a 5.9% error rate, or conversely, they are about 93.8% and 94.1% accurate respectively. In relative terms, therefore, our stateful model outperforms the stateless model by a slight margin.

The source code for this example is provided in the files `econs_data.py` that parses the dataset, and `econs_stateful.py` that defines and trains the stateless and stateful models, available from the code download for this chapter.

Other RNN variants

We will round up this chapter by looking at some more variants of the RNN cell. RNN is an area of active research and many researchers have suggested variants for specific purposes.

One popular LSTM variant is adding *peephole connections*, which means that the gate layers are allowed to peek at the cell state. This was introduced by Gers and Schmidhuber (for more information refer to the article: *Learning Precise Timing with LSTM Recurrent Networks*, by F. A. Gers, N. N. Schraudolph, and J. Schmidhuber, Journal of Machine Learning Research, pp. 115-43) in 2002.

Another LSTM variant, that ultimately led to the GRU, is to use coupled forget and output gates. Decisions about what information to forget and what to acquire are made together, and the new information replaces the forgotten information.

Keras provides only the three basic variants, namely the SimpleRNN, LSTM, and GRU layers. However, that isn't necessarily a problem. Gref conducted an experimental survey (for more information refer to the article: *LSTM: A Search Space Odyssey*, by K. Greff, arXiv:1503.04069, 2015) of many LSTM variants, and concluded that none of the variants improved significantly over the standard LSTM architecture. So the components provided in Keras are usually sufficient to solve most problems.

In case you do need the capability to construct your own layer, you can build custom Keras layers. We will look at how to build a custom layer in the next chapter. There is also an open source framework called recurrent shop (`https://github.com/datalogai/recurrentshop`) that allows you to build complex recurrent neural networks with Keras.

Summary

In this chapter, we looked at the basic architecture of recurrent neural networks and how they work better than traditional neural networks over sequence data. We saw how RNNs can be used to learn an author's writing style and generate text using the learned model. We also saw how this example can be extended to predicting stock prices or other time series, speech from noisy audio, and so on, as well as generate music that was composed by a learned model.

We looked at different ways to compose our RNN units and these topologies can be used to model and solve specific problems such as sentiment analysis, machine translation, image captioning, and classification, and so on.

We then looked at one of the biggest drawbacks of the SimpleRNN architecture, that of vanishing and exploding gradients. We saw how the vanishing gradient problem is handled using the LSTM (and GRU) architectures. We also looked at the LSTM and GRU architectures in some detail. We also saw two examples of predicting sentiment using an LSTM-based model, and predicting POS tags using a GRU-based sequence-to-sequence architecture.

We then learned about stateful RNNs and how they can be used in Keras. We also saw an example of learning a stateful RNN to predict CO levels in the atmosphere.

Finally, we learned about some RNN variants that are not available in Keras, and briefly explored how to build them.

In the next chapter, we will look at models that don't quite fit into the basic molds we have looked at so far. We will also look at composing these basic models larger and more complex ones using the Keras functional API, as well as look at some examples of customizing Keras to our needs.

7
Additional Deep Learning Models

So far, most of the discussion has been focused around different models that do classification. These models are trained using object features and their labels to predict labels for hitherto unseen objects. The models also had a fairly simple architecture, all the ones we have seen so far have a linear pipeline modeled by the Keras sequential API.

In this chapter, we will focus on more complex architectures where the pipelines are not necessarily linear. Keras provides the functional API to deal with these sorts of architectures. We will learn how to define our networks using the functional API in this chapter. Note that the functional API can be used to build linear architectures as well.

The simplest extension of classification networks are regression networks. The two broad subcategories under supervised machine learning are classification and regression. Instead of predicting a category, the network now predicts a continuous value. You saw an example of a regression network when we discussed stateless versus stateful RNNs. Many regression problems can be solved using classification models with very little effort. We will see an example of such a network to predict atmospheric benzene in this chapter.

Yet another class of models deal with learning the structure of the data from unlabeled data. These are called **unsupervised** (or more correctly, self-supervised) models. They are similar to classification models, but the labels are available implicitly within the data. We have already seen examples of this kind of model; for example, the CBOW and skip-gram word2vec models are self-supervised models. Autoencoders are another example of this type of model. We will learn about autoencoders and describe an example that builds compact vector representations of sentences.

We will then look at how to compose the networks we have seen so far into larger computation graphs. These graphs are often built to achieve some custom objective that is not achievable by a sequential model alone, and may have multiple inputs and outputs and connections to external components. We will see an example of composing such a network for question answering.

We then take a detour to look at the Keras backend API, and how we can use this API to build custom components to extend Keras' functionality.

Going back to models for unlabeled data, another class of models that don't require labels are generative models. These models are trained using a set of existing objects and attempt to learn the distribution these objects come from. Once the distribution is learned, we can draw samples from this distribution that look like the original training data. We have seen an example of this where we trained a character RNN model to generate text similar to *Alice in Wonderland* in the previous chapter. The idea is already covered, so we won't cover this particular aspect of generative models here. However, we will look at how we can leverage the idea of a trained network learning the data distribution to create interesting visual effects using a VGG-16 network pre-trained on ImageNet data.

To summarize, we will learn the following topics in this chapter:

- The Keras functional API
- Regression networks
- Autoencoders for unsupervised learning
- Composing complex networks with the functional API
- Customizing Keras
- Generative networks

Let's get started.

Keras functional API

The Keras functional API defines each layer as a function and provides operators to compose these functions into a larger computational graph. A function is some sort of transformation with a single input and single output. For example, the function *y = f(x)* defines a function *f* with input *x* and output *y*. Let us consider the simple sequential model from Keras (for more information refer to: `https://keras.io/getting-started/sequenti al-model-guide/`):

```
from keras.models import Sequential
from keras.layers.core import dense, Activation

model = Sequential([
    dense(32, input_dim=784),
    Activation("sigmoid"),
    dense(10),
    Activation("softmax"),
])

model.compile(loss="categorical_crossentropy", optimizer="adam")
```

As you can see, the sequential model represents the network as a linear pipeline, or list, of layers. We can also represent the network as the composition of the following nested functions. Here *x* is the input tensor of shape *(None, 784)* and *y* is the output tensor of *(None, 10)*. Here *None* refers to the as-yet undetermined batch size:

$$y = \sigma_K(f(\sigma_2(g(x))))$$

Where:

$$g(x) = W_g x + b_g$$

$$\sigma_2(x) = \frac{1}{1 + e^{-x}}$$

$$f(x) = W_f x + b_f$$

$$\sigma_K(x) = \frac{e^x}{\sum_{k=1}^{K} e^{x_k}}$$

The network can be redefined using the Keras functional API as follows. Notice how the predictions variable is a composition of the same functions we defined in equation form previously:

```
from keras.layers import Input
from keras.layers.core import dense
from keras.models import Model
from keras.layers.core import Activation

inputs = Input(shape=(784,))

x = dense(32)(inputs)
x = Activation("sigmoid")(x)
x = dense(10)(x)
predictions = Activation("softmax")(x)

model = Model(inputs=inputs, outputs=predictions)

model.compile(loss="categorical_crossentropy", optimizer="adam")
```

Since a model is a composition of layers that are also functions, a model is also a function. Therefore, you can treat a trained model as just another layer by calling it on an appropriately shaped input tensor. Thus, if you have built a model that does something useful like image classification, you can easily extend it to work with a sequence of images using Keras's `TimeDistributed` wrapper:

```
sequence_predictions = TimeDistributed(model)(input_sequences)
```

The functional API can be used to define any network that can be defined using the sequential API. In addition, the following types of network can only be defined using the functional API:

- Models with multiple inputs and outputs
- Models composed of multiple submodels
- Models that used shared layers

Models with multiple inputs and outputs are defined by composing the inputs and outputs separately, as shown in the preceding example, and then passing in an array of input functions and an array of output functions in the input and output parameters of the `Model` constructor:

```
model = Model(inputs=[input1, input2], outputs=[output1, output2])
```

Models with multiple inputs and outputs also generally consist of multiple subnetworks, the results of whose computations are merged into the final result. The merge function provides multiple ways to merge intermediate results such as vector addition, dot product, and concatenation. We will see examples of merging in our question answering example later in this chapter.

Another good use for the functional API are models that use shared layers. Shared layers are defined once, and referenced in each pipeline where their weights need to be shared.

We will use the functional API almost exclusively in this chapter, so you will see quite a few examples of its use. The Keras website has many more usage examples for the functional API.

Regression networks

The two major techniques of supervised learning are classification and regression. In both cases, the model is trained with data to predict known labels. In case of classification, these labels are discrete values such as genres of text or image categories. In case of regression, these labels are continuous values, such as stock prices or human intelligence quotients (IQ).

Most of the examples we have seen show deep learning models being used to perform classification. In this section, we will look at how to perform regression using such a model.

Recall that classification models have a dense layer with a nonlinear activation at the end, the output dimension of which corresponds to the number of classes the model can predict. Thus, an ImageNet image classification model has a dense (1,000) layer at the end, corresponding to 1,000 ImageNet classes it can predict. Similarly, a sentiment analysis model has a dense layer at the end, corresponding to positive or negative sentiment.

Regression models also have a dense layer at the end, but with a single output, that is, an output dimension of one, and no nonlinear activation. Thus the dense layer just returns the sum of the activations from the previous layer. In addition, the loss function used is typically **mean squared error** (**MSE**), but some of the other objectives (listed on the Keras objectives page at: `https://keras.io/losses/`) can be used as well.

Keras regression example — predicting benzene levels in the air

In this example, we will predict the concentration of benzene in the atmosphere given some other variables such as concentrations of carbon monoxide, nitrous oxide, and so on in the atmosphere as well as temperature and relative humidity. The dataset we will use is the air quality dataset from the UCI Machine Learning Repository (https://archive.ics.uci.edu/ml/datasets/Air+Quality). The dataset contains 9,358 instances of hourly averaged readings from an array of five metal oxide chemical sensors. The sensor array was located in a city in Italy, and the recordings were made from March 2004 to February 2005.

As usual, first we import all our necessary libraries:

```
from keras.layers import Input
from keras.layers.core import dense
from keras.models import Model
from sklearn.preprocessing import StandardScaler
import matplotlib.pyplot as plt
import numpy as np
import os
import pandas as pd
```

The dataset is provided as a CSV file. We load the input data into a Pandas (for more information refer to: http://pandas.pydata.org/) data frame. Pandas is a popular data analysis library built around data frames, a concept borrowed from the R language. We use Pandas here to read the dataset for two reasons. First, the dataset contains empty fields where they could not be recorded for some reason. Second, the dataset uses commas for decimal points, a custom common in some European countries. Pandas has built-in support to handle both situations, along with a few other conveniences, as we will see soon:

```
DATA_DIR = "../data"
AIRQUALITY_FILE = os.path.join(DATA_DIR, "AirQualityUCI.csv")

aqdf = pd.read_csv(AIRQUALITY_FILE, sep=";", decimal=",", header=0)

# remove first and last 2 cols
del aqdf["Date"]
del aqdf["Time"]
del aqdf["Unnamed: 15"]
del aqdf["Unnamed: 16"]

# fill NaNs in each column with the mean value
aqdf = aqdf.fillna(aqdf.mean())

Xorig = aqdf.as_matrix()
```

The preceding example removes the first two columns, which contains the observation date and time, and the last two columns which seem to be spurious. Next we replace the empty fields with the average value for the column. Finally, we export the data frame as a matrix for downstream use.

One thing to note is that each column of the data has different scales since they measure different quantities. For example, the concentration of tin oxide is in the 1,000 range, while non-methanic hydrocarbons is in the 100 range. In many situations our features are homogeneous so scaling is not an issue, but in cases like this it is generally a good practice to scale the data. Scaling here consists of subtracting from each column the mean of the column and dividing by its standard deviation:

$$z = \frac{x - \mu}{\sigma}$$

To do this, we use the `StandardScaler` class provided by the `scikit-learn` library, shown as follows. We store the mean and standard deviations because we will need this later when reporting results or predicting against new data. Our target variable is the fourth column in our input dataset, so we split this scaled data into input variables X and target variable y:

```
scaler = StandardScaler()
Xscaled = scaler.fit_transform(Xorig)
# store these off for predictions with unseen data
Xmeans = scaler.mean_
Xstds = scaler.scale_

y = Xscaled[:, 3]
X = np.delete(Xscaled, 3, axis=1)
```

We then split the data into the first 70% for training and the last 30% for testing. This gives us 6,549 records for training and 2,808 records for testing:

```
train_size = int(0.7 * X.shape[0])
Xtrain, Xtest, ytrain, ytest = X[0:train_size], X[train_size:],
    y[0:train_size], y[train_size:]
```

Next we define our network. This is a simple two layer dense network that takes a vector of 12 features as input and outputs a scaled prediction. The hidden dense layer has eight neurons. We initialize weight matrices for both dense layers with a specific initialization scheme called *glorot uniform*. For a full list of initialization schemes, please refer to the Keras initializations here: `https://keras.io/initializers/`. The loss function used is mean squared error (`mse`) and the optimizer is `adam`:

```
readings = Input(shape=(12,))
x = dense(8, activation="relu",
kernel_initializer="glorot_uniform")(readings)
benzene = dense(1, kernel_initializer="glorot_uniform")(x)

model = Model(inputs=[readings], outputs=[benzene])
model.compile(loss="mse", optimizer="adam")
```

We train this model for 20 epochs and batch size of 10:

```
NUM_EPOCHS = 20
BATCH_SIZE = 10

history = model.fit(Xtrain, ytrain, batch_size=BATCH_SIZE,
epochs=NUM_EPOCHS,
    validation_split=0.2)
```

This results in a model that has a mean squared error of 0.0003 (approximately 2% RMSE) on the training set and 0.0016 (approximately 4% RMSE) on the validation set, as shown in the logs of the training step here:

```
Epoch 8/20
5239/5239 [==============================] - 0s - loss: 0.0015 - val_loss: 0.0024
Epoch 9/20
5239/5239 [==============================] - 0s - loss: 0.0012 - val_loss: 0.0020
Epoch 10/20
5239/5239 [==============================] - 0s - loss: 9.5742e-04 - val_loss: 0.0018
Epoch 11/20
5239/5239 [==============================] - 0s - loss: 8.2761e-04 - val_loss: 0.0019
Epoch 12/20
5239/5239 [==============================] - 0s - loss: 7.1237e-04 - val_loss: 0.0021
Epoch 13/20
5239/5239 [==============================] - 0s - loss: 6.4492e-04 - val_loss: 0.0018
Epoch 14/20
5239/5239 [==============================] - 0s - loss: 6.0119e-04 - val_loss: 0.0019
Epoch 15/20
5239/5239 [==============================] - 0s - loss: 5.1915e-04 - val_loss: 0.0017
Epoch 16/20
5239/5239 [==============================] - 0s - loss: 4.4686e-04 - val_loss: 0.0014
Epoch 17/20
5239/5239 [==============================] - 0s - loss: 5.6912e-04 - val_loss: 0.0019
Epoch 18/20
5239/5239 [==============================] - 0s - loss: 3.6897e-04 - val_loss: 0.0013
Epoch 19/20
5239/5239 [==============================] - 0s - loss: 3.6652e-04 - val_loss: 0.0012
Epoch 20/20
5239/5239 [==============================] - 0s - loss: 3.2395e-04 - val_loss: 0.0016
```

We also look at some values of benzene concentrations that were originally recorded and compare them to those predicted by our model. Both actual and predicted values are rescaled from their scaled *z*-values to actual values:

```
ytest_ = model.predict(Xtest).flatten()
for i in range(10):
    label = (ytest[i] * Xstds[3]) + Xmeans[3]
    prediction = (ytest_[i] * Xstds[3]) + Xmeans[3]
    print("Benzene Conc. expected: {:.3f}, predicted: {:.3f}".format(label,
prediction))
```

The side-by-side comparison shows that the predictions are quite close to the actual values:

Benzene Conc. expected: 4.600, predicted: 5.254
Benzene Conc. expected: 5.500, predicted: 4.932
Benzene Conc. expected: 6.500, predicted: 5.664
Benzene Conc. expected: 10.300, predicted: 8.482
Benzene Conc. expected: 8.900, predicted: 6.705
Benzene Conc. expected: 14.000, predicted: 12.928
Benzene Conc. expected: 9.200, predicted: 7.128
Benzene Conc. expected: 8.200, predicted: 5.983
Benzene Conc. expected: 7.200, predicted: 6.256
Benzene Conc. expected: 5.500, predicted: 5.184

Finally, we graph the actual values against the predictions for our entire test set. Once more, we see that the network predicts values that are very close to the expected values:

```
plt.plot(np.arange(ytest.shape[0]), (ytest * Xstds[3]) / Xmeans[3],
    color="b", label="actual")
plt.plot(np.arange(ytest_.shape[0]), (ytest_ * Xstds[3]) / Xmeans[3],
    color="r", alpha=0.5, label="predicted")
plt.xlabel("time")
plt.ylabel("C6H6 concentrations")
plt.legend(loc="best")
plt.show()
```

The output of the preceding example is as follows:

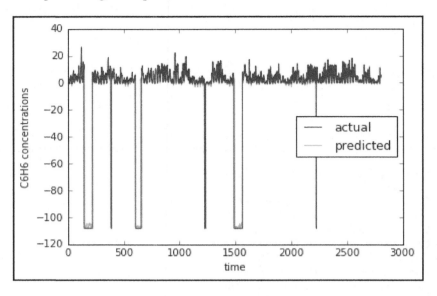

Unsupervised learning — autoencoders

Autoencoders are a class of neural network that attempt to recreate the input as its target using back-propagation. An autoencoder consists of two parts, an encoder and a decoder. The encoder will read the input and compress it to a compact representation, and the decoder will read the compact representation and recreate the input from it. In other words, the autoencoder tries to learn the identity function by minimizing the reconstruction error.

Even though the identity function does not seem like a very interesting function to learn, the way in which this is done makes it interesting. The number of hidden units in the autoencoder is typically less than the number of input (and output) units. This forces the encoder to learn a compressed representation of the input which the decoder reconstructs. If there is structure in the input data in the form of correlations between input features, then the autoencoder will discover some of these correlations, and end up learning a low dimensional representation of the data similar to that learned using **principal component analysis (PCA)**.

Once the autoencoder is trained, we would typically just discard the decoder component and use the encoder component to generate compact representations of the input. Alternatively, we could use the encoder as a feature detector that generates a compact, semantically rich representation of our input and build a classifier by attaching a softmax classifier to the hidden layer.

The encoder and decoder components of an autoencoder can be implemented using either dense, convolutional, or recurrent networks, depending on the kind of data that is being modeled. For example, dense networks might be a good choice for autoencoders used to build **collaborative filtering (CF)** models (for more information refer to the articles: *AutoRec: Autoencoders Meet Collaborative Filtering*, by S. Sedhain, Proceedings of the 24th International Conference on World Wide Web, ACM, 2015 and *Wide & Deep Learning for Recommender Systems*, by H. Cheng, Proceedings of the 1st Workshop on Deep Learning for Recommender Systems, ACM, 2016), where we learn a compressed model of user preferences based on actual sparse user ratings. Similarly, convolutional neural networks may be appropriate for the use case covered in the article: *See: Using Deep Learning to Remove Eyeglasses from Faces*, by M. Runfeldt. and recurrent networks a good choice for autoencoders building on text data, such as deep patient (for more information refer to the article: *Deep Patient: An Unsupervised Representation to Predict the Future of Patients from the Electronic Health Records*, by R. Miotto, Scientific Reports 6, 2016) and skip-thought vectors ((for more information refer to the article: *Skip-Thought Vectors*, by R. Kiros, Advances in Neural Information Processing Systems, 2015).

Autoencoders can also be stacked by successively stacking encoders that compress their input to smaller and smaller representations, and stacking decoders in the opposite sequence. Stacked autoencoders have greater expressive power and the successive layers of representations capture a hierarchical grouping of the input, similar to the convolution and pooling operations in convolutional neural networks.

Stacked autoencoders used to be trained layer by layer. For example, in the network shown next, we would first train layer *X* to reconstruct layer *X'* using the hidden layer *H1* (ignoring *H2*). We would then train the layer *H1* to reconstruct layer *H1'* using the hidden layer *H2*. Finally, we would stack all the layers together in the configuration shown and fine tune it to reconstruct *X'* from *X*. With better activation and regularization functions nowadays, however, it is quite common to train these networks in totality:

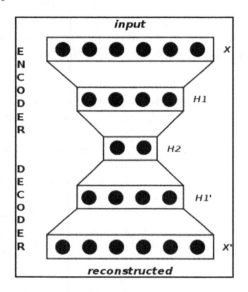

The Keras blog post, *Building Autoencoders in Keras* (`https://blog.keras.io/building-au toencoders-in-keras.html`) has great examples of building autoencoders that reconstructs MNIST digit images using fully connected and convolutional neural networks. It also has a good discussion on denoising and variational autoencoders, which we will not cover here.

Keras autoencoder example — sentence vectors

In this example, we will build and train an LSTM-based autoencoder to generate sentence vectors for documents in the Reuters-21578 corpus (`https://archive.ics.uci.edu/ml/da tasets/Reuters-21578+Text+Categorization+Collection`). We have already seen in Chapter 5, *Word Embeddings*, how to represent a word using word embeddings to create vectors that represent its meaning in the context of other words it appears with. Here, we will see how to build similar vectors for sentences. Sentences are a sequence of words, so a sentence vector represents the meaning of the sentence.

The easiest way to build a sentence vector is to just add up the word vectors and divide by the number of words. However, this treats the sentence as a bag of words, and does not take the order of words into account. Thus the sentences *The dog bit the man* and *The man bit the dog* would be treated as identical under this scenario. LSTMs are designed to work with sequence input and do take the order of words into consideration thus providing a better and more natural representation for the sentence.

First we import the necessary libraries:

```
from sklearn.model_selection import train_test_split
from keras.callbacks import ModelCheckpoint
from keras.layers import Input
from keras.layers.core import RepeatVector
from keras.layers.recurrent import LSTM
from keras.layers.wrappers import Bidirectional
from keras.models import Model
from keras.preprocessing import sequence
from scipy.stats import describe
import collections
import matplotlib.pyplot as plt
import nltk
import numpy as np
import os
```

The data is provided as a set of SGML files. We have already parsed and consolidated this data into a single text file in Chapter 6, *Recurrent Neural Network — RNN*, for our GRU-based POS tagging example. We will reuse this data to first convert each block of text into a list of sentences, one sentence per line:

```
sents = []
fsent = open(sent_filename, "rb")
for line in fsent:
    docid, sent_id, sent = line.strip().split("t")
    sents.append(sent)
fsent.close()
```

To build up our vocabulary, we read this list of sentences again, word by word. Each word is normalized as it is added. The normalization is to replace any token that looks like a number with the digit 9 and to lowercase them. The result is the word frequency table, word_freqs. We also compute the sentence length for each sentence and create a list of parsed sentences by rejoining the tokens with space so it is easier to parse in a subsequent step:

```
def is_number(n):
    temp = re.sub("[.,-/]", "", n)
    return temp.isdigit()
```

```
word_freqs = collections.Counter()
sent_lens = []
parsed_sentences = []
for sent in sentences:
    words = nltk.word_tokenize(sent)
    parsed_words = []
    for word in words:
        if is_number(word):
            word = "9"
        word_freqs[word.lower()] += 1
        parsed_words.append(word)
    sent_lens.append(len(words))
    parsed_sentences.append(" ".join(parsed_words))
```

This gives us some information about the corpus that will help us figure out good values for our constants for our LSTM network:

```
sent_lens = np.array(sent_lens)
print("number of sentences: {:d}".format(len(sent_lens)))
print("distribution of sentence lengths (number of words)")
print("min:{:d}, max:{:d}, mean:{:.3f}, med:{:.3f}".format(
np.min(sent_lens), np.max(sent_lens), np.mean(sent_lens),
np.median(sent_lens)))
print("vocab size (full): {:d}".format(len(word_freqs)))
```

This gives us the following information about the corpus:

number of sentences: 131545
distribution of sentence lengths (number of words)
min: 1, max: 429, mean: 22.315, median: 21.000
vocab size (full): 50751

Based on this information, we set the following constants for our LSTM model. We choose our VOCAB_SIZE as 5000, that is, our vocabulary covers the most frequent 5,000 words that cover over 93% of the words used in the corpus. The remaining words are treated as **out of vocabulary (OOV)** and replaced with the token UNK. At prediction time, any word that the model hasn't seen will also be assigned the token UNK. SEQUENCE_LEN is set to approximately twice the median length of sentences in the training set, and indeed, approximately 110 million of our 131 million sentences are shorter than this setting. Sentences that are shorter than SEQUENCE_LENGTH will be padded by a special PAD character, and those that are longer will be truncated to fit the limit:

```
VOCAB_SIZE = 5000
SEQUENCE_LEN = 50
```

Since the input to our LSTM will be numeric, we need to build lookup tables that go back and forth between words and word IDs. Since we limit our vocabulary size to 5,000 and we have to add the two pseudo-words PAD and UNK, our lookup table contains entries for the most frequently occurring 4,998 words plus PAD and UNK:

```
word2id = {}
word2id["PAD"] = 0
word2id["UNK"] = 1
for v, (k, _) in enumerate(word_freqs.most_common(VOCAB_SIZE - 2)):
    word2id[k] = v + 2
id2word = {v:k for k, v in word2id.items()}
```

The input to our network is a sequence of words, where each word is represented by a vector. Simplistically, we could just use a one-hot encoding for each word, but that makes the input data very large. So we encode each word using its 50-dimensional GloVe embeddings. The embedding is generated into a matrix of shape (VOCAB_SIZE, EMBED_SIZE) where each row represents the GloVe embedding for a word in our vocabulary. The PAD and UNK rows (0 and 1 respectively) are populated with zeros and random uniform values respectively:

```
EMBED_SIZE = 50

def lookup_word2id(word):
    try:
        return word2id[word]
    except KeyError:
        return word2id["UNK"]

def load_glove_vectors(glove_file, word2id, embed_size):
    embedding = np.zeros((len(word2id), embed_size))
    fglove = open(glove_file, "rb")
    for line in fglove:
        cols = line.strip().split()
        word = cols[0]
        if embed_size == 0:
            embed_size = len(cols) - 1
        if word2id.has_key(word):
            vec = np.array([float(v) for v in cols[1:]])
        embedding[lookup_word2id(word)] = vec
    embedding[word2id["PAD"]] = np.zeros((embed_size))
    embedding[word2id["UNK"]] = np.random.uniform(-1, 1, embed_size)
    return embedding

embeddings = load_glove_vectors(os.path.join(
    DATA_DIR, "glove.6B.{:d}d.txt".format(EMBED_SIZE)), word2id,
EMBED_SIZE)
```

Our autoencoder model takes a sequence of GloVe word vectors and learns to produce another sequence that is similar to the input sequence. The encoder LSTM compresses the sequence into a fixed size context vector, which the decoder LSTM uses to reconstruct the original sequence. A schematic of the network is shown here:

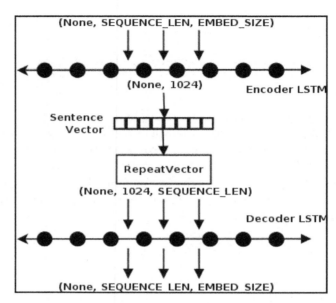

Because the input is quite large, we will use a generator to produce each batch of input. Our generator produces batches of tensors of shape (BATCH_SIZE, SEQUENCE_LEN, EMBED_SIZE). Here BATCH_SIZE is 64, and since we are using 50-dimensional GloVe vectors, EMBED_SIZE is 50. We shuffle the sentences at the beginning of each epoch, and return batches of 64 sentences. Each sentence is represented as a vector of GloVe word vectors. If a word in the vocabulary does not have a corresponding GloVe embedding, it is represented by a zero vector. We construct two instances of the generator, one for training data and one for test data, consisting of 70% and 30% of the original dataset respectively:

```
BATCH_SIZE = 64

def sentence_generator(X, embeddings, batch_size):
    while True:
        # loop once per epoch
        num_recs = X.shape[0]
        indices = np.random.permutation(np.arange(num_recs))
        num_batches = num_recs // batch_size
        for bid in range(num_batches):
            sids = indices[bid * batch_size : (bid + 1) * batch_size]
            Xbatch = embeddings[X[sids, :]]
```

```
                 yield Xbatch, Xbatch

train_size = 0.7
Xtrain, Xtest = train_test_split(sent_wids, train_size=train_size)
train_gen = sentence_generator(Xtrain, embeddings, BATCH_SIZE)
test_gen = sentence_generator(Xtest, embeddings, BATCH_SIZE)
```

Now we are ready to define the autoencoder. As we have shown in the diagram, it is composed of an encoder LSTM and a decoder LSTM. The encoder LSTM reads a tensor of shape (BATCH_SIZE, SEQUENCE_LEN, EMBED_SIZE) representing a batch of sentences. Each sentence is represented as a padded fixed-length sequence of words of size SEQUENCE_LEN. Each word is represented as a 300-dimensional GloVe vector. The output dimension of the encoder LSTM is a hyperparameter LATENT_SIZE, which is the size of the sentence vector that will get out of the encoder part of the trained autoencoder later. The vector space of dimensionality LATENT_SIZE represents the latent space that encodes the meaning of the sentence. The output of the LSTM is a vector of size (LATENT_SIZE) for each sentence, so for the batch the shape of the output tensor is (BATCH_SIZE, LATENT_SIZE). This is now fed to a RepeatVector layer, which replicates this across the entire sequence, that is., the output tensor from this layer has the shape (BATCH_SIZE, SEQUENCE_LEN, LATENT_SIZE). This tensor is now fed into the decoder LSTM, whose output dimension is the EMBED_SIZE, so the output tensor has shape (BATCH_SIZE, SEQUENCE_LEN, EMBED_SIZE), that is, the same shape as the input tensor.

We compile this model with the SGD optimizer and the mse loss function. The reason we use MSE is that we want to reconstruct a sentence that has a similar meaning, that is, something that is close to the original sentence in the embedded space of dimension LATENT_SIZE:

```
inputs = Input(shape=(SEQUENCE_LEN, EMBED_SIZE), name="input")
encoded = Bidirectional(LSTM(LATENT_SIZE), merge_mode="sum",
    name="encoder_lstm")(inputs)
decoded = RepeatVector(SEQUENCE_LEN, name="repeater")(encoded)
decoded = Bidirectional(LSTM(EMBED_SIZE, return_sequences=True),
    merge_mode="sum",
    name="decoder_lstm")(decoded)

autoencoder = Model(inputs, decoded)

autoencoder.compile(optimizer="sgd", loss="mse")
```

We train the autoencoder for 10 epochs using the following code. 10 epochs were chosen because the MSE loss converges within this time. We also save the best model retrieved so far based on the MSE loss:

```
num_train_steps = len(Xtrain) // BATCH_SIZE
num_test_steps = len(Xtest) // BATCH_SIZE
checkpoint = ModelCheckpoint(filepath=os.path.join(DATA_DIR,
    "sent-thoughts-autoencoder.h5"), save_best_only=True)
history = autoencoder.fit_generator(train_gen,
    steps_per_epoch=num_train_steps,
    epochs=NUM_EPOCHS,
    validation_data=test_gen,
    validation_steps=num_test_steps,
    callbacks=[checkpoint])
```

The results of the training are shown as follows. As you can see, the training MSE reduces from 0.14 to 0.1 and the validation MSE reduces from 0.12 to 0.1:

```
Epoch 1/10
92032/92032 [==============================] - 542s - loss: 0.1368 - val_loss: 0.1239
Epoch 2/10
92032/92032 [==============================] - 540s - loss: 0.1203 - val_loss: 0.1164
Epoch 3/10
92032/92032 [==============================] - 546s - loss: 0.1139 - val_loss: 0.1107
Epoch 4/10
92032/92032 [==============================] - 547s - loss: 0.1087 - val_loss: 0.1064
Epoch 5/10
92032/92032 [==============================] - 542s - loss: 0.1053 - val_loss: 0.1038
Epoch 6/10
92032/92032 [==============================] - 543s - loss: 0.1034 - val_loss: 0.1020
Epoch 7/10
92032/92032 [==============================] - 544s - loss: 0.1021 - val_loss: 0.1025
Epoch 8/10
92032/92032 [==============================] - 545s - loss: 0.1011 - val_loss: 0.1002
Epoch 9/10
92032/92032 [==============================] - 545s - loss: 0.1003 - val_loss: 0.0993
Epoch 10/10
92032/92032 [==============================] - 545s - loss: 0.0997 - val_loss: 0.1009
```

Or, graphically it shows as follows:

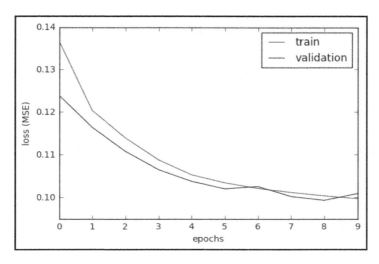

Since we are feeding in a matrix of embeddings, the output will also be a matrix of word embeddings. Since the embedding space is continuous and our vocabulary is discrete, not every output embedding will correspond to a word. The best we can do is to find a word that is closest to the output embedding in order to reconstruct the original text. This is a bit cumbersome, so we will evaluate our autoencoder in a different way.

Since the objective of the autoencoder is to produce a good latent representation, we compare the latent vectors produced from the encoder using the original input versus the output of the autoencoder. First, we extract the encoder component into its own network:

```
encoder = Model(autoencoder.input,
    autoencoder.get_layer("encoder_lstm").output)
```

Then we run the autoencoder on the test set to return the predicted embeddings. We then send both the input embedding and the predicted embedding through the encoder to produce sentence vectors from each, and compare the two vectors using *cosine* similarity. Cosine similarities close to one indicate high similarity and those close to zero indicate low similarity. The following code runs against a random subset of 500 test sentences and produces some sample values of cosine similarities between the sentence vectors generated from the source embedding and the corresponding target embedding produced by the autoencoder:

```
def compute_cosine_similarity(x, y):
    return np.dot(x, y) / (np.linalg.norm(x, 2) * np.linalg.norm(y, 2))

k = 500
```

```
cosims = np.zeros((k))
i = 0
for bid in range(num_test_steps):
    xtest, ytest = test_gen.next()
    ytest_ = autoencoder.predict(xtest)
    Xvec = encoder.predict(xtest)
    Yvec = encoder.predict(ytest_)
    for rid in range(Xvec.shape[0]):
        if i >= k:
            break
        cosims[i] = compute_cosine_similarity(Xvec[rid], Yvec[rid])
        if i <= 10:
            print(cosims[i])
        i += 1
    if i >= k:
        break
```

The first 10 values of cosine similarities are shown as follows. As we can see, the vectors seem to be quite similar:

```
0.982818722725
0.970908224583
0.98131018877
0.974798440933
0.968060493469
0.976065933704
0.96712064743
0.949920475483
0.973583400249
0.980291545391
0.817819952965
```

A histogram of the distribution of values of cosine similarities for the sentence vectors from the first 500 sentences in the test set are shown as follows. As previously, it confirms that the sentence vectors generated from the input and output of the autoencoder are very similar, showing that the resulting sentence vector is a good representation of the sentence:

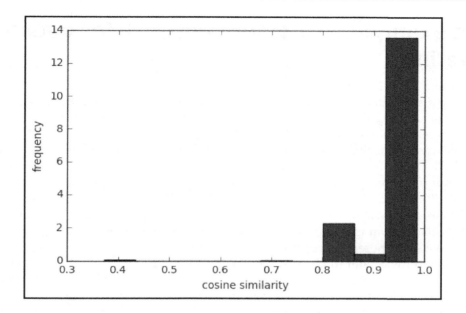

Composing deep networks

We have looked extensively at these three basic deep learning networks—the **fully connected network (FCN)**, the CNN and the RNN models. While each of these have specific use cases for which they are most suited, you can also compose larger and more useful models by combining these models as Lego-like building blocks and using the Keras functional API to glue them together in new and interesting ways.

Such models tend to be somewhat specialized to the task for which they were built, so it is impossible to generalize about them. Usually, however, they involve learning from multiple inputs or generating multiple outputs. One example could be a question answering network, where the network learns to predict answers given a story and a question. Another example could be a siamese network that calculates similarity between a pair of images, where the network is trained to predict either a binary (similar/not similar) or categorical (gradations of similarity) label using a pair of images as input. Yet another example could be an object classification and localization network where it learns to predict the image category as well as where the image is located in the picture jointly from the image. The first two examples are examples of composite networks with multiple inputs, and the last is an example of a composite network with multiple outputs.

Keras example — memory network for question answering

In this example, we will build a memory network for question answering. Memory networks are a specialized architecture that consist of a memory unit in addition to other learnable units, usually RNNs. Each input updates the memory state and the final output is computed by using the memory along with the output from the learnable unit. This architecture was suggested in 2014 via the paper (for more information refer to: *Memory Networks*, by J. Weston, S. Chopra, and A. Bordes, arXiv:1410.3916, 2014). A year later, another paper (for more information refer to: *Towards AI-Complete Question Answering: A Set of Prerequisite Toy Tasks*, by J. Weston, arXiv:1502.05698, 2015) put forward the idea of a synthetic dataset and a standard set of 20 question answering tasks, each with a higher degree of difficulty than the previous one, and applied various deep learning networks to solve these tasks. Of these, the memory network achieved the best results across all the tasks. This dataset was later made available to the general public through Facebook's bAbI project (https://research.fb.com/projects/babi/). The implementation of our memory network resembles most closely the one described in this paper (for more information refer to: *End-To-End Memory Networks*, by S. Sukhbaatar, J. Weston, and R. Fergus, Advances in Neural Information Processing Systems, 2015), in that all the training happens jointly in a single network. It uses the bAbI dataset to solve the first question answering task.

First, we will import the necessary libraries:

```
from keras.layers import Input
from keras.layers.core import Activation, dense, Dropout, Permute
from keras.layers.embeddings import Embedding
from keras.layers.merge import add, concatenate, dot
from keras.layers.recurrent import LSTM
from keras.models import Model
from keras.preprocessing.sequence import pad_sequences
from keras.utils import np_utils
import collections
import itertools
import nltk
import numpy as np
import matplotlib.pyplot as plt
import os
```

The bAbI data for the first question answering task consists of 10,000 short sentences each for the training and the test sets. A story consists of two to three sentences, followed by a question. The last sentence in each story has the question and the answer appended to it at the end. The following block of code parses each of the training and test files into a list of triplets of story, question and answer:

```
DATA_DIR = "../data"
TRAIN_FILE = os.path.join(DATA_DIR, "qa1_single-supporting-fact_train.txt")
TEST_FILE = os.path.join(DATA_DIR, "qa1_single-supporting-fact_test.txt")

def get_data(infile):
    stories, questions, answers = [], [], []
    story_text = []
    fin = open(TRAIN_FILE, "rb")
    for line in fin:
        line = line.decode("utf-8").strip()
        lno, text = line.split(" ", 1)
        if "t" in text:
            question, answer, _ = text.split("t")
            stories.append(story_text)
            questions.append(question)
            answers.append(answer)
            story_text = []
        else:
            story_text.append(text)
    fin.close()
    return stories, questions, answers

data_train = get_data(TRAIN_FILE)
data_test = get_data(TEST_FILE)
```

Our next step is to run through the texts in the generated lists and build our vocabulary. This should be quite familiar to us by now, since we have used a similar idiom a few times already. Unlike the previous time, our vocabulary is quite small, only 22 unique words, so we will not have any out of vocabulary words:

```
def build_vocab(train_data, test_data):
    counter = collections.Counter()
    for stories, questions, answers in [train_data, test_data]:
        for story in stories:
            for sent in story:
                for word in nltk.word_tokenize(sent):
                    counter[word.lower()] += 1
            for question in questions:
                for word in nltk.word_tokenize(question):
                    counter[word.lower()] += 1
            for answer in answers:
```

```
                    for word in nltk.word_tokenize(answer):
                        counter[word.lower()] += 1
        word2idx = {w:(i+1) for i, (w, _) in enumerate(counter.most_common())}
        word2idx["PAD"] = 0
    idx2word = {v:k for k, v in word2idx.items()}
        return word2idx, idx2word

    word2idx, idx2word = build_vocab(data_train, data_test)

    vocab_size = len(word2idx)
```

The memory network is based on RNNs, where each sentence in the story and question is treated as a sequence of words, so we need to find out the maximum length of the sequence for our story and question. The following block of code does this. We find that the maximum length of a story is 14 words and the maximum length of a question is just four words:

```
def get_maxlens(train_data, test_data):
    story_maxlen, question_maxlen = 0, 0
    for stories, questions, _ in [train_data, test_data]:
        for story in stories:
            story_len = 0
            for sent in story:
                swords = nltk.word_tokenize(sent)
                story_len += len(swords)
            if story_len > story_maxlen:
                story_maxlen = story_len
        for question in questions:
            question_len = len(nltk.word_tokenize(question))
            if question_len > question_maxlen:
                question_maxlen = question_len
    return story_maxlen, question_maxlen

story_maxlen, question_maxlen = get_maxlens(data_train, data_test)
```

As previously, the input to our RNNs is a sequence of word IDs. So we need to use our vocabulary dictionary to convert the (story, question, and answer) triplet into a sequence of integer word IDs. The next block of code does this and zero pads the resulting sequences of story and answer to the maximum sequence lengths we computed previously. At this point, we have lists of padded word ID sequences for each triplet in the training and test sets:

```
def vectorize(data, word2idx, story_maxlen, question_maxlen):
    Xs, Xq, Y = [], [], []
    stories, questions, answers = data
    for story, question, answer in zip(stories, questions, answers):
        xs = [[word2idx[w.lower()] for w in nltk.word_tokenize(s)]
                for s in story]
```

```
                xs = list(itertools.chain.from_iterable(xs))
                xq = [word2idx[w.lower()] for w in nltk.word_tokenize(question)]
                Xs.append(xs)
                Xq.append(xq)
                Y.append(word2idx[answer.lower()])
        return pad_sequences(Xs, maxlen=story_maxlen),
            pad_sequences(Xq, maxlen=question_maxlen),
            np_utils.to_categorical(Y, num_classes=len(word2idx))

Xstrain, Xqtrain, Ytrain = vectorize(data_train, word2idx, story_maxlen,
question_maxlen)
Xstest, Xqtest, Ytest = vectorize(data_test, word2idx, story_maxlen,
question_maxlen)
```

We want to define the model. The definition is longer than we have seen previously, so it may be convenient to refer to the diagram as you look through the definition:

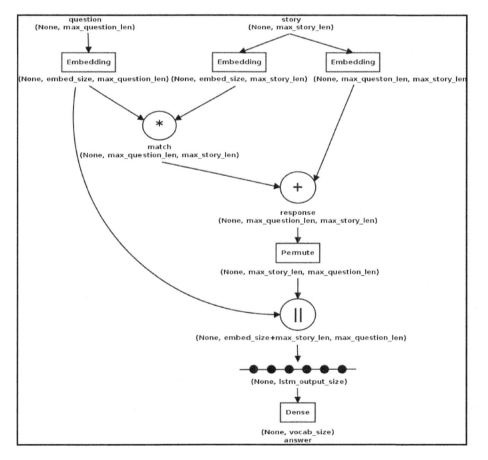

There are two inputs to our model, the sequence of word IDs for the question and that for the sentence. Each of these is passed into an Embedding layer to convert the word IDs to a vector in the 64-dimensional embedding space. Additionally the story sequence is passed through an additional embedding that projects it to an embedding of size `max_question_length`. All these embedding layers start with random weights and are trained jointly with the rest of the network.

The first two embeddings (story and question) are merged using a dot product to form the network's memory. These represent words in the story and question that are identical or close to each other in the embedding space. The output of the memory is merged with the second story embedding and summed to form the network response, which is once again merged with the embedding for the question to form the response sequence. This response sequence is sent through an LSTM, the context vector of which is sent to a dense layer to predict the answer, which can be one of the words in the vocabulary.

The model is trained using the RMSprop optimizer and categorical cross-entropy as the loss function:

```
EMBEDDING_SIZE = 64
LATENT_SIZE = 32

# inputs
story_input = Input(shape=(story_maxlen,))
question_input = Input(shape=(question_maxlen,))

# story encoder memory
story_encoder = Embedding(input_dim=vocab_size,
output_dim=EMBEDDING_SIZE,
    input_length=story_maxlen)(story_input)
story_encoder = Dropout(0.3)(story_encoder)

# question encoder
question_encoder = Embedding(input_dim=vocab_size,
output_dim=EMBEDDING_SIZE,
    input_length=question_maxlen)(question_input)
question_encoder = Dropout(0.3)(question_encoder)

# match between story and question
match = dot([story_encoder, question_encoder], axes=[2, 2])

# encode story into vector space of question
story_encoder_c = Embedding(input_dim=vocab_size,
output_dim=question_maxlen,
    input_length=story_maxlen)(story_input)
story_encoder_c = Dropout(0.3)(story_encoder_c)
```

```
# combine match and story vectors
response = add([match, story_encoder_c])
response = Permute((2, 1))(response)

# combine response and question vectors
answer = concatenate([response, question_encoder], axis=-1)
answer = LSTM(LATENT_SIZE)(answer)
answer = Dropout(0.3)(answer)
answer = dense(vocab_size)(answer)
output = Activation("softmax")(answer)

model = Model(inputs=[story_input, question_input], outputs=output)
model.compile(optimizer="rmsprop", loss="categorical_crossentropy",
    metrics=["accuracy"])
```

We train this network for 50 epochs with a batch size of 32 and achieve an accuracy of over 81% on the validation set:

```
BATCH_SIZE = 32
NUM_EPOCHS = 50
history = model.fit([Xstrain, Xqtrain], [Ytrain], batch_size=BATCH_SIZE,
    epochs=NUM_EPOCHS,
    validation_data=([Xstest, Xqtest], [Ytest]))
```

Here is the trace of the training logs:

```
Epoch 38/50
10000/10000 [==============================] - 5s - loss: 0.4636 - acc: 0.7952 - val_loss: 0.4499 - val_acc: 0.8071
Epoch 39/50
10000/10000 [==============================] - 5s - loss: 0.4603 - acc: 0.7993 - val_loss: 0.4489 - val_acc: 0.8083
Epoch 40/50
10000/10000 [==============================] - 5s - loss: 0.4590 - acc: 0.8003 - val_loss: 0.4475 - val_acc: 0.8086
Epoch 41/50
10000/10000 [==============================] - 5s - loss: 0.4592 - acc: 0.7997 - val_loss: 0.4472 - val_acc: 0.8099
Epoch 42/50
10000/10000 [==============================] - 5s - loss: 0.4611 - acc: 0.7966 - val_loss: 0.4466 - val_acc: 0.8099
Epoch 43/50
10000/10000 [==============================] - 5s - loss: 0.4577 - acc: 0.8025 - val_loss: 0.4437 - val_acc: 0.8114
Epoch 44/50
10000/10000 [==============================] - 5s - loss: 0.4576 - acc: 0.8023 - val_loss: 0.4431 - val_acc: 0.8136
Epoch 45/50
10000/10000 [==============================] - 5s - loss: 0.4575 - acc: 0.8013 - val_loss: 0.4422 - val_acc: 0.8127
Epoch 46/50
10000/10000 [==============================] - 5s - loss: 0.4587 - acc: 0.7998 - val_loss: 0.4420 - val_acc: 0.8127
Epoch 47/50
10000/10000 [==============================] - 6s - loss: 0.4574 - acc: 0.8005 - val_loss: 0.4412 - val_acc: 0.8126
Epoch 48/50
10000/10000 [==============================] - 5s - loss: 0.4559 - acc: 0.8023 - val_loss: 0.4408 - val_acc: 0.8168
Epoch 49/50
10000/10000 [==============================] - 6s - loss: 0.4550 - acc: 0.8003 - val_loss: 0.4395 - val_acc: 0.8154
Epoch 50/50
10000/10000 [==============================] - 5s - loss: 0.4577 - acc: 0.7985 - val_loss: 0.4407 - val_acc: 0.8139
```

The change in training and validation loss and accuracy for this training run is shown graphically in this graph:

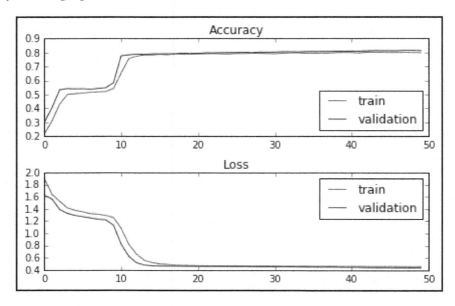

We ran the model against the first 10 stories from our test set to verify how good the predictions were:

```
ytest = np.argmax(Ytest, axis=1)
Ytest_ = model.predict([Xstest, Xqtest])
ytest_ = np.argmax(Ytest_, axis=1)

for i in range(NUM_DISPLAY):
    story = " ".join([idx2word[x] for x in Xstest[i].tolist() if x != 0])
    question = " ".join([idx2word[x] for x in Xqtest[i].tolist()])
    label = idx2word[ytest[i]]
    prediction = idx2word[ytest_[i]]
    print(story, question, label, prediction)
```

As you can see, the predictions were mostly correct:

Story	Question	Answer	Predicted
mary moved to the bathroom . john went to the hallway .	where is mary ?	bathroom	bathroom
daniel went back to the hallway . sandra moved to the garden .	where is daniel ?	hallway	hallway
john moved to the office . sandra journeyed to the bathroom .	where is daniel ?	hallway	kitchen
mary moved to the hallway . daniel travelled to the office .	where is daniel ?	office	office
john went back to the garden . john moved to the bedroom .	where is sandra ?	bathroom	bedroom
sandra travelled to the office . sandra went to the bathroom .	where is sandra ?	bathroom	bathroom
mary went to the bedroom . daniel moved to the hallway .	where is sandra ?	bathroom	garden
john went to the garden . john travelled to the office .	where is sandra ?	bathroom	bathroom
daniel journeyed to the bedroom . daniel travelled to the hallway .	where is john ?	office	kitchen
john went to the bedroom . john travelled to the office .	where is daniel ?	hallway	kitchen

Customizing Keras

Just as composing our basic building blocks into larger architectures enables us to build interesting deep learning models, sometimes we need to look at the other end of the spectrum. Keras has a lot of functionality built in already, so it is very likely that you can build all your models with the provided components and not feel the need for customization at all. In case you do need customization, Keras has you covered.

As you will recall, Keras is a high level API that delegates to either a TensorFlow or Theano backend for the computational heavy lifting. Any code you build for your customization will call out to one of these backends. In order to keep your code portable across the two backends, your custom code should use the Keras backend API (https://keras.io/backend/), which provides a set of functions that act like a facade over your chosen backend. Depending on the backend selected, the call to the backend facade will translate to the appropriate TensorFlow or Theano call. The full list of functions available and their detailed descriptions can be found on the Keras backend page.

In addition to portability, using the backend API also results in more maintainable code, since Keras code is generally more high-level and compact compared to equivalent TensorFlow or Theano code. In the unlikely case that you do need to switch to using the backend directly, your Keras components can be used directly inside TensorFlow (not Theano though) code as described in this Keras blog (https://blog.keras.io/keras-as-a-simplified-interface-to-tensorflow-tutorial.html).

Customizing Keras typically means writing your own custom layer or custom distance function. In this section, we will demonstrate how to build some simple Keras layers. You will see more examples of using the backend functions to build other custom Keras components, such as objectives (loss functions), in subsequent sections.

Keras example — using the lambda layer

Keras provides a lambda layer; it can wrap a function of your choosing. For example, if you wanted to build a layer that squares its input tensor element-wise, you can say simply:

```
model.add(lambda(lambda x: x ** 2))
```

You can also wrap functions within a lambda layer. For example, if you want to build a custom layer that computes the element-wise euclidean distance between two input tensors, you would define the function to compute the value itself, as well as one that returns the output shape from this function, like so:

```
def euclidean_distance(vecs):
    x, y = vecs
    return K.sqrt(K.sum(K.square(x - y), axis=1, keepdims=True))

def euclidean_distance_output_shape(shapes):
    shape1, shape2 = shapes
    return (shape1[0], 1)
```

You can then call these functions using the lambda layer shown as follows:

```
lhs_input = Input(shape=(VECTOR_SIZE,))
lhs = dense(1024, kernel_initializer="glorot_uniform",
activation="relu")(lhs_input)

rhs_input = Input(shape=(VECTOR_SIZE,))
rhs = dense(1024, kernel_initializer="glorot_uniform",
activation="relu")(rhs_input)

sim = lambda(euclidean_distance,
output_shape=euclidean_distance_output_shape)([lhs, rhs])
```

Keras example — building a custom normalization layer

While the lambda layer can be very useful, sometimes you need more control. As an example, we will look at the code for a normalization layer that implements a technique called **local response normalization**. This technique normalizes the input over local input regions, but has since fallen out of favor because it turned out not to be as effective as other regularization methods such as dropout and batch normalization, as well as better initialization methods.

Building custom layers typically involves working with the backend functions, so it involves thinking about the code in terms of tensors. As you will recall, working with tensors is a two step process. First, you define the tensors and arrange them in a computation graph, and then you run the graph with actual data. So working at this level is harder than working in the rest of Keras. The Keras documentation has some guidelines for building custom layers (https://keras.io/layers/writing-your-own-keras-layers/), which you should definitely read.

One of the ways to make it easier to develop code in the backend API is to have a small test harness that you can run to verify that your code is doing what you want it to do. Here is a small harness I adapted from the Keras source to run your layer against some input and return a result:

```
from keras.models import Sequential
from keras.layers.core import Dropout, Reshape

def test_layer(layer, x):
    layer_config = layer.get_config()
    layer_config["input_shape"] = x.shape
    layer = layer.__class__.from_config(layer_config)
    model = Sequential()
    model.add(layer)
    model.compile("rmsprop", "mse")
    x_ = np.expand_dims(x, axis=0)
    return model.predict(x_)[0]
```

And here are some tests with `layer` objects provided by Keras to make sure that the harness runs okay:

```
from keras.layers.core import Dropout, Reshape
from keras.layers.convolutional import ZeroPadding2D
import numpy as np

x = np.random.randn(10, 10)
```

```
layer = Dropout(0.5)
y = test_layer(layer, x)
assert(x.shape == y.shape)

x = np.random.randn(10, 10, 3)
layer = ZeroPadding2D(padding=(1,1))
y = test_layer(layer, x)
assert(x.shape[0] + 2 == y.shape[0])
assert(x.shape[1] + 2 == y.shape[1])

x = np.random.randn(10, 10)
layer = Reshape((5, 20))
y = test_layer(layer, x)
assert(y.shape == (5, 20))
```

Before we begin building our local response normalization layer, we need to take a moment to understand what it really does. This technique was originally used with Caffe, and the Caffe documentation (`http://caffe.berkeleyvision.org/tutorial/layers/lrn.html`) describes it as a kind of *lateral inhibition* that works by normalizing over local input regions. In `ACROSS_CHANNEL` mode, the local regions extend across nearby channels but have no spatial extent. In `WITHIN_CHANNEL` mode, the local regions extend spatially, but are in separate channels. We will implement the `WITHIN_CHANNEL` model as follows. The formula for local response normalization in the `WITHIN_CHANNEL` model is given by:

$$LRN(x_i) = \frac{x_i}{(k + \frac{\alpha}{n}\sum_i x_i)^\beta}$$

The code for the custom layer follows the standard structure. The `__init__` method is used to set the application specific parameters, that is, the hyperparameters associated with the layer. Since our layer only does a forward computation and doesn't have any learnable weights, all we do in the build method is to set the input shape and delegate to the superclass's build method, which takes care of any necessary book-keeping. In layers where learnable weights are involved, this method is where you would set the initial values.

The call method does the actual computation. Notice that we need to account for dimension ordering. Another thing to note is that the batch size is usually unknown at design times, so you need to write your operations so that the batch size is not explicitly invoked. The computation itself is fairly straightforward and follows the formula closely. The sum in the denominator can also be thought of as average pooling over the row and column dimension with a padding size of *(n, n)* and a stride of *(1, 1)*. Because the pooled data is averaged already, we no longer need to divide the sum by *n*.

The last part of the class is the `get_output_shape_for` method. Since the layer normalizes each element of the input tensor, the output size is identical to the input size:

```
from keras import backend as K
from keras.engine.topology import Layer, InputSpec

class LocalResponseNormalization(Layer):

    def __init__(self, n=5, alpha=0.0005, beta=0.75, k=2, **kwargs):
        self.n = n
        self.alpha = alpha
        self.beta = beta
        self.k = k
        super(LocalResponseNormalization, self).__init__(**kwargs)

    def build(self, input_shape):
        self.shape = input_shape
        super(LocalResponseNormalization, self).build(input_shape)

    def call(self, x, mask=None):
        if K.image_dim_ordering == "th":
            _, f, r, c = self.shape
        else:
            _, r, c, f = self.shape
        squared = K.square(x)
        pooled = K.pool2d(squared, (n, n), strides=(1, 1),
            padding="same", pool_mode="avg")
        if K.image_dim_ordering == "th":
            summed = K.sum(pooled, axis=1, keepdims=True)
            averaged = self.alpha * K.repeat_elements(summed, f, axis=1)
        else:
            summed = K.sum(pooled, axis=3, keepdims=True)
            averaged = self.alpha * K.repeat_elements(summed, f, axis=3)
        denom = K.pow(self.k + averaged, self.beta)
        return x / denom

    def get_output_shape_for(self, input_shape):
        return input_shape
```

You can test this layer during development using the test harness we described here. It is easier to run this instead of trying to build a whole network to put this into, or worse, waiting till you have fully specified the layer before running it:

```
x = np.random.randn(225, 225, 3)
layer = LocalResponseNormalization()
y = test_layer(layer, x)
assert(x.shape == y.shape)
```

While building custom Keras layers seems to be fairly commonplace among experienced Keras developers, there are not too many examples available on the Internet. This is probably because custom layers are usually built to serve a specific narrow purpose and may not be widely useful. The variability also means that one single example cannot demonstrate all the possibilities of what you can do with the API. Now that you have a good idea of how to build a custom Keras layer, you might find it instructive to look at Keunwoo Choi's `melspectogram` (`https://keunwoochoi.wordpress.com/2016/11/18/fo r-beginners-writing-a-custom-keras-layer/`) and Shashank Gupta's `NodeEmbeddingLayer` (`http://shashankg7.github.io/2016/10/12/Custom-Layer-In-K eras-Graph-Embedding-Case-Study.html`).

Generative models

Generative models are models that learn to create data similar to data it is trained on. We saw one example of a generative model that learns to write prose similar to *Alice in Wonderland* in `Chapter 6`, *Recurrent Neural Network — RNN*. In that example, we trained a model to predict the 11th character of text given the first 10 characters. Yet another type of generative model is **generative adversarial models (GAN)** that have recently emerged as a very powerful class of models—you saw examples of GANs in `Chapter 4`, *Generative Adversarial Networks and WaveNet*. The intuition for generative models is that it learns a good internal representation of its training data, and is therefore able to generate similar data during the *prediction* phase.

Another perspective on generative models is the probabilistic one. A typical classification or regression network, also called a discriminative model, learns a function that maps the input data X to some label or output y, that is, these models learn the conditional probability $P(y | X)$. On the other hand, a generative model learns the joint probability and labels simultaneously, that is, $P(x, y)$. This knowledge can then be used to create probable new (X, y) samples. This gives generative models the ability to explain the underlying structure of input data even when there are no labels. This is a very important advantage in the real world, since unlabeled data is more abundant than labeled data.

Simple generative models such as the example mentioned above can be extended to audio as well, for example, models that learn to generate and play music. One interesting one is described in the WaveNet paper (for more information refer to: *WaveNet: A Generative Model for Raw Audio*, by A. van den Oord, 2016.) which describes a network built using atrous convolutional layers and provides a Keras implementation on GithHub (`https://github.c om/basveeling/wavenet`).

Keras example — deep dreaming

In this example, we will look at a slightly different generative network. We will see how to take a pre-trained convolutional network and use it to generate new objects in an image. Networks trained to discriminate between images learn enough about the images to generate them as well. This was first demonstrated by Alexander Mordvintsev of Google and described in this Google Research blog post (https://research.googleblog.com /2015/06/inceptionism-going-deeper-into-neural.html). It was originally called *inceptionalism* but the term *deep dreaming* became more popular to describe the technique.

Deep dreaming takes the backpropagated gradient activations and adds it back to the image, running the same process over and over in a loop. The network optimizes the loss function in the process, but we get to see how it does so in the input image (three channels) rather than in a high dimensional hidden layer that cannot easily be visualized.

There are many variations to this basic strategy, each of which leads to new and interesting effects. Some variations are blurring, adding constraints on the total activations, decaying the gradient, infinitely zooming into the image by cropping and scaling, adding jitter by randomly moving the image around, and so on. In our example, we will show the simplest approach—we will optimize the gradient of the mean of the selected layer's activation for each of the pooling layers of a pre-trained VGG-16 and observe the effect on our input image.

First, as usual, we will declare our imports:

```
from keras import backend as K
from keras.applications import vgg16
from keras.layers import Input
import matplotlib.pyplot as plt
import numpy as np
import os
```

Next we will load up our input image. This image may be familiar to you from blog posts about deep learning. The original image is from here (https://www.flickr.com/photos/b illgarrett-newagecrap/14984990912):

```
DATA_DIR = "../data"
IMAGE_FILE = os.path.join(DATA_DIR, "cat.jpg")
img = plt.imread(IMAGE_FILE)
plt.imshow(img)
```

The output of the preceding example is as follows:

Next we define a pair of functions to preprocess and deprocess the image to and from a four-dimensional representation suitable for input to a pre-trained VGG-16 network:

```
def preprocess(img):
    img4d = img.copy()
    img4d = img4d.astype("float64")
    if K.image_dim_ordering() == "th":
        # (H, W, C) -> (C, H, W)
        img4d = img4d.transpose((2, 0, 1))
        img4d = np.expand_dims(img4d, axis=0)
        img4d = vgg16.preprocess_input(img4d)
    return img4d

def deprocess(img4d):
    img = img4d.copy()
    if K.image_dim_ordering() == "th":
        # (B, C, H, W)
        img = img.reshape((img4d.shape[1], img4d.shape[2],
img4d.shape[3]))
        # (C, H, W) -> (H, W, C)
        img = img.transpose((1, 2, 0))
    else:
        # (B, H, W, C)
```

```
        img = img.reshape((img4d.shape[1], img4d.shape[2], img4d.shape[3]))
    img[:, :, 0] += 103.939
    img[:, :, 1] += 116.779
    img[:, :, 2] += 123.68
    # BGR -> RGB
    img = img[:, :, ::-1]
    img = np.clip(img, 0, 255).astype("uint8")
return img
```

These two functions are inverses of each other, that is, passing the image through `preprocess` and then through `deprocess` will return the original image.

Next, we load up our pre-trained VGG-16 network. This network has been pre-trained on ImageNet data and is available from the Keras distribution. You already learned how to work with pre-trained models in `Chapter 3`, *Deep Learning with ConvNets*. We select the version whose fully connected layers have been removed already. Apart from saving us the trouble of having to remove them ourselves, this also allows us to pass in any shape of image, since the reason we need to specify the image width and height in our input is because this determines the size of the weight matrices in the fully connected layers. Because CNN transformations are local in nature, the size of the image doesn't affect the sizes of the weight matrices for the convolutional and pooling layers. So the only constraint on image size is that it must be constant within the batch:

```
img_copy = img.copy()
print("Original image shape:", img.shape)
p_img = preprocess(img_copy)
batch_shape = p_img.shape
dream = Input(batch_shape=batch_shape)
model = vgg16.VGG16(input_tensor=dream, weights="imagenet",
include_top=False)
```

We will need to refer to the CNN's layer objects by name in our following calculations, so let us construct a dictionary. We also need to understand the layer naming convention, so we dump it out:

```
layer_dict = {layer.name : layer for layer in model.layers}
print(layer_dict)
```

The output of the preceding example is as follows:

{'block1_conv1': <keras.layers.convolutional.Convolution2D at 0x11b847690>,
 'block1_conv2': <keras.layers.convolutional.Convolution2D at 0x11b847f90>,
 'block1_pool': <keras.layers.pooling.MaxPooling2D at 0x11c45db90>,
 'block2_conv1': <keras.layers.convolutional.Convolution2D at 0x11c45ddd0>,
 'block2_conv2': <keras.layers.convolutional.Convolution2D at 0x11b88f810>,
 'block2_pool': <keras.layers.pooling.MaxPooling2D at 0x11c2d2690>,

```
'block3_conv1': <keras.layers.convolutional.Convolution2D at 0x11c47b890>,
'block3_conv2': <keras.layers.convolutional.Convolution2D at 0x11c510290>,
'block3_conv3': <keras.layers.convolutional.Convolution2D at 0x11c4afa10>,
'block3_pool': <keras.layers.pooling.MaxPooling2D at 0x11c334a10>,
'block4_conv1': <keras.layers.convolutional.Convolution2D at 0x11c345b10>,
'block4_conv2': <keras.layers.convolutional.Convolution2D at 0x11c345950>,
'block4_conv3': <keras.layers.convolutional.Convolution2D at 0x11d52c910>,
'block4_pool': <keras.layers.pooling.MaxPooling2D at 0x11d550c90>,
'block5_conv1': <keras.layers.convolutional.Convolution2D at 0x11d566c50>,
'block5_conv2': <keras.layers.convolutional.Convolution2D at 0x11d5b1910>,
'block5_conv3': <keras.layers.convolutional.Convolution2D at 0x11d5b1710>,
'block5_pool': <keras.layers.pooling.MaxPooling2D at 0x11fd68e10>,
'input_1': <keras.engine.topology.InputLayer at 0x11b847410>}
```

We then compute the loss at each of the five pooling layers and compute the gradient of the mean activation for three steps each. The gradient is added back to the image and the image displayed at each of the pooling layers for each step:

```
num_pool_layers = 5
num_iters_per_layer = 3
step = 100

for i in range(num_pool_layers):
    # identify each pooling layer
    layer_name = "block{:d}_pool".format(i+1)
    # build loss function that maximizes the mean activation in layer
    layer_output = layer_dict[layer_name].output
    loss = K.mean(layer_output)
    # compute gradient of image wrt loss and normalize
    grads = K.gradients(loss, dream)[0]
    grads /= (K.sqrt(K.mean(K.square(grads))) + 1e-5)
    # define function to return loss and grad given input image
    f = K.function([dream], [loss, grads])
    img_value = p_img.copy()
    fig, axes = plt.subplots(1, num_iters_per_layer, figsize=(20, 10))
    for it in range(num_iters_per_layer):
        loss_value, grads_value = f([img_value])
        img_value += grads_value * step
        axes[it].imshow(deprocess(img_value))
    plt.show()
```

The resulting images are shown as follows:

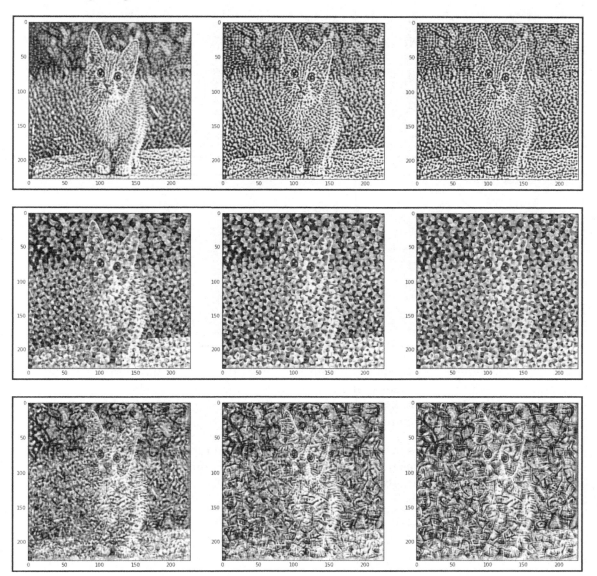

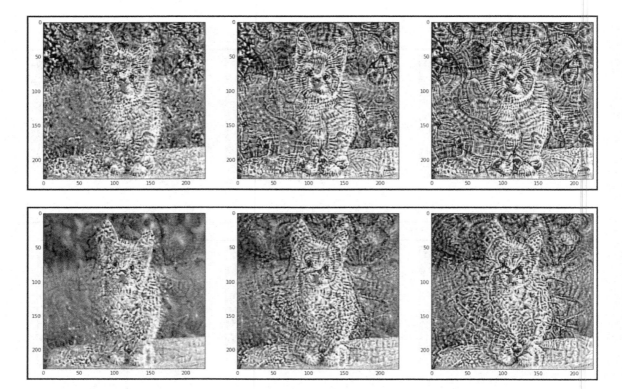

As you can see, the process of deep dreaming amplifies the effect of the gradient on the chosen layer, resulting in images that are quite surreal. Later layers backpropagate gradients that result in more distortion, reflecting their larger receptive fields and their capacity to recognize more complex features.

To convince ourselves that a trained network really learns a representation of the various categories of the image it was trained on, let us consider a completely random image, shown next, and pass it through the pre-trained network:

```
img_noise = np.random.randint(100, 150, size=(227, 227, 3), dtype=np.uint8)
plt.imshow(img_noise)
```

The output of the preceding example is as follows:

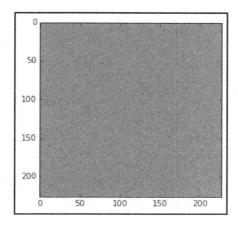

Passing this image through the preceding code results in very specific patterns at each layer, as shown next, showing that the network is trying to find a structure in the random data:

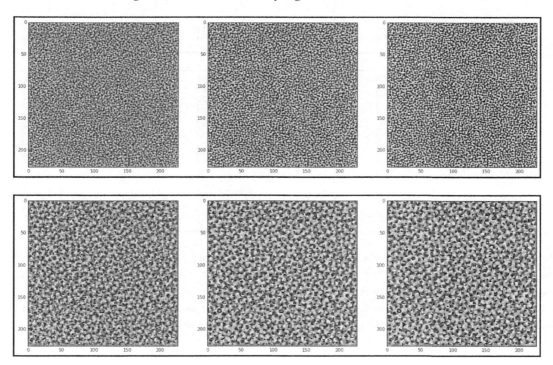

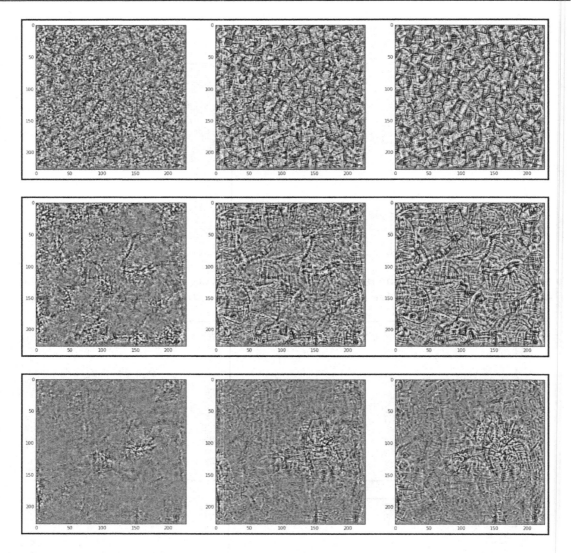

We can repeat our experiment with the noise image as input and compute the loss from a single filter instead of taking the mean across all the filters. The filter we choose is for the ImageNet label African elephant (24). Thus, we replace the value of the loss in the previous code with the following. So instead of computing the mean across all filters, we calculate the loss as the output of the filter representing the African elephant class:

```
loss = layer_output[:, :, :, 24]
```

We get back what looks very much like repeating images of the trunk of an elephant in the `block4_pool` output, as shown here:

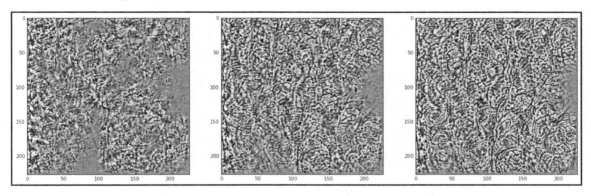

Keras example — style transfer

An extension of deep dreaming was described in this paper (for more information refer to: *Image Style Transfer Using Convolutional Neural Networks*, by L. A. Gatys, A. S. Ecker, and M. Bethge, Proceedings of the IEEE Conference on Computer Vision and Pattern Recognition, 2016), which showed that trained neural networks, such as the VGG-16, learn both content and style, and these two can be manipulated independently. Thus an image of an object (content) could be styled to look like a painting by combining it with the image of a painting (style).

Let us start, as usual, by importing our libraries:

```
from keras.applications import vgg16
from keras import backend as K
from scipy.misc import imresize
import matplotlib.pyplot as plt
import numpy as np
import os
```

Our example will demonstrate styling our image of a cat with this image of a reproduction of Claude Monet's *The Japanese Bridge* by Rosalind Wheeler (https://goo.gl/0VXC39):

```
DATA_DIR = "../data"
CONTENT_IMAGE_FILE = os.path.join(DATA_DIR, "cat.jpg")
STYLE_IMAGE_FILE = os.path.join(DATA_DIR, "JapaneseBridgeMonetCopy.jpg")
RESIZED_WH = 400

content_img_value = imresize(plt.imread(CONTENT_IMAGE_FILE), (RESIZED_WH,
RESIZED_WH))
style_img_value = imresize(plt.imread(STYLE_IMAGE_FILE), (RESIZED_WH,
```

```
RESIZED_WH))

plt.subplot(121)
plt.title("content")
plt.imshow(content_img_value)

plt.subplot(122)
plt.title("style")
plt.imshow(style_img_value)

plt.show()
```

The output of the preceding example is as follows:

As previously, we declare our two functions to convert back and forth from the image and the four-dimensional tensor that the CNN expects:

```
def preprocess(img):
    img4d = img.copy()
    img4d = img4d.astype("float64")
    if K.image_dim_ordering() == "th":
        # (H, W, C) -> (C, H, W)
        img4d = img4d.transpose((2, 0, 1))
    img4d = np.expand_dims(img4d, axis=0)
    img4d = vgg16.preprocess_input(img4d)
    return img4d

def deprocess(img4d):
    img = img4d.copy()
    if K.image_dim_ordering() == "th":
        # (B, C, H, W)
        img = img.reshape((img4d.shape[1], img4d.shape[2], img4d.shape[3]))
        # (C, H, W) -> (H, W, C)
```

```
        img = img.transpose((1, 2, 0))
    else:
        # (B, H, W, C)
        img = img.reshape((img4d.shape[1], img4d.shape[2], img4d.shape[3]))
    img[:, :, 0] += 103.939
    img[:, :, 1] += 116.779
    img[:, :, 2] += 123.68
    # BGR -> RGB
    img = img[:, :, ::-1]
    img = np.clip(img, 0, 255).astype("uint8")
    return img
```

We declare tensors to hold the content image and the style image, and another tensor to hold the combined image. The content and style images are then concatenated into a single input tensor. The input tensor will be fed to the pre-trained VGG-16 network:

```
content_img = K.variable(preprocess(content_img_value))
style_img = K.variable(preprocess(style_img_value))
if K.image_dim_ordering() == "th":
    comb_img = K.placeholder((1, 3, RESIZED_WH, RESIZED_WH))
else:
    comb_img = K.placeholder((1, RESIZED_WH, RESIZED_WH, 3))

# concatenate images into single input
input_tensor = K.concatenate([content_img, style_img, comb_img], axis=0)
```

We instantiate an instance of a pre-trained VGG-16 network, pre-trained with the ImageNet data, and with the fully connected layers excluded:

```
model = vgg16.VGG16(input_tensor=input_tensor, weights="imagenet",
include_top=False)
```

As previously, we construct a layer dictionary to map the layer name to the output layer of the trained VGG-16 network:

```
layer_dict = {layer.name : layer.output for layer in model.layers}
```

The next block defines the code for computing the content_loss, the style_loss, and the variational_loss. Finally, we define our loss as a linear combination of these three losses:

```
def content_loss(content, comb):
    return K.sum(K.square(comb - content))

def gram_matrix(x):
    if K.image_dim_ordering() == "th":
        features = K.batch_flatten(x)
    else:
```

```python
            features = K.batch_flatten(K.permute_dimensions(x, (2, 0, 1)))
        gram = K.dot(features, K.transpose(features))
        return gram

    def style_loss_per_layer(style, comb):
        S = gram_matrix(style)
        C = gram_matrix(comb)
        channels = 3
        size = RESIZED_WH * RESIZED_WH
        return K.sum(K.square(S - C)) / (4 * (channels ** 2) * (size ** 2))

    def style_loss():
        stl_loss = 0.0
        for i in range(NUM_LAYERS):
            layer_name = "block{:d}_conv1".format(i+1)
            layer_features = layer_dict[layer_name]
            style_features = layer_features[1, :, :, :]
            comb_features = layer_features[2, :, :, :]
            stl_loss += style_loss_per_layer(style_features, comb_features)
        return stl_loss / NUM_LAYERS

    def variation_loss(comb):
        if K.image_dim_ordering() == "th":
            dx = K.square(comb[:, :, :RESIZED_WH-1, :RESIZED_WH-1] -
                          comb[:, :, 1:, :RESIZED_WH-1])
            dy = K.square(comb[:, :, :RESIZED_WH-1, :RESIZED_WH-1] -
                          comb[:, :, :RESIZED_WH-1, 1:])
        else:
            dx = K.square(comb[:, :RESIZED_WH-1, :RESIZED_WH-1, :] -
                          comb[:, 1:, :RESIZED_WH-1, :])
            dy = K.square(comb[:, :RESIZED_WH-1, :RESIZED_WH-1, :] -
                          comb[:, :RESIZED_WH-1, 1:, :])
        return K.sum(K.pow(dx + dy, 1.25))

    CONTENT_WEIGHT = 0.1
    STYLE_WEIGHT = 5.0
    VAR_WEIGHT = 0.01
    NUM_LAYERS = 5

    c_loss = content_loss(content_img, comb_img)
    s_loss = style_loss()
    v_loss = variation_loss(comb_img)
    loss = (CONTENT_WEIGHT * c_loss) + (STYLE_WEIGHT * s_loss) + (VAR_WEIGHT *
    v_loss)
```

Here the content loss is the root mean square distance (also known as **L2 distance**) between the features of the content image extracted from the target layer and the combination image. Minimizing this has the effect of keeping the styled image close to the original one.

The style loss is the L2 distance between the gram matrices of the base image representation and the style image. A gram matrix of a matrix M is the transpose of M multiplied by M, that is, $MT * M$. This loss measures how often features appear together in the content image representation and the style image. One practical implication of this is that the content and style matrices must be square.

The total variation loss measures the difference between neighboring pixels. Minimizing this has the effect that neighboring pixels will be similar so the final image is smooth rather than *jumpy*.

We calculate the gradient and the loss function, and run our network in reverse for five iterations:

```
grads = K.gradients(loss, comb_img)[0]
f = K.function([comb_img], [loss, grads])

NUM_ITERATIONS = 5
LEARNING_RATE = 0.001

content_img4d = preprocess(content_img_value)
for i in range(NUM_ITERATIONS):
    print("Epoch {:d}/{:d}".format(i+1, NUM_ITERATIONS))
    loss_value, grads_value = f([content_img4d])
    content_img4d += grads_value * LEARNING_RATE
    plt.imshow(deprocess(content_img4d))
    plt.show()
```

The output from the last two iterations is shown as follows. As you can see, it has picked up the impressionistic fuzziness and even the texture of the canvas in the final images:

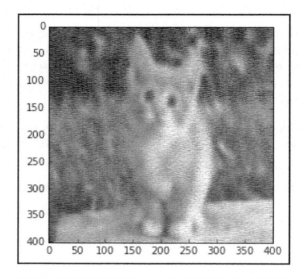

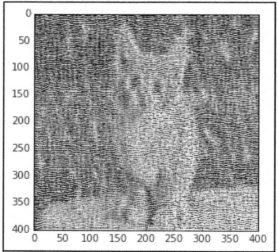

Summary

In this chapter, we covered some deep learning networks that were not covered in earlier chapters. We started with a brief look into the Keras functional API, which allows us to build networks that are more complex than the sequential networks we have seen so far. We then looked at regression networks, which allow us to do predictions in a continuous space, and opens up a whole new range of problems we can solve. However, a regression network is really a very simple modification of a standard classification network. The next area we looked at was autoencoders, which are a style of network that allows us to do unsupervised learning and make use of the massive amount of unlabeled data that all of us have access to nowadays. We also learned how to compose the networks we had already learned about as giant Lego-like building blocks into larger and more interesting networks. We then moved from building large networks using smaller networks, to learning how to customize individual layers in a network using the Keras backend layer. Finally, we looked at generative models, another class of models that learn to mimic the input it is trained on, and looked at some novel uses for this kind of model.

In the next chapter, we will turn our attention to another learning style called reinforcement learning, and explore its concepts by building and training a network in Keras to play a simple computer game.

8
AI Game Playing

In previous chapters, we looked at supervised learning techniques such as regression and classification, and unsupervised learning techniques such as GANs, autoencoders and generative models. In the case of supervised learning, we train the network with the expected input and output and expect it to predict the output given a new input. In the case of unsupervised learning, we show the network some input and expect it to learn the structure of the data so that it can apply this knowledge to a new input.

In this chapter, we will learn about reinforcement learning, or more specifically deep reinforcement learning, that is, the application of deep neural networks to reinforcement learning. Reinforcement learning has its roots in behavioral psychology. An agent is trained by rewarding it for correct behavior and punishing it for incorrect behavior. In the context of deep reinforcement learning, a network is shown some input and is given a positive or negative reward based on whether it produces the correct output from that input. Thus, in reinforcement learning, we have sparse and time-delayed labels. Over many iterations, the network learns to produce the correct output.

The pioneer in the deep reinforcement learning space was a small British company called DeepMind, which in 2013 published a paper (for more information refer to: *Playing Atari with Deep Reinforcement Learning*, by V. Mnih, arXiv:1312.5602, 2013.) describing how a **convolutional neural network (CNN)** could be taught to play Atari 2600 video games by showing it screen pixels and giving it a reward when the score increases. The same architecture was used to learn seven different Atari 2600 games, in six of which the model outperformed all previous approaches, and it outperformed a human expert in three.

Unlike the learning strategies we learned about previously, where each network learns about a single discipline, reinforcement learning seems to be a general learning algorithm that can be applied to a variety of environments; it may even be the first step to general artificial intelligence. DeepMind has since been acquired by Google, and the group has been on the forefront of AI research. A subsequent paper (for more information refer to: *Human-Level Control through Deep Reinforcement Learning*, by V. Mnih, Nature 518.7540, 2015: 529-533.) was featured in the prestigious Nature journal in 2015, where they applied the same model to 49 different games.

In this chapter, we will explore the theoretical framework that underlies deep reinforcement learning. We'll then apply this framework to build a network using Keras that learns to play a game of catch. We'll briefly look at some ideas that can make this network better as well as some promising new areas of research in this space.

To sum up, we will learn the following core concepts around reinforcement learning in this chapter:

- Q-learning
- Exploration versus exploitation
- Experience replay

Reinforcement learning

Our objective is to build a neural network to play the game of catch. Each game starts with a ball being dropped from a random position from the top of the screen. The objective is to move a paddle at the bottom of the screen using the left and right arrow keys to catch the ball by the time it reaches the bottom. As games go, this is quite simple. At any point in time, the state of this game is given by the *(x, y)* coordinates of the ball and paddle. Most arcade games tend to have many more moving parts, so a general solution is to provide the entire current game screen image as the state. The following screenshot shows four consecutive screenshots of our catch game:

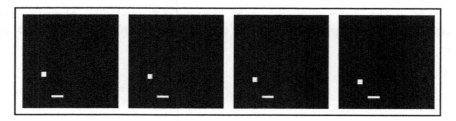

Astute readers might note that our problem could be modeled as a classification problem, where the input to the network are the game screen images and the output is one of three actions--move left, stay, or move right. However, this would require us to provide the network with training examples, possibly from recordings of games played by experts. An alternative and simpler approach might be to build a network and have it play the game repeatedly, giving it feedback based on whether it succeeds in catching the ball or not. This approach is also more intuitive and is closer to the way humans and animals learn.

The most common way to represent such a problem is through a **markov decision process** (**MDP**). Our game is the environment within which the agent is trying to learn. The state of the environment at time step t is given by s_t (and contains the location of the ball and paddle). The agent can perform certain actions (such as moving the paddle left or right). These actions can sometimes result in a reward r_t, which can be positive or negative (such as an increase or decrease in the score). Actions change the environment and can lead to a new state s_{t+1}, where the agent can perform another action a_{t+1}, and so on. The set of states, actions and rewards, together with the rules for transitioning from one state to the other, make up a markov decision process. A single game is one episode of this process, and is represented by a finite sequence of states, actions, and rewards:

$$s_0, a_0, r_1, s_1, a_1, r_2, s_2, \ldots, s_{n-1}, a_{n-1}, r_n, s_n$$

Since, this is a markov decision process, the probability of state s_{t+1} depends only on current state s_t and action a_t.

Maximizing future rewards

As an agent, our objective is to maximize the total reward from each game. The total reward can be represented as follows:

$$R = \sum_{i=1}^{n} r_i$$

In order to maximize the total reward, the agent should try to maximize the total reward from any time point t in the game. The total reward at time step t is given by R_t and is represented as:

$$R_t = \sum_{i=t}^{n} r_i = r_t + r_{t+1} + \ldots + r_n$$

However, it is harder to predict the value of the rewards the further we go into the future. In order to take this into consideration, our agent should try to maximize the total discounted future reward at time *t* instead. This is done by discounting the reward at each future time step by a factor γ over the previous time step. If γ is *0*, then our network does not consider future rewards at all, and if γ is *1*, then our network is completely deterministic. A good value for γ is around *0.9*. Factoring the equation allows us to express the total discounted future reward at a given time step recursively as the sum of the current reward and the total discounted future reward at the next time step:

$$R_t = r_t + \gamma r_{t+1} + \gamma^2 r_{t+2} + ... + \gamma^{n-t} r_n$$
$$= r_t + \gamma(r_{t+1} + \gamma(r_{t+2} + ...))$$
$$= r_t + \gamma R_{t+1}$$

Q-learning

Deep reinforcement learning utilizes a model-free reinforcement learning technique called **Q-learning**. Q-learning can be used to find an optimal action for any given state in a finite markov decision process. Q-learning tries to maximize the value of the Q-function which represents the maximum discounted future reward when we perform action *a* in state *s*:

$$Q(s_t, a_t) = max(R_{t+1})$$

Once we know the Q-function, the optimal action *a* at a state *s* is the one with the highest Q-value. We can then define a policy Ïє(s) that gives us the optimal action at any state:

$$\Pi(s) = argmax_a \, Q(s, a)$$

We can define the Q-function for a transition point (s_t, a_t, r_t, s_{t+1}) in terms of the Q-function at the next point $(s_{t+1}, a_{t+1}, r_{t+1}, s_{t+2})$ similar to how we did with the total discounted future reward. This equation is known as the **Bellman equation**:

$$Q(s_t, a_t) = r + \gamma \, max_{a_{t+1}} \, Q(s_{t+1}, a_{t+1})$$

The Q-function can be approximated using the Bellman equation. You can think of the Q-function as a lookup table (called a **Q-table**) where the states (denoted by *s*) are rows and actions (denoted by *a*) are columns, and the elements (denoted by *Q(s, a)*) are the rewards that you get if you are in the state given by the row and take the action given by the column. The best action to take at any state is the one with the highest reward. We start by randomly initializing the Q-table, then carry out random actions and observe the rewards to update the Q-table iteratively according to the following algorithm:

```
initialize Q-table Q
observe initial state s
repeat
    select and carry out action a
    observe reward r and move to new state s'
    Q(s, a) = Q(s, a) + α(r + γ max_a' Q(s', a') - Q(s, a))
    s = s'
until game over
```

You will realize that the algorithm is basically doing stochastic gradient descent on the Bellman equation, backpropagating the reward through the state space (or episode) and averaging over many trials (or epochs). Here α is the learning rate that determines how much of the difference between the previous Q-value and the discounted new maximum Q-value should be incorporated.

The deep Q-network as a Q-function

We know that our Q-function is going to be a neural network, the natural question is: what kind? For our simple example game, each state is represented by four consecutive black and white screen images of size *(80, 80)*, so the total number of possible states (and the number of rows of our Q-table) is $2^{80x80x4}$. Fortunately, many of these states represent impossible or highly improbable pixel combinations. Since convolutional neural networks have local connectivity (that is, each neuron is connected to only a local region of its input), it avoids these impossible or improbable pixel combinations. In addition, neural networks are generally very good at coming up with good features for structured data such as images. Hence a CNN can be used to model a Q-function very effectively.

The DeepMind paper (for more information refer to: *Playing Atari with Deep Reinforcement Learning*, by V. Mnih, arXiv:1312.5602, 2013.), also uses three layers of convolutions followed by two fully connected layers. Unlike traditional CNNs used for image classification or recognition, there are no pooling layers. This is because pooling layers makes the network less sensitive to the location of specific objects in the image. In case of games this information is likely to be required to compute the reward, and thus cannot be discarded.

The following diagram, shows the structure of the deep Q-network that is used for our example. It follows the same structure as the original DeepMind paper except for the input and output layer shapes. The shape for each of our inputs is *(80, 80, 4)*: four black and white consecutive screenshots of the game console, each *80 x 80* pixels in size. Our output shape is *(3)*, corresponding to the Q-value for each of three possible actions (move left, stay, move right):

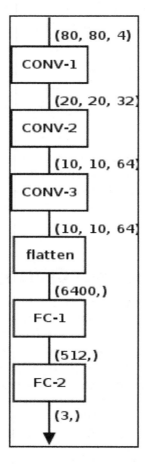

Since our output are the three Q-values, this is a regression task, and we can optimize this by minimizing the difference of the squared error between the current value of *Q(s, a)* and its computed value in terms of the sum of the reward and the discounted Q-value *Q(s', a')* one step into the future. The current value is already known at the beginning of the iteration and the future value is computed based on the reward returned by the environment:

$$L = \frac{1}{2} \left[r + \gamma \ max \ Q(s', a') - Q(s, a) \right]^2$$

Balancing exploration with exploitation

Deep reinforcement learning is an example of online learning, where the training and prediction steps are interspersed. Unlike batch learning techniques where the best predictor is generated by learning on the entire training data, a predictor trained with online learning is continuously improving as it trains on new data.

Thus in the initial epochs of training, a deep Q-network gives random predictions which can give rise to poor Q-learning performance. To alleviate this, we can use a simple exploration method such as ε-greedy. In case of ε-greedy exploration, the agent chooses the action suggested by the network with probability *1-ε* or an action uniformly at random otherwise. That is why this strategy is called exploration/exploitation.

As the number of epochs increases and the Q-function converges, it begins to return more consistent Q-values. The value of ε can be attenuated to account for this, so as the network begins to return more consistent predictions, the agent chooses to exploit the values returned by the network over choosing random actions. In case of DeepMind, the value of ε decreases over time from *1* to *0.1*, and in our example it decreases from *0.1* to *0.001*.

Thus, ε-greedy exploration ensures that in the beginning the system balances the unreliable predictions made from the Q-network with completely random moves to explore the state space, and then settles down to less aggressive exploration (and more aggressive exploitation) as the predictions made by the Q-network improve.

Experience replay, or the value of experience

Based on the equations that represent the Q-value for a state action pair (s_t, a_t) in terms of the current reward r_t and the discounted maximum Q-value for the next time step (s_{t+1}, a_{t+1}), our strategy would logically be to train the network to predict the best next state s' given the current state (s, a, r). It turns out that this tends to drive the network into a local minimum. The reason for this is that consecutive training samples tend to be very similar.

To counter this, during game play, we collect all the previous moves (s, a, r, s') into a large fixed size queue called the **replay memory**. The replay memory represents the experience of the network. When training the network, we generate random batches from the replay memory instead of the most recent (batch of) transactions. Since the batches are composed of random experience tuples (s, a, r, s') that are out of order, the network trains better and avoids getting stuck in local minima.

Experiences could be collected from human gameplay as well instead of (or in addition to) from previous moves during game play by the network. Yet another approach is to collect experiences by running the network in *observation* mode for a while in the beginning, when it generates completely random actions ($\varepsilon = 1$) and extracts the reward and next state from the game and collects them into its experience replay queue.

Example - Keras deep Q-network for catch

The objective of our game is to catch a ball released from a random location from the top of the screen with a paddle at the bottom of the screen by moving the paddle horizontally using the left and right arrow keys. The player wins if the paddle can catch the ball and loses if the balls falls off the screen before the paddle gets to it. The game has the advantage of being very simple to understand and build, and is modeled after the game of catch described by Eder Santana in his blog post (for more information refer to: *Keras Plays Catch, a Single File Reinforcement Learning Example*, by Eder Santana, 2017.) on deep reinforcement learning. We built the original game using Pygame (https://www.pygame.org/news), a free and open source library for building games. This game allows the player to move the paddle using the left and right arrow keys. The game is available as game.py in the code bundle for this chapter in case you want to get a feel for it.

Installing Pygame:

Pygame runs on top of Python, and is available for Linux (various flavors), macOS, Windows, as well as some phone operating systems such as Android and Nokia. The full list of distributions can be found at: `http://www.pygame.org/download.shtml`. Pre-built versions are available for 32-bit and 64-bit versions of Linux and Windows and 64-bit version of macOS. On these platforms, you can install Pygame with `pip install pygame` command.

If a pre-built version does not exist for your platform, you can also build it from source using instructions available at: `http://www.pygame.org/wiki/GettingStarted`.

Anaconda users can find pre-built Pygame versions on the conda-forge:

```
conda install binstar
conda install anaconda-client
conda install -c https://conda.binstar.org/tlatorre
pygame # Linux
conda install -c https://conda.binstar.org/quasiben
pygame # Mac
```

In order to train our neural network, we need to make some changes to the original game so the network can play instead of the human player. We want to wrap the game to allow the network to communicate with it via an API instead of the keyboard left and right arrow keys. Let us look at the code for this wrapped game.

As usual, we start with the imports:

```
from __future__ import division, print_function
import collections
import numpy as np
import pygame
import random
import os
```

We define our class. Our constructor can optionally set the wrapped version of the game to run in *headless* mode, that is, without needing to display a Pygame screen. This is useful where you have to run on a GPU box in the cloud and only have access to a text based terminal. You can comment this line out if you are running the wrapped game locally where you have access to a graphics terminal. Next we call the `pygame.init()` method to initialize all Pygame components. Finally, we set a bunch of class level constants:

```
class MyWrappedGame(object):

    def __init__(self):
        # run pygame in headless mode
```

```
os.environ["SDL_VIDEODRIVER"] = "dummy"

pygame.init()

# set constants
self.COLOR_WHITE = (255, 255, 255)
self.COLOR_BLACK = (0, 0, 0)
self.GAME_WIDTH = 400
self.GAME_HEIGHT = 400
self.BALL_WIDTH = 20
self.BALL_HEIGHT = 20
self.PADDLE_WIDTH = 50
self.PADDLE_HEIGHT = 10
self.GAME_FLOOR = 350
self.GAME_CEILING = 10
self.BALL_VELOCITY = 10
self.PADDLE_VELOCITY = 20
self.FONT_SIZE = 30
self.MAX_TRIES_PER_GAME = 1
self.CUSTOM_EVENT = pygame.USEREVENT + 1
self.font = pygame.font.SysFont("Comic Sans MS", self.FONT_SIZE)
```

The reset() method defines the operations that need to be called at the start of each game, such as clearing out the state queue, setting the ball, and paddle to their starting positions, initializing the scores, and so on:

```
def reset(self):
    self.frames = collections.deque(maxlen=4)
    self.game_over = False
    # initialize positions
    self.paddle_x = self.GAME_WIDTH // 2
    self.game_score = 0
    self.reward = 0
    self.ball_x = random.randint(0, self.GAME_WIDTH)
    self.ball_y = self.GAME_CEILING
    self.num_tries = 0

    # set up display, clock, etc
    self.screen = pygame.display.set_mode((self.GAME_WIDTH,
self.GAME_HEIGHT))
    self.clock = pygame.time.Clock()
```

In the original game, there is a Pygame event queue into which the left and right arrow key events raised by the player as he moves the paddle, as well as internal events raised by Pygame components are written to. The central part of the game code is basically a loop (called the **event loop**), that reads the event queue and reacts to it.

In the wrapped version, we have moved the event loop to the caller. The `step()` method describes what happens in a single pass in the loop. The method takes an integer 0, 1, or 2 representing an action (respectively move left, stay, and move right), and then it sets variables that control the position of the ball and paddle at this time step. The `PADDLE_VELOCITY` variable represents a *speed* that moves the paddle that many pixels to the left or right when the move left and move right actions are sent. If the ball has dropped past the paddle, it checks whether there is a collision. If there is, the paddle *catches* the ball and the player (the neural network) wins, otherwise the player loses. The method then redraws the screen and appends it to the fixed length `deque` that contains the last four frames of the game screen. Finally, it returns the state (given by the last four frames), the reward for the current action and a flag that tells the caller if the game is over:

```
def step(self, action):
    pygame.event.pump()

    if action == 0: # move paddle left
        self.paddle_x -= self.PADDLE_VELOCITY
        if self.paddle_x < 0:
            # bounce off the wall, go right
            self.paddle_x = self.PADDLE_VELOCITY
    elif action == 2: # move paddle right
        self.paddle_x += self.PADDLE_VELOCITY
        if self.paddle_x > self.GAME_WIDTH - self.PADDLE_WIDTH:
            # bounce off the wall, go left
            self.paddle_x = self.GAME_WIDTH - self.PADDLE_WIDTH -
self.PADDLE_VELOCITY
    else: # don't move paddle
        pass

    self.screen.fill(self.COLOR_BLACK)
    score_text = self.font.render("Score: {:d}/{:d}, Ball: {:d}"
        .format(self.game_score, self.MAX_TRIES_PER_GAME,
                self.num_tries), True, self.COLOR_WHITE)
    self.screen.blit(score_text,
        ((self.GAME_WIDTH - score_text.get_width()) // 2,
        (self.GAME_FLOOR + self.FONT_SIZE // 2)))

    # update ball position
    self.ball_y += self.BALL_VELOCITY
    ball = pygame.draw.rect(self.screen, self.COLOR_WHITE,
        pygame.Rect(self.ball_x, self.ball_y, self.BALL_WIDTH,
        self.BALL_HEIGHT))
    # update paddle position
    paddle = pygame.draw.rect(self.screen, self.COLOR_WHITE,
        pygame.Rect(self.paddle_x, self.GAME_FLOOR,
                    self.PADDLE_WIDTH, self.PADDLE_HEIGHT))
```

```
# check for collision and update reward
self.reward = 0
if self.ball_y >= self.GAME_FLOOR - self.BALL_WIDTH // 2:
    if ball.colliderect(paddle):
        self.reward = 1
    else:
        self.reward = -1

self.game_score += self.reward
self.ball_x = random.randint(0, self.GAME_WIDTH)
self.ball_y = self.GAME_CEILING
self.num_tries += 1

pygame.display.flip()

# save last 4 frames
self.frames.append(pygame.surfarray.array2d(self.screen))

if self.num_tries >= self.MAX_TRIES_PER_GAME:
    self.game_over = True

self.clock.tick(30)
return np.array(list(self.frames)), self.reward, self.game_over
```

We will look at the code to train our network to play the game.

As usual, first we import the libraries and objects that we need. In addition to third-party components from Keras and SciPy, we also import the wrapped_game class we described previously:

```
from __future__ import division, print_function
from keras.models import Sequential
from keras.layers.core import Activation, Dense, Flatten
from keras.layers.convolutional import Conv2D
from keras.optimizers import Adam
from scipy.misc import imresize
import collections
import numpy as np
import os

import wrapped_game
```

We define two convenience functions. The first converts the set of four input images to a form suitable for use by the network. The input comes in a set of four 800 x 800 images, so the shape of the input is *(4, 800, 800)*. However, the network expects its input as a four-dimensional tensor of shape *(batch size, 80, 80, 4)*. At the very beginning of the game, we don't have four frames, so we fake it by stacking the first frame four times. The shape of the output tensor returned from this function is *(80, 80, 4)*.

The `get_next_batch()` function samples `batch_size` state tuples from the experience replay queue, and gets the reward and predicted next state from the neural network. It then calculates the value of the Q-function at the next time step and returns it:

```python
def preprocess_images(images):
    if images.shape[0] < 4:
        # single image
        x_t = images[0]
        x_t = imresize(x_t, (80, 80))
        x_t = x_t.astype("float")
        x_t /= 255.0
        s_t = np.stack((x_t, x_t, x_t, x_t), axis=2)
    else:
        # 4 images
        xt_list = []
        for i in range(images.shape[0]):
            x_t = imresize(images[i], (80, 80))
            x_t = x_t.astype("float")
            x_t /= 255.0
            xt_list.append(x_t)
        s_t = np.stack((xt_list[0], xt_list[1], xt_list[2], xt_list[3]),
                       axis=2)
    s_t = np.expand_dims(s_t, axis=0)
    return s_t


def get_next_batch(experience, model, num_actions, gamma, batch_size):
    batch_indices = np.random.randint(low=0, high=len(experience),
        size=batch_size)
    batch = [experience[i] for i in batch_indices]
    X = np.zeros((batch_size, 80, 80, 4))
    Y = np.zeros((batch_size, num_actions))
    for i in range(len(batch)):
        s_t, a_t, r_t, s_tp1, game_over = batch[i]
        X[i] = s_t
        Y[i] = model.predict(s_t)[0]
        Q_sa = np.max(model.predict(s_tp1)[0])
        if game_over:
            Y[i, a_t] = r_t
        else:
```

```
            Y[i, a_t] = r_t + gamma * Q_sa
    return X, Y
```

We define our network. This is the network that models the Q-function for our game. Our network is very similar to the one proposed in the DeepMind paper. The only difference is the size of the input and the output. Our input shape is *(80, 80, 4)* while theirs was *(84, 84, 4)* and our output is *(3)* corresponding to the three actions for which the value of the Q-function needs to be computed, whereas their was *(18)*, corresponding to the actions possible from Atari.

There are three convolutional layers and two fully connected (dense) layers. All layers, except the last have the ReLU activation unit. Since we are predicting values of Q-functions, it is a regression network and the last layer has no activation unit:

```
# build the model
model = Sequential()
model.add(Conv2D(32, kernel_size=8, strides=4,
                 kernel_initializer="normal",
                 padding="same",
                 input_shape=(80, 80, 4)))
model.add(Activation("relu"))
model.add(Conv2D(64, kernel_size=4, strides=2,
                 kernel_initializer="normal",
                 padding="same"))
model.add(Activation("relu"))
model.add(Conv2D(64, kernel_size=3, strides=1,
                 kernel_initializer="normal",
                 padding="same"))
model.add(Activation("relu"))
model.add(Flatten())
model.add(Dense(512, kernel_initializer="normal"))
model.add(Activation("relu"))
model.add(Dense(3, kernel_initializer="normal"))
```

As we have described previously, our loss function is the squared difference between the current value of *Q(s, a)* and its computed value in terms of the sum of the reward and the discounted Q-value *Q(s', a')* one step into the future, so the mean squared error (MSE) loss function works very well. For the optimizer, we choose Adam, a good general-purpose optimizer, instantiated with a low learning rate:

```
model.compile(optimizer=Adam(lr=1e-6), loss="mse")
```

We define some constants for our training. The NUM_ACTIONS constant defines the number of output actions that the network can send to the game. In our case, these actions are 0, 1, and 2, corresponding to move left, stay, and move right. The GAMMA value is the discount factor γ for future rewards. The INITIAL_EPSILON and FINAL_EPSILON refer to starting and ending values for the ε parameter in ε-greedy exploration. The MEMORY_SIZE is the size of the experience replay queue. The NUM_EPOCHS_OBSERVE refer to the number of epochs where the network is allowed to explore the game by sending it completely random actions and seeing the rewards. The NUM_EPOCHS_TRAIN variable refers to the number of epochs the network will undergo online training. Each epoch corresponds to a single game or episode. The total number of games played for a training run is the sum of the NUM_EPOCHS_OBSERVE and NUM_EPOCHS_TRAIN values. The BATCH_SIZE is the size of the mini-batch that we will use for training:

```
# initialize parameters
DATA_DIR = "../data"
NUM_ACTIONS = 3 # number of valid actions (left, stay, right)
GAMMA = 0.99 # decay rate of past observations
INITIAL_EPSILON = 0.1 # starting value of epsilon
FINAL_EPSILON = 0.0001 # final value of epsilon
MEMORY_SIZE = 50000 # number of previous transitions to remember
NUM_EPOCHS_OBSERVE = 100
NUM_EPOCHS_TRAIN = 2000

BATCH_SIZE = 32
NUM_EPOCHS = NUM_EPOCHS_OBSERVE + NUM_EPOCHS_TRAIN
```

We instantiate the game and the experience replay queue. We also open up a log file and initialize some variables in preparation for training:

```
game = wrapped_game.MyWrappedGame()
experience = collections.deque(maxlen=MEMORY_SIZE)

fout = open(os.path.join(DATA_DIR, "rl-network-results.tsv"), "wb")
num_games, num_wins = 0, 0
epsilon = INITIAL_EPSILON
```

Next up, we set up the loop that controls the number of epochs of training. As noted previously, each epoch corresponds to a single game, so we reset the game state at this point. A game corresponds to a single episode of a ball falling from the ceiling and either getting caught by the paddle or being missed. The loss is the squared difference between the predicted and actual Q-value for the game.

We start the game off by sending it a dummy action (in our case, a *stay*) and get back the initial state tuple for the game:

```
for e in range(NUM_EPOCHS):
    game.reset()
    loss = 0.0

    # get first state
    a_0 = 1 # (0 = left, 1 = stay, 2 = right)
    x_t, r_0, game_over = game.step(a_0)
    s_t = preprocess_images(x_t)
```

The next block is the main loop of the game. This is the event loop in the original game that we moved to the calling code. We save the current state because we will need that for our experience replay queue, then decide what action signal to send the wrapped game. If we are in observation mode, we will just generate a random number corresponding to one of our actions, otherwise we will use ε-greedy exploration to either select a random action or use our neural network (which we are also training) to predict the action we should send:

```
while not game_over:
    s_tm1 = s_t

    # next action
    if e <= NUM_EPOCHS_OBSERVE:
        a_t = np.random.randint(low=0, high=NUM_ACTIONS, size=1)[0]
    else:
        if np.random.rand() <= epsilon:
            a_t = np.random.randint(low=0, high=NUM_ACTIONS, size=1)[0]
        else:
            q = model.predict(s_t)[0]
            a_t = np.argmax(q)
```

Once we know our action, we send it to the game by calling `game.step()`, which returns the new state, the reward and a Boolean flag indicating the game is over. If the reward is positive (indicating that the ball was caught), we increment the number of wins, and we store this *(state, action, reward, new state, game over)* tuple in our experience replay queue:

```
# apply action, get reward
x_t, r_t, game_over = game.step(a_t)
s_t = preprocess_images(x_t)
# if reward, increment num_wins
if r_t == 1:
    num_wins += 1
# store experience
experience.append((s_tm1, a_t, r_t, s_t, game_over))
```

We then draw a random mini-batch from our experience replay queue and train our network. For each session of training, we compute the loss. The sum of the losses for all the trainings in each epoch is the loss for the entire epoch:

```
if e > NUM_EPOCHS_OBSERVE:
    # finished observing, now start training
    # get next batch
    X, Y = get_next_batch(experience, model, NUM_ACTIONS, GAMMA,
BATCH_SIZE)
    loss += model.train_on_batch(X, Y)
```

When the network is relatively untrained, its predictions are not very good, so it makes sense to explore the state space more in an effort to reduce the chances of getting stuck in a local minima. However, as the network gets more and more trained, we reduce the value of ε gradually so the model gets to predict more and more of the actions the network sends to the game:

```
# reduce epsilon gradually
if epsilon > FINAL_EPSILON:
    epsilon -= (INITIAL_EPSILON - FINAL_EPSILON) / NUM_EPOCHS
```

We write out a per epoch log both on console and into a log file for later analysis. After 100 epochs of training, we save the current state of the model so that we can recover in case we decide to stop training for any reason. We also save our final model so that we can use it to play our game later:

```
print("Epoch {:04d}/{:d} | Loss {:.5f} | Win Count {:d}"
    .format(e + 1, NUM_EPOCHS, loss, num_wins))
fout.write("{:04d}t{:.5f}t{:d}n".format(e + 1, loss, num_wins))

if e % 100 == 0:
    model.save(os.path.join(DATA_DIR, "rl-network.h5"), overwrite=True)

fout.close()
model.save(os.path.join(DATA_DIR, "rl-network.h5"), overwrite=True)
```

We trained the game by making it observe 100 games, followed by playing 1,000, 2,000, and 5,000 games respectively. The last few lines of the log file for the 5,000 game run are shown next. As you can see, towards the end of the training, the network gets quite skilled at playing the game:

```
Epoch 5075/5100 | Loss 0.02603 | Win Count 2548
Epoch 5076/5100 | Loss 0.06248 | Win Count 2549
Epoch 5077/5100 | Loss 0.09836 | Win Count 2550
Epoch 5078/5100 | Loss 0.05955 | Win Count 2551
Epoch 5079/5100 | Loss 0.07357 | Win Count 2552
Epoch 5080/5100 | Loss 0.05425 | Win Count 2553
Epoch 5081/5100 | Loss 0.05961 | Win Count 2553
Epoch 5082/5100 | Loss 0.05737 | Win Count 2553
Epoch 5083/5100 | Loss 0.06699 | Win Count 2554
Epoch 5084/5100 | Loss 0.04265 | Win Count 2555
Epoch 5085/5100 | Loss 0.06579 | Win Count 2556
Epoch 5086/5100 | Loss 0.06825 | Win Count 2557
Epoch 5087/5100 | Loss 0.09329 | Win Count 2557
Epoch 5088/5100 | Loss 0.06124 | Win Count 2558
Epoch 5089/5100 | Loss 0.15128 | Win Count 2559
Epoch 5090/5100 | Loss 0.03769 | Win Count 2560
Epoch 5091/5100 | Loss 0.06348 | Win Count 2560
Epoch 5092/5100 | Loss 0.03817 | Win Count 2561
Epoch 5093/5100 | Loss 0.05225 | Win Count 2562
Epoch 5094/5100 | Loss 0.04986 | Win Count 2563
Epoch 5095/5100 | Loss 0.06316 | Win Count 2564
Epoch 5096/5100 | Loss 0.07558 | Win Count 2564
Epoch 5097/5100 | Loss 0.04027 | Win Count 2565
Epoch 5098/5100 | Loss 0.03801 | Win Count 2566
Epoch 5099/5100 | Loss 0.02446 | Win Count 2567
Epoch 5100/5100 | Loss 0.04321 | Win Count 2568
```

The plot of loss and win count over epoch, shown in the following graph, also tells a similar story. While it does look like the loss could converge further with more training, it has gone down from *0.6* to around *0.1* in *5000* epochs of training. Similarly, the plot of the number of wins curve upward, showing that the network is learning faster as the number of epochs increases:

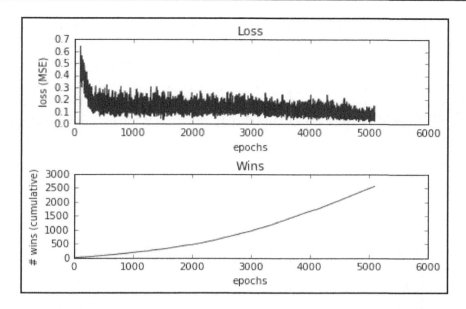

Finally, we evaluate the skill of our trained model by making it play a fixed number of games (100 in our case) and seeing how many it can win. Here is the code to do this. As previously, we start with our imports:

```
from __future__ import division, print_function
from keras.models import load_model
from keras.optimizers import Adam
from scipy.misc import imresize
import numpy as np
import os
import wrapped_game
```

We load up the model we had saved at the end of training and compile it. We also instantiate our `wrapped_game`:

```
DATA_DIR = "../data"
model = load_model(os.path.join(DATA_DIR, "rl-network.h5"))
model.compile(optimizer=Adam(lr=1e-6), loss="mse")

game = wrapped_game.MyWrappedGame()
```

We then loop over 100 games. We instantiate each game by calling its `reset()` method, and start it off. Then, for each game, until it is over, we call on the model to predict the action with the best Q-function. We report a running total of how many games it won.

We ran the test with each of our models. The first one that was trained for 1,000 games won 42 of 100 games, the one trained for 2,000 games won 74 of 100 games, and the one trained for 5,000 games won 87 of 100 games. This clearly shows that the network is improving with training:

```
num_games, num_wins = 0, 0
for e in range(100):
    game.reset()

    # get first state
    a_0 = 1 # (0 = left, 1 = stay, 2 = right)
    x_t, r_0, game_over = game.step(a_0)
    s_t = preprocess_images(x_t)

    while not game_over:
        s_tm1 = s_t
        # next action
        q = model.predict(s_t)[0]
        a_t = np.argmax(q)
        # apply action, get reward
        x_t, r_t, game_over = game.step(a_t)
        s_t = preprocess_images(x_t)
        # if reward, increment num_wins
        if r_t == 1:
            num_wins += 1

    num_games += 1
    print("Game: {:03d}, Wins: {:03d}".format(num_games, num_wins),
end="r")
print("")
```

If you run the evaluation code with the call to run it in headless mode commented out, you can watch the network playing the game and it's quite amazing to watch. Given that the Q-value predictions start off as random values and that it's mainly the sparse reward mechanism that provides the guidance to the network during training, it is almost unreasonable that the network learns to play the game this effectively. But as with other areas of deep learning, the network does in fact learn to play quite well.

The example presented previously is fairly simple, but it illustrates the process by which deep reinforcement learning models work, and hopefully has helped create a mental model using which you can approach more complex implementations. One implementation you might find interesting is Ben Lau's implementation of FlappyBird (for more information refer to: *Using Keras and Deep Q-Network to Play FlappyBird*, by Ben Lau, 2016. and GitHub page: `https://github.com/yanpanlau/Keras-FlappyBird`) using Keras. The Keras-RL project (`https://github.com/matthiasplappert/keras-rl`), a Keras library for deep reinforcement learning, also has some very good examples.

Since the original proposal from DeepMind, there have been other improvements suggested, such as double Q-learning (for more information refer to: *Deep Reinforcement Learning with Double Q-Learning*, by H. Van Hasselt, A. Guez, and D. Silver, AAAI. 2016), prioritized experience replay (for more information refer to: *Prioritized Experience Replay*, by T. Schaul, arXiv:1511.05952, 2015), and dueling network architectures (for more information refer to: *Dueling Network Architectures for Deep Reinforcement Learning*, by Z. Wang, arXiv:1511.06581, 2015). Double Q-learning uses two networks - the primary network chooses the action and the target network chooses the target Q-value for the action. This reduces possible overestimation of Q-values by the single network, and allows the network to train quicker and better. Prioritized experience replay increases the probability of sampling experience tuples with a higher expected learning progress. Dueling network architectures decompose the Q-function into state and action components and combine them back separately.

All of the code discussed in this section, including the base game that can be played by a human player, is available in the code bundle accompanying this chapter.

The road ahead

In January 2016, DeepMind announced the release of AlphaGo (for more information refer to: *Mastering the Game of Go with Deep Neural Networks and Tree Search*, by D. Silver, Nature 529.7587, pp. 484-489, 2016), a neural network to play the game of Go. Go is regarded as a very challenging game for AIs to play, mainly because at any point in the game, there are an average of approximately 10^{170} possible (for more information refer to: `http://ai-depot.com/LogicGames/Go-Complexity.html`) moves (compared with approximately 10^{50} for chess). Hence determining the best move using brute force methods is computationally infeasible. At the time of publication, AlphaGo had already won 5-0 in a 5-game competition against the current European Go champion, Fan Hui. This was the first time that any computer program had defeated a human player at Go. Subsequently, in March 2016, AlphaGo won 4-1 against Lee Sedol, the world's second professional Go player.

There were several notable new ideas that went into AlphaGo. First, it was trained using a combination of supervised learning from human expert games and reinforcement learning by playing one copy of AlphaGo against another. You have seen applications of both these ideas in previous chapters.

Second, AlphaGo was composed of a value network and a policy network. During each move, AlphaGo uses Monte Carlo simulation, a process used to predict the probability of different outcomes in the future in the presence of random variables, to imagine many alternative games starting from the current position. The value network is used to reduce the depth of the tree search to estimate win/loss probability without having to compute all the way to the end of the game, sort of like an intuition about how good the move is. The policy network is used to reduce the breadth of the search by guiding the search towards actions that promise the maximum immediate reward (or Q-value). For a more detailed description, please refer to the blog post: *AlphaGo: Mastering the ancient game of Go with Machine Learning*, Google Research Blog, 2016.

While AlphaGo was a major improvement over the original DeepMind network, it was still playing a game where all the players can see all the game pieces, that is, they are still games of perfect information. In January, 2017, researchers at Carnegie Mellon University announced Libratus (for more information refer to: *AI Takes on Top Poker Players*, by T. Revel, New Scientist 223.3109, pp. 8, 2017), an AI that plays Poker. Simultaneously, another group comprised of researchers from the University of Alberta, Charles University of Prague, and Czech Technical University (also from Prague), have proposed the DeepStack architecture (for more information refer to: *DeepStack: Expert-Level Artificial Intelligence in No-Limit Poker*, by M. Moravaak, arXiv:1701.01724, 2017) to do the same thing. Poker is a game of imperfect information, since a player cannot see the opponent's cards. So, in addition to learning how to play the game, the Poker playing AI also needs to develop an intuition about the opponent's game play.

Rather than use a built-in strategy for its intuition, Libratus has an algorithm that computes this strategy by trying to achieve a balance between risk and reward, also known as the Nash equilibrium. From January 11, 2017 to January 31, 2017, Libratus was pitted against four top human Poker players (for more information refer to: *Upping the Ante: Top Poker Pros Face Off vs. Artificial Intelligence*, Carnegie Mellon University, January 2017), and beat them resoundingly.

DeepStack's intuition is trained using reinforcement learning, using examples generated from random Poker situations. It has played 33 professional Poker players from 17 countries and has a win rating that makes it an *order of magnitude* better than a good player rating (for more information refer to: *The Uncanny Intuition of Deep Learning to Predict Human Behavior*, by C. E. Perez, Medium corporation, Intuition Machine, February 13, 2017).

As you can see, these are very exciting times indeed. Advances that started with deep learning networks able to play arcade games have led to networks that can effectively read your mind, or at least anticipate (sometimes non-rational) human behavior and win at games of bluffing. The possibilities with deep learning seem to be just limitless.

Summary

In this chapter, we have learned the concepts behind reinforcement learning, and how it can be used to build deep learning networks with Keras that learn how to play arcade games based on reward feedback. From there, we moved on to briefly discuss advances in this field, such as networks that have been taught to play harder games such as Go and Poker at a superhuman level. While game playing might seem like a frivolous application, these ideas are the first step towards general artificial intelligence, where a network learns from experience rather than large amounts of training data.

Conclusion

Congratulations on making it to the end of the book! Let us take a moment and see how far we have come since we started.

If you are like most readers, you started with some knowledge of Python and some background in machine learning, but you were interested in learning more about deep learning and wanted to be able to apply these deep learning skills using Python.

You learned how to install Keras on your machine and started using it to build simple deep learning models. You then learned about the original deep learning model, the multi-layer perceptron, also called the **fully connected network (FCN)**. You learned how to build this network using Keras.

You also learned about the many tunable parameters that you need to tweak to get good results from your network. With Keras, a lot of the hard work has been done for you since it comes with sensible defaults, but there are occasions where this knowledge will be helpful to you.

Continuing on from there, you were introduced to **convolutional neural network (CNN)**, originally built to exploit feature locality of images, although you can also use them for other types of data such as text, audio or video. Once again, you saw how to build a CNN using Keras. You also saw the functionality that Keras provides to build CNNs easily and intuitively. You saw how to use pre-trained image networks to make predictions about your own images, via the process of transfer learning and fine-tuning.

From there, you learned about **generative adversarial network (GAN)**, which are a pair of networks (usually CNN) that attempt to work against each other and, in the process, make each other stronger. GANs are a cutting-edge technology in the deep learning space; a lot of recent work is going on around GANs.

From there, we turned our attention to text and we learned about **word embeddings**, which have become the most common technology used for the vector representation of text in the last couple of years. We looked at various popular word embedding algorithms and saw how to use pre-trained word embeddings to represent collections of words, as well as support for word embeddings in Keras and gensim.

We then looked at **recurrent neural network (RNN)**, a class of neural network optimized for handing sequence data such as text or time series. We learned about the shortcomings of the basic RNN model and how these are alleviated in the more powerful variants such as the **long short term model (LSTM)** and **gated recurrent unit (GRU)**. We looked at a few examples where these components are used. We also looked briefly at Stateful RNN models and where they might be used.

Next up, we looked at a few additional models that don't quite fit the molds of the models we have spoken so far. Among them are **autoencoders**, a model for unsupervised learning—**regression networks** that predict a continuous value rather than a discrete label. We introduced the **Keras functional API**, which allows us to build complex networks with multiple inputs and outputs and share components among multiple pipelines. We looked at ways to customize Keras to add functionality that doesn't currently exist.

Finally, we looked at training deep learning networks using **reinforcement learning** in the context of playing arcade games, which many consider a first step toward a general artificial intelligence. We provided a Keras example of training a simple game. We then briefly described advances in this field in the context of networks playing even harder games such as Go and Poker at a superhuman level.

We believe you are now equipped with the skills to solve new machine learning problems using deep learning and Keras. This is an important and valuable skill in your journey to becoming a deep learning expert.

We would like to thank you for letting us help you on your journey to deep learning mastery.

Keras 2.0 — what is new

According to Francois Chollet, Keras was released two years ago, in March, 2015. It then proceeded to grow from one user to one hundred thousand. The following image, taken from the Keras blog, shows the growth of number of Keras users over time.

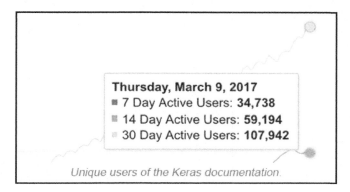

Thursday, March 9, 2017
- 7 Day Active Users: **34,738**
- 14 Day Active Users: **59,194**
- 30 Day Active Users: **107,942**

Unique users of the Keras documentation.

One important update with Keras 2.0 is that the API will now be a part of TensorFlow, starting with TensorFlow 1.2. Indeed, Keras is becoming more and more the *lingua franca* for deep learning, a *spec* used in an increasing number of deep learning contexts. For instance, Skymind is implementing Keras spec in Scala for ScalNet, and Keras.js is doing the same for JavaScript for running of deep learning directly in the browser. Efforts are also underway to provide a Keras API for MXNET and CNTK deep learning toolkits.

Installing Keras 2.0

Installing Keras 2.0 is very simple via the `pip install keras --upgrade` followed by `pip install tensorflow --upgrade`.

API changes

The Keras 2.0 changes implied the need to rethink some APIs. For full details, please refer to the release notes (`https://github.com/fchollet/keras/wiki/Keras-2.0-release-notes`). This module `legacy.py` summarizes the most impactful changes and prevents warnings when using Keras 1.x calls:

```
""
Utility functions to avoid warnings while testing both Keras 1 and 2.
"""
import keras
keras_2 = int(keras.__version__.split(".")[0]) > 1 # Keras > 1

def fit_generator(model, generator, epochs, steps_per_epoch):
    if keras_2:
        model.fit_generator(generator, epochs=epochs,
steps_per_epoch=steps_per_epoch)
    else:
        model.fit_generator(generator, nb_epoch=epochs,
samples_per_epoch=steps_per_epoch)

def fit(model, x, y, nb_epoch=10, *args, **kwargs):
    if keras_2:
        return model.fit(x, y, *args, epochs=nb_epoch, **kwargs)
    else:
        return model.fit(x, y, *args, nb_epoch=nb_epoch, **kwargs)

def l1l2(l1=0, l2=0):
    if keras_2:
        return keras.regularizers.L1L2(l1, l2)
    else:
        return keras.regularizers.l1l2(l1, l2)

def Dense(units, W_regularizer=None, W_initializer='glorot_uniform',
**kwargs):
    if keras_2:
        return keras.layers.Dense(units, kernel_regularizer=W_regularizer,
kernel_initializer=W_initializer, **kwargs)
    else:
        return keras.layers.Dense(units, W_regularizer=W_regularizer,
                                  init=W_initializer, **kwargs)

def BatchNormalization(mode=0, **kwargs):
    if keras_2:
        return keras.layers.BatchNormalization(**kwargs)
    else:
        return keras.layers.BatchNormalization(mode=mode, **kwargs)
```

```
def Convolution2D(units, w, h, W_regularizer=None,
W_initializer='glorot_uniform', border_mode='same', **kwargs):
    if keras_2:
        return keras.layers.Conv2D(units, (w, h), padding=border_mode,
                                   kernel_regularizer=W_regularizer,
                                   kernel_initializer=W_initializer,
                                   **kwargs)
    else:
        return keras.layers.Conv2D(units, w, h, border_mode=border_mode,
W_regularizer=W_regularizer, init=W_initializer, **kwargs)

def AveragePooling2D(pool_size, border_mode='valid', **kwargs):
    if keras_2:
        return keras.layers.AveragePooling2D(pool_size=pool_size,
                                             padding=border_mode, **kwargs)
    else:
        return keras.layers.AveragePooling2D(pool_size=pool_size,
                                             border_mode=border_mode,
**kwargs)
```

There are also a number of breaking changes. In particular:

- The maxout dense, time distributed dense, and highway legacy layers have been removed
- The batch normalization layer no longer supports the mode argument, because Keras internals have changed
- Custom layers have to be updated
- Any undocumented Keras functionality could have broken

In addition, the Keras code base has been instrumented to detect the use of the Keras 1.x API calls and show deprecation warnings that show how to change the call to conform to the Keras 2 API. If you have some volume of Keras 1.x code already and are hesitant to try Keras 2 because of the fear of non-breaking changes, these deprecation warnings from the Keras 2 code base can be very helpful in making the transition.

Index

Made in the USA
Monee, IL
06 December 2019